With Compliments
& Thanks
Sidney

A GARLAND OF LEGENDS

*"Lawrence of Arabia"
and
"The Arab Revolt"*

Other books by the Author

A Bibliography of the Printed Works of James Parkes
with selected quotations
1977
(together with Diana Bailey)

A GARLAND OF LEGENDS

*"Lawrence of Arabia"
and
"The Arab Revolt"*

Sidney Sugarman

Published in 1992 by
The SPA Ltd,
Units 7/10 Hanley Workshops,
Hanley Road, Hanley Swan,
Worcs.

in conjunction with Sidney Sugarman

© SIDNEY SUGARMAN 1992

This book is copyright. No part of it may be reproduced in any form without permission in writing from the publishers except by a reviewer who wishes to quote brief passages in connection with a review written for inclusion in a newspaper, magazine, radio or television broadcast.

British Library Cataloguing in Publication Data
A catalogue record for this book is available from the British Library

ISBN 1 85421 201 X

Designed and Produced by Images Design and Print Ltd.
Printed and bound in Great Britain by Hartnolls Ltd, Bodmin, Cornwall.

Contents

		Page
List of Illustrations		7
Acknowledgements		9
Introduction		11
Author's Notes	Author's Note on the English Spelling of Arabic Names	15
Chapter One	Anglo-French conflicts in the Middle East. The Francophobia of Lawrence.	17
Chapter Two	Britain prepares her groundwork. War Office Intelligence Department in Cairo, and Lawrence's "motives".	23
Chapter Three	Lawrence's sexual orientation: a non-hysterical study.	31
Chapter Four	Turkey plans war. Storrs and McMahon consider the Sharif's expectations and promises.	37
Chapter Five	Lawrence's views of the Sharif's campaign: His transfer to the Arab Bureau	49
Chapter Six	Storr's account of October 1916. Arab demands: gold and Hashemite rule.	57
Chapter Seven	Abdullah's account. The Hejaz becomes a Kingdom.	63
Chapter Eight	Lawrence's account. He is appointed Liaison Officer to Feisal.	69
Chapter Nine	The evanescent "revolt", and the picturesque procession to Wejh.	75
Chapter Ten	A leisurely excursion with Aqaba in mind, and an unexplained diversion.	81
Chapter Eleven	The price of Arab co-operation: backstairs dealings with the Turks.	89

Chapter Twelve	Mudowwara; Lawrence announces his design, and his failure.	95
Chapter Thirteen	The River Yarmuk Bridge survives Lawrence's plan for its destruction.	101
Chapter Fourteen	Tafileh: a farcical battle, a parodied report, and a serious embezzlement.	111
Chapter Fifteen	Maan; more mountains of gold. Allenby suffers defeat at Es Salt.	123
Chapter Sixteen	Deraa, another Lawrence miscarriage. A disputed massacre at Tafas. Flagellation, sadism and masochism.	131
Chapter Seventeen	Lawrence's views on the love-life of the desert warriors. Castigation and obscenity.	141
Chapter Eighteen	Lawrence and the "Arab Revolt." Major Jarvis and the Generals offer their views.	147
Chapter Nineteen	Damascus surrenders: The allies enter. Lawrence's loyalty called into question.	155
Chapter Twenty	The letters Lawrence "hated" to write. Lawrence abandons his Arabian identity.	165
Chapter Twenty One	The genesis of the legend	171
Chapter Twenty Two	"With Lawrence of Arabia": Lowell Thomas composes a novel history. Lawrence's own responsibility for the legend.	179
Chapter Twenty Three	"Objective truth"; Britain's actions and Lawrence's part in them.	189
Chapter Twenty Four	War in Mesopotamia. The tragedy of Kut.	195
Chapter Twenty Five	A catalogue of dreadful atrocities: the martyrdom of the British captives.	207
Chapter Twenty Six	Triumph of an Arab Revolt; The British create the Arab State of Iraq.	213
Chapter Twenty Seven	The Hashemite brothers are awarded their awaited thrones. Death of Lawrence.	225
Postscript		233
Reference Notes		236
Bibliography		247
Index		251

List of Illustrations

	Page
Lawrence of Arabia with the Emir Feisal.	61
Lawrence, taken at Akaba.	82
Lawrence drives a Talbot car in the desert.	102
Map of Lawrence's Desert Campaigns.	120
Lawrence of Arabia.	130
Posing for posterity. "as I looked a perfect idiot . . . " (see page 176) (Letter to H.R. Hadley, September 2nd 1920).	173
"With Lawrence of Arabia".	180
Film: "Lawrence of Arabia" (1962).	181
Irish born actor, 27 year old Peter O' Toole in the title role of Sam Spiegel's film production of the famous Lawrence of Arabia.	191
Lawrence of Arabia (Thomas Edward Lawrence).	191

ACKNOWLEDGEMENTS

I am indebted to Tony Harold and his group of dedicated professionals, and in particular to Alison Uren in the exercise of her editorial talents; to Diana Bailey, for her deep involvement from the very beginning and her rewardingly diligent researches in the Public Record Office; to George Paul for his critical encouragement and his valued percipience; and not least to my resident proof-reader, my wife Tessa, for her forbearance and help.

Photographs by courtesy of
The Hulton Picture Company & Topham Picture Source.

INTRODUCTION

"It is a bold person who sets out to explode myths", wrote Gillian Reynolds. "The myths would not be there in the first place if they did not meet the romantic longings of many a human heart and so they have a power which fascinates and grows."

The aim of this book is to assemble the facts and present the real history lying buried beneath two myths: "Lawrence of Arabia" and "The Arab Revolt". Many readers will be familiar with the legends which intertwine the complex historical and political events of 1916-1918, not least because Lawrence himself, in the *Seven Pillars of Wisdom*, laid the foundation for the creation of a legendary personality. While this may not have been his intention, his account of his exploits is so extravagant and dramatic that the book gives a vivid impression of fiction. Nevertheless it must be admitted that eventually he both resented and rejected the legend and its creation, and did not shrink from recording his several failures.

The other legend in the twisted garland is of a different order, meriting relegation to the realms of obscure mythology. It has come down to us under the stirring caption of "The Arab Revolt," but however deeply we delve into the history of that alleged event there emerges only the account of a feeble and opportunist attempt on the part of a single noble Arab family to grasp a measure of power at a crucial point in the course of a war between two major forces.

That story, attending the creation of the Kingdom of the Hejaz, is central to the theme of this present work. It begins on the 5th June, 1916, when Ali and Feisal, sons of the Sharif of Mecca, led a force of several thousand tribesmen against the Turkish garrison in Medina. The attack was repulsed, and after suffering heavy losses the tribesmen withdrew to positions well beyond the range of Turkish reprisal.

During the course of that retreat, the Sharif Hussein was able to launch an attack against Mecca, from which the bulk of the Turkish garrison had moved to their summer station at Taif, seventy miles to the south-east. The remaining handful of troops in the town were disposed of: the force at Taif, contained there by Abdullah, the second son of the Sharif, held out until the third week in September, when, despairing of relief, it capitulated. This last action marked the end of Sharif Hussein's 'revolt' but before the end of the year he had with a stroke of his pen created the Kingdom of the Hejaz, with himself as ruler.

This arbitrary feat failed to achieve for him the support of any of the other Arab peoples – those of Syria and Palestine, the Shammar, the Yemen, the Nejd and the other adjacent territories. Indeed it has to be recorded that these Arabs mustered in their tens of thousands – by both conscription and enlistment – in every rank of the Turkish armies to fight *against* the British and their allies. It was only at the end of fighting, when they could with certainty witness the complete destruction of the masters they had served for centuries, that they swarmed to join the ranks of the victors.

Over the succeeding years, constant reiteration together with Lawrence's own epic account of the desert campaigns of 1917-1918 assisted to establish the belief that there had in fact been a widespread revolt against the Turks, and that this alleged uprising had been a major contribution towards the subsequent Allied victory. Furthermore, the story went, not only was this revolt instigated by the British but had also been encouraged through promises of independence for the Arabs at the end of the war.

That these fictions should have been promulgated and exploited during the negotiations between the interested parties at the Peace Conference in 1919 and in other places is not surprising. Feisal officially represented only his father, but claimed to speak on behalf of 'the Arab nation', an entity which did not in fact exist; it was natural that he would make every effort to impress the delegates at the conference with romantic accounts of Arab sacrifices and Arab victories.

In the real history of the period there is, however, recorded a very full account of *an* Arab revolt – that powerful onslaught which the Arabs of Mesopotamia had directed against those British forces which had entered their country with pretensions of their redemption from Turkish oppression. The bloody consequences of this Arab revolt have no place in myth or legend. The invaders had invested mountains of gold and thousands of their soldiers' lives: but not entirely in vain, for an independent Arab state of Iraq ultimately emerged from the carnage to become one of the most powerful – and sadly the most menacing – of the states which were carved out of the carcass of the shattered Ottoman Empire.

That the myth of 'The Arab Revolt' in its widely accepted sense could survive the facts is in itself astonishing yet at the same time suggests that myths may do more than "meet romantic longings". They may, for instance, be fostered by those who seek to justify Arab claims to rewards even greater than those already harvested from the Allied sacrifices of the First World War. But what must be beyond the understanding of those who endeavour to formulate an objective view of history is the seemingly insatiable chorus who bleat unceasingly about 'broken promises' and 'Arabs betrayed'.

For them the battle is never over, and if they should yet again muster their motley forces their escutcheons may well be decorated with the intertwined *Garland of Legends*. In the meantime, the Arabs, as James MacManus wrote in *The Times* of January 16th,

1991, ". . . remain in limbo between the ancient and modern worlds, trapped in a twilight zone of popular myths and images which offer only the comforting thought that the West is the source of all evil".

Author's Note on the English Spelling of Arabic Names

Readers – and, more especially, proof-readers – will have frequent occasion to remark on the varied English renderings of Arabic names: e.g., Akaba and Aqaba, Feisal, Faisul, Faysal, Feysul and so on. This is an irritant for which I know of no acceptable remedy. While I might have my own preferred spelling, when I quote another writer it would be improper for me to adjust his version. Storrs, who had the reputation of an Arabic scholar, always wrote "Abdallah" where today it is invariably written "Abdullah"; while Lawrence and Aldington and others dispensed with the final "h". This state of anarchy did in no way displease Lawrence, who, as you will find on page 117 of this book, flaunts five different versions of an Arab character's name on a single page: I suspect in a spirit of deliberate impishness. In *Seven Pillars of Wisdom* he has Feisal and Feysul on the same page, and defends this practice in the Preface, stating: "I spell my names anyhow, to show what rot the systems are". "The systems" he explains as follows:

"The general practice of orientalists in recent years has been to adopt one of the various sets of conventional signs for the letters and vowel marks of the Arabic alphabet, transliterating Mohamed as Muhammad, muezzin as mu'edhdin, and Koran as Qur'an or Kur'an. This method is useful to those who know what it means, but this book follows the old fashion of writing the best phonetic approximations according to ordinary English spelling. The same place-name will be found spelt in several different ways, not only because the sound of many Arabic words can legitimately be represented in English in a variety of ways, but also because the natives of a district often differ as to the pronunciation of any place-name which has not already become famous or fixed by literary usage. (For example a locality near Akaba is called Abu Lissan, Aba el Lissan or Abu Lissal.)" (*Seven Pillars of Wisdom*, 1935, p.24)

Sidney Sugarman

CHAPTER ONE

Anglo-French conflicts in the Middle East.
The Francophobia of Lawrence.

Lawrence first drifted into my ken some years ago when I was engaged in gathering material for a book which would record the full story of the centuries-old conflict between the English and the French. Before long it became increasingly evident that any adequate – let alone complete – history would need not a book but a substantial library, for the earlier years of strife athwart the English Channel were succeeded in the following centuries by rivalries which raged fiercely in many parts of the emergent world. Repeatedly, wherever the French had attempted to establish themselves as traders or colonisers, the British soon followed to challenge their primacy. The French had penetrated Canada early in the seventeenth century, founding their first colony there in 1604, and beginning the settlement of Quebec four years later. In the following century they extended their explorations southwards, but, by the Peace of Paris in 1763, they not only surrendered their Canadian possessions to Britain but were also driven from New Orleans, Detroit and their settlements on the Great Lakes, the Ohio and the Mississippi. Crozet's possession of New Zealand on behalf of France in 1772 was ultimately followed by Capt. William Hobson's annexation of the country to Australia in 1840. In India the French surrendered Pondicherry to British land and sea forces in 1761, heralding the beginnings of British rule in India.

With India under British control it became important to establish staging points on the sea routes to the Middle East. In 1783 the British defeated a combined French-Spanish fleet at Gibraltar, and in the same year the Treaty of Versailles confirmed Britain's possession of the Rock. Gibraltar became a "Crown Colony" in 1840. Malta, where the French knights had held sway for centuries, and which Napoleon had occupied in 1798, came under British rule after the Union Jack was hoisted there in 1799. At the eastern end of the approaches to India, Britain entered into treaties with the Arab states bordering the Persian Gulf, ostensibly with the purpose of suppressing Arab piracy, in 1820; and in the years which followed the entire Gulf area became an area of British influence. Aden was acquired in 1839, and in the same year Britain established the first European consulate in Jerusalem.

France's interests in the Holy Land dated from the period of the Crusades of the 11th to the 13th centuries. In 1535 François I and the Ottoman Sultan Suleiman I signed a treaty which conferred on France the privileges of the capitulations and recognition of her position as the protector of Latin Christianity in the Ottoman Empire. The capitulations were further extended in 1740, and again by Napoleon in 1802. Napoleon had invaded Palestine in 1798 but was forced in the next year to retreat, and in 1801 his army there had surrendered to the British. In Lebanon, because the Maronite Church there was in communion with Rome and was thus entitled to French protection, France intervened when its members were persecuted between 1842 and 1845, and again in 1860, when after serious anti-Christian riots she was successful in persuading the Sultan to permit the establishment of Lebanon as an autonomous region.

Despite the failure of Napoleon's expedition France succeeded in Egypt and increased her influence with the Ottoman Sultans. She became deeply involved in the country's economy, especially in the railways and in banking. The Suez Canal was built by French engineers and largely with French capital, but in 1875 Disraeli purchased all of the Khedive's Suez Canal shares for Britain. Seven years later the Dual Control of Egypt by Britain and France came to an end, and was followed by the British military occupation of the country. After the declaration of the First World War in 1914, Britain declared Egypt to be a British Protectorate, but her military occupation of the country was maintained for many years after that war. The "Anglo-Egyptian Sudan" came under British rule in 1888.

Cyprus, the most easterly of the Mediterranean staging-posts, had been occupied by Britain in 1878. Thus in little more than one hundred years, the sea route to India was secured, extending some 5,000 miles from Gibraltar eastwards through the Mediterranean, the Suez Canal, the Red Sea and the Arabian Sea to Karachi and Bombay. It curved around the vast land mass of the Arabian Peninsula without touching its coast line until it reached Aden; Britain was content to leave the Turkish domination of the peninsula unchallenged – provided that no other European power intervened. But in 1914 the Great War brought the Germans into Syria, and the ultimate consequence of that situation was the British domination of Arabia, for by the end of that war, less than one hundred years after the signing of the Trucial Coast Agreements, Britain was in control of Palestine to the west of Arabia and Mesopotamia at its eastern end. Between these two countries the vast territories of the Hejaz, under the Hashemite King Hussein, and the even greater areas ruled by Ibn Saud, found themselves largely reliant on British support and subsidies.

Throughout the period of the war the British and the French, united in an entente cordiale in the face of a common enemy, put aside their ancient rivalries. If from the French there were still heard small whispers about "Perfidious Albion", these for the most part remained sufficiently muted. In the second year of the war the two allies had entered into an agreement – the Sykes-Picot Agreement[1] – concerning the division of the Ottoman Empire after an Allied victory. But when the time arrived for the implementation of the agreed terms, Britain demanded the French acceptance of a number of modifications, none of which were to France's advantage. Britain was no longer content with the small coastal strip stretching from Haifa to Acre: she now insisted on a mandate which would give her control of the whole area of Palestine; while Mosul, which was known to possess valuable oil deposits, would be detached from the French sphere of interest centred on Syria and transferred also into British Mandatory rule. Cilicia, hitherto provisionally awarded to France, would remain part of Turkey. The French protested, but were powerless to do more than that. Most of the European fighting had taken place on French soil, and she had suffered tremendous economic ruination as well as nearly three million human casualties. Besides, the troops now occupying Mesopotamia, Syria and Palestine were overwhelmingly British. The French had little alternative but to accept, if not to agree.

A sceptical observer may have ventured that with the disappearance of the common danger the traditional British challenge to French primacy might now be resumed. During the war, there had indeed been some indiscreet whispers of hostility to the idea of French aspirations in the Middle East. These are revealed in a letter written by Lawrence, then a very junior officer of some three months' standing in the Military Intelligence Office in Cairo, to D.G. Hogarth, the archaeologist whom Lawrence regarded as his mentor and who was later appointed Director of the Arab Bureau, with the rank of Lieutenant-Commander, RNVR. Dated "March, 1915", it announced: "We can rush right up to Damascus, & biff the French out of all hope of Syria . . . Won't the French be mad if we win through?" In an earlier letter[2] to Hogarth he had advocated a British occupation of Alexandretta, a port in the Syrian vilayet of Aleppo, on the grounds that "In the hands of France it will provide a sure base for naval attacks on Egypt". Small wonder that David Garnett, the editor of *The Letters of T.E. Lawrence of Arabia*, was prompted to remark in his introduction that Lawrence "was planning a strategy in the Middle East which was to liberate Syria from the Turks and involve England in violent friction with her chief ally, France. Indeed his letters putting forward his plan for seizing Alexandretta and making it an English naval base might lead one to think that England and France were on the brink of war".[3]

Garnett, writing those words shortly before the outbreak of the Second World War, could hardly have foreseen that within a few years

British and French forces would indeed be facing each other in battle. In 1941, after Petain's Minister of War had informed the Vichy Commander-in-Chief in Syria, General Dentz, that the use of air bases in the Levant had been conceded to Germany, the instruction was added, that "English aircraft must be attacked by all possible means". On May 15th 1941, Petain announced a policy of closer collaboration with Hitler in Europe and Africa and Dentz was further enjoined that he must be prepared to place the ports of Beirut, Tripoli and Latakia at the disposal of the Germans. Faced with the prospect of Syria falling into German hands, the British saw no alternative but to mount an invasion of Syria, which their forces entered on June 8th. Vichy resistance ended on July 14th.[4]

CHAPTER TWO

*Britain prepares her groundwork.
War Office Intelligence Department in Cairo,
and Lawrence's "motives".*

In his history of *The Palestine Campaigns* Field Marshal Earl Wavell found it necessary to comment on "the lack of good maps", adding in a footnote: "The best map available was the survey made by Lord Kitchener in 1878 when a subaltern in the Royal Engineers. It was excellent as far as it went, but the detail was not always sufficiently accurate for tactical purposes".[1]

This was originally published as a one-inch map in 26 sheets, and was followed in October 1882 by a "Special Edition" on a smaller scale for the Committee of the Palestine Exploration Fund, "Illustrating the Old Testament, the Apocrypha and Josephus". It was headed "Map of Western Palestine from Surveys conducted by Lieuts. C.R. Condor and H.H. Kitchener, R.E." Its northern boundary was the Litani River to the latitude of Mount Hermon, and the eastern followed the River Jordan and the western shores of the Dead Sea and the Sea of Galilee, but in the south the map ended at a line which ran from just below Gaza down to Beersheba.

1882 was, as we have noted, the year in which the Dual Control by Britain and France in Egypt came to an end and the British military occupation commenced. Part of Sinai had come under the administration of Egypt at the time when Egypt had the status of an

Ottoman Pashalik, but its eastern boundaries had never been clearly defined, so that when, in 1906, the Turks attempted to establish a garrison at Taba (south and west of Aqaba) the British felt able to challenge the move. The dispute which followed became known as the "Aqaba Incident", and was resolved after the British mounted a demonstration of force to which the Turks were not able to offer effective resistance. The Sultan had to submit to a British ultimatum and accept the inclusion of the whole Sinai Peninsula in Egypt, with the eastern land boundary running from Rafah on the Mediterranean down to Aqaba. This measure brought the whole area under the department of the Survey of Egypt, enabling the British War Office to organise a military survey.

By the end of 1913 this survey was approaching completion, giving the British possession of a series of detailed maps covering an area stretching from the Litani and Jordan Rivers to the Suez Canal, but with a gap below latitude 31 between the Wadi el Arish (about 30 miles west of Rafah) and the Wadi Araba, which ran south to Aqaba. The eastern part of this uncharted area lay in Turkish territory, where the Turks could hardly be expected, after the "Aqaba Incident", to welcome a team of British officers on a mapping expedition. The obvious solution to this problem was to invoke the same prescription which thirty years earlier had produced the Map of Western Palestine. The Palestine Exploration Fund would be called upon to send an archaeologist who would conduct a survey which could be related to the holy scriptures. Leonard Woolley, who had worked with Lawrence at an archaeological site at Carchemish until June, 1913, was selected for the task. Lawrence accompanied him as his assistant, and they reached Gaza on January 6th, 1914. At Beersheba they were joined by Captain Newcombe of the Royal Engineers, and for the following four or five weeks the three worked on both sides of the border, with Newcombe doing the survey while the two archaeologists prepared notes for the P.E.F. report.

Some years later Lawrence wrote: "Turkey was sore about the Sinai survey, which it felt had been a military game. Kitchener, the only begetter of the survey, insisted on the Palestine Exploration Fund's bringing out its record of our archaeological researching, p.d.q. (pretty damn quick) as whitewash". It is doubtful whether the Turks were reassured by this ploy. However, the Turkish Governor at Aqaba informed Newcombe at some time in February that orders from Constantinople forbidding the survey had been received. Kitchener immediately gave orders for its withdrawal, and Lawrence returned first to Syria and then to Carchemish for a few weeks.

He was back in London by June, and after completing his part of *The Wilderness of Zin* (the report for the P.E.F., with Woolley as co-author) he wrote to "A Friend" in the autumn of 1914 to say he was working on "a complete map of Sinai, showing all road and wells, with capacity of latter, and a rough outline of hills". Admitting that he was not in possession of all the information required for a proper completion of the job, he nevertheless produced (he confessed) "a map of Sinai in three colours. Some of it was accurate, and the rest I invented".[2]

Such initiative may have been considered by some of his friends as clever, or even praiseworthy, but unhappily these maps became available to the soldiers who planned and led the attacks on Gaza in 1917, where desperate and bloody battles were fought. Wavell has described the fighting which took place on the 8th and 9th of November in that year. "The two attacking brigades lost in this section 700 men. In this as in other operations the lack of accurate maps was much felt".[3]

We may assume that Lawrence completed the work on the book and the maps by October 19th, because that is the date of a letter he wrote to Mrs Fontana, the wife of the British consul in Aleppo, informing her "Woolley and I are doing (– nothing – but we have good intentions)."[4] Later he wrote elsewhere that about this time he and Woolley had been in touch with Newcombe "when the book was finished, and asked his advice about a war job". This may have been a reference to the "good intentions" he mentions in the letter to Mrs Fontana.

It seems that Newcombe was unable to do anything for them. Woolley refused to go on doing "nothing", and obtained a commission in the Artillery: Newcombe was sent out to France.[5] What followed next must be derived from a number of conflicting accounts. After Liddell Hart had completed his typescript for the "*T.E. Lawrence*" biography he was informed by Lawrence that he had at that time obtained an appointment to see Colonel Hedley, the head of the Geographical Section of the General Staff (Intelligence) of the War Office through the good offices of Hogarth. However, Hedley has denied that he was approached by anybody acting on Lawrence's behalf, saying instead that Lawrence turned up "one day in September" at a time when all his officers, with but one exception, had been called away to active service, and the remaining one was within a week of departing to France. Hedley knew about the Sinai job, and was pleased to have Lawrence in his otherwise deserted office.[6] However, all accounts agree that Lawrence commenced work at the Geographical Section as a civilian and soon afterwards was told by Hedley that he would have to be commissioned. He told Liddell Hart that he went off to the Army and Navy Stores and fitted himself out with a second-lieutenant's uniform without waiting until his appointment was gazetted.[7] It appears that he was not required to pass a medical examination.

There is a reason for devoting what may appear to be inordinate attention to the relatively unimportant details of Lawrence's admission to the commissioned ranks. When Lawrence later wrote about his wartime experiences, he referred more than once to his "motives" for his entrance into the arena. The autumn and following winter of 1914 witnessed the enrolment into the fighting services of tens of thousands of volunteers. As we have already seen, Woolley refused to wait to be recruited, and there must have been many others of similar mind. Two of Lawrence's younger brothers enlisted: Frank, who was an undergraduate at Jesus College when war broke out, was killed on the Western Front in the following May, and Will, in the Royal Flying Corps, lost his life in September. In December, 1914, Lawrence wrote to his friend, the poet James Elroy Flecker: "Not many dons have taken commissions – but 95% of the undergraduates have taken or applied for them". In every town and village Kitchener's fore-finger emphasised the country's urgent need, and men everywhere flocked into the recruiting centres.

We have no knowledge of their "motive". Many were doubtless motivated by the spirit of adventure, others possibly by genuine patriotism: for the most part they remained silent on the question. But in a letter, now in the Bodleian Library, Lawrence wrote about his "motives", giving the first one as: "Personal. I liked a particular Arab very much, and I thought that freedom for the race would be an acceptable present".[8] And the last page of his *Seven Pillars of Wisdom* takes the form of a postscript, again concerned with motivation, telling, cryptically, that the capture of Damascus "disclosed the exhaustion of my main springs of action. The strongest motive throughout had been a personal one."

In a letter to Robert Graves he explained that his dedicatory poem in *Seven Pillars* (which is addressed, enigmatically, to "S.A.") "had been inspired by one who provided a disproportionate share of the motive for the Arabian adventure[9]", and Graves later said that in 1927 he had been told "by one of Lawrence's oldest friends" that "S.A." was Sheikh Achmed, an Arab with whom Lawrence had a sort of blood brotherhood before the war".[10] Professor A.W. Lawrence, T.E.'s younger brother, has affirmed that he shared this belief.

These references all point to a youth known as Dahoum, whose real name, according to Suleiman Mousa, the author of an Arab biography of Lawrence, was Sheikh Ahmed. Mousa describes him as "the water boy" and reports Woolley's observation that "the Arabs at Carchemish believed that Lawrence was a homosexual because of his close friendship with Dahoum, who was handsome, gracefully built and not yet fifteen".[11] Are we then asked to believe that Lawrence had planned to go to war because of his love for an Arab youth, and to defeat the Turks so that he would be able to present the resultant "freedom for the race" as "an acceptable present?"

There is scant evidence from any available records, or from his own letters, that in the months which followed his enlistment he was making any purposeful contribution to implement this declared motive. In January 1915 he wrote to Hogarth: "Blank. Am in an office all day, adding together scraps of information, & writing geographies from memory of little details. It is the dullest job to hear of, but not so bad in action."[12]

Despite this boredom he seemed to be in the privileged position of being able to dispense inside military information to chosen friends, confiding to Hogarth in his letter of January 15th that "the preparations of the Turks seem to be slacking off". Perhaps he was nearer the truth when on the 20th of the preceding month he had written to Hogarth: "*Intelligence Dept., War Office, Cairo* . . . There wasn't an Intelligence department it seemed, and they thought all was well without it . . . It promises to be good fun",[13] because on the 26th and 27th January the Turks impertinently launched heavy attacks on the Suez Canal defences. Although these were repulsed the Turks struck again a week later, and on this occasion they succeeded in crossing the Canal.[14]

The Turkish preparations for these actions involved the transport of heavy guns and considerable bridging equipment across more than one hundred miles of desert:[15] unquestionably a considerable achievement and certainly no evidence that they were "slacking off", and it is difficult to understand how such activity could have escaped the notice of any Intelligence Department worthy of the name. Furthermore, they were not only at this time dangerously active in the Canal Zone, but on the distant side of the Peninsula they were actually preparing an invasion of Persia's western frontiers: involving a threat not only to the right flank of the Anglo-Indian troops in the south of Mesopotamia but also to the British oil interests in Persia. In the event they were successful in penetrating into Persia to a depth of sixty miles in the first week of February.[16] Some slacking off!

In the Epilogue in Liddell Hart's biography of Lawrence the author ventures: "he has a confidence that sometimes savours of arrogance . . ."[17,] and it must be admitted that Lawrence displayed no diffidence in his frequent attempts to share his inaccurate knowledge with his friends. He confided in a letter, dated 19.x.1914, to Mrs Fontana: "Turkey seems at last to have made up its mind to lie down and be at peace with all the world". Unfortunately, ten days later Turkey attacked Russia and declared war on the British Empire. A letter to Hogarth written in 1915, and dated 18th March, is replete with dubious political insight, reporting, among other things, that "Ibn Rashid has been heavily defeated by Ibn Saoud (Ibn Saud)", but Arnold Wilson, then Political Officer with the British Expeditionary Forces in Mesopotamia, has a different version, writing: "Unfortunately the collision was a stalemate and Ibn Saud recoiled from the contest severely crippled".[18]

Unabashed, Lawrence was telling Hogarth a month later (in a letter dated April 20th, 1915) "Poor old Turkey is only hanging together. People always talk of the splendid show she has made lately, but it really is too pitiful for words. Everything about her is very sick, and I almost think it will be good to make an end of her".[19] It seems incredible that an officer in the War Office Intelligence Department in Cairo should not have been aware of the defeats in the previous weeks which "poor old Turkey" had succeeded in inflicting on the British Forces in Mesopotamia. General Robinson had been defeated in a battle which took place on March 2nd, suffering casualties of 62 killed and 127 wounded,[20] and this was followed by a further series of defeats which cost the British an additional 1,257 casualties.[21]

Even more significant is the fact that at the very time he was writing that commiserating appraisal of "poor old Turkey", G.H.Q. in Egypt was planning the historic landing at Gallipoli. General Hamilton, in charge of the operation, had estimated that he would be facing some 34,000 troops who would be supported by 100 guns. Once again one is reminded of Lawrence's expectation of "good fun" and his humorous remark: "There wasn't an Intelligence Dept. it seemed", for Hamilton found, to his tremendous cost, that not only was the Turkish force far more numerous than his information had led him to believe, but also they possessed almost three times the estimated number of guns.

This is not the place to recount in detail the tragic disasters which the unfortunate Allied attackers suffered: the full story has been told elsewhere. It is sufficient to recall that in the first week alone the Allies lost 15,000 men, and by the time the operation was called off the total losses were enormous.

Inevitably Lawrence's uninhibited pronouncements attracted comment from his associates. Liddell Hart wrote that "there was continuous irritation in the complete assurance, almost dogmatic, with which Lawrence used to utter verdicts on any matter that came within his own range of knowledge"; while General Wingate[22] commented that "he appears to me to be a visionary and his amateur soldiering has evidently given him an exaggerated idea of the soundness of his views on purely military matters."

CHAPTER THREE

Lawrence's sexual orientation: a non-hysterical study.

In their introduction to *The Secret Lives of Lawrence of Arabia* the authors, Phillip Knightley and Colin Simpson, wrote: "We make no apology for what some may consider an intrusion (into the most controversial part of Lawrence's private life). The actions of a public figure may be influenced by his private behaviour".[1] Dr John Mack, the author of *A Prince of our Disorder* (another Lawrence biography) deals with the same issue in his chapter on "*Intimacy, Sexuality and Penance*", writing that "a man's sexuality, like the rest of his personal or intimate life, remains his private business, and the biographer may be required to have some justification beyond the potential interest for making its details public".[2] In explaining his own approach to the question he virtually paraphrases the comment of Knightley and Simpson quoted above, writing that: "The biographer's justification for exploring the sexual (or any other intimate aspect of the life of the person being studied) is his belief that it is vitally related to his public life . . ."

In a further chapter, "*Lawrence Assayed*", Mack expounds: "Early in the development of this study I sought to demonstrate the contributions that a thorough study of the psychology of an individual historical figure might make to the understanding of historical events and change".[3] Lawrence, of course, provided the necessary justification for such a study when he confessed that his motive for entering the Middle East conflict was in fact "a personal" one inspired by his affection for a particular Arab. It follows inevitably that his sexual orientation would be called into question.

The recurring speculation concerning his possible homosexuality is fuelled by Lawrence's own writings, for he constantly returns to the theme. For the most part this question has been investigated in a rational manner, but the readers of the 1985 edition of the *Oxford Companion to English Literature* were informed that "Aldington's (*Life of Lawrence*) in 1955 caused outrage by its iconoclastic portrayal of him as a [*sic*] hysterical homosexual". But in fact Aldington wrote, in a chapter devoted to a study of Lawrence's affections: "A circumstance which has to be recorded is that Lawrence had no known love affairs. He was never married or engaged, and, from the sexual point of view, there are no women recorded in his life. He himself claimed that he had lived his life in complete sexual ignorance of women".[4]

In the same chapter Aldington proceeds to discuss "the strong friendship in pre-war days between Lawrence and the Arab boy nicknamed Dahoum, otherwise Sheik Ahmed, and how greatly their living together aroused the suspicions of the Arab villagers".[5] Yet, despite his unconcealed hostility to Lawrence, Aldington's conclusion is that: "The opinions of those who without any concrete evidence assert that Lawrence was a homosexual cancel out the opinions of those who thought he wasn't. So far as I can discover, there is no legal or medical evidence whatsoever".[6] This is hardly an "iconoclastic portrayal of a hysterical homosexual".

While the *Oxford Companion* is manifestly unjust in its comments on Aldington's alleged views, not everyone would agree with Aldington's statement that "Lawrence had no known love affairs". The opening lines of the dedicatory poem in *Seven Pillars* of Wisdom which is addressed to "S.A." are:

> *I loved you, so I drew these tides of men into my hands*
> *and wrote my will across the sky in stars*
> *To earn you Freedom, the seven pillared worthy house,*
> *that your eyes might be shining for me*
> *When we came.*

Surely a clear declaration of love, though not necessarily of homosexual love. One here finds the need for an acceptable definition. Clifford Longley, writing in *The Times* of January 4, 1988, offers: "A homosexual is someone whose sexual feelings are in the direction of his own sex" (a definition with which few surely would quarrel), and then suggests that such a person may, for a number of understandable reasons "commit himself to a life of chastity while still experiencing these attractions and affections". In the view of some of his biographers and friends that is precisely what Lawrence chose to do.

Nevertheless his love affair with Dahoum, whether or not homosexual, is fully testified by Lawrence's own statements. Mack refuses – or at least refrains from – acknowledgement of the association as a "love affair", preferring to describe it as "the most valued relationship of all for Lawrence" in the years before the outbreak of the war. Knightley and Simpson describe Dahoum as "a key figure in Lawrence's private life"[7]: later they express their conviction that "S.A. (*of the Dedication Poem*) is Salim Ahmed, the man nicknamed Dahoum" and that "not only was Salim Ahmed the strongest private motivation for Lawrence's actions in the Middle East, but that his influence lived on to affect Lawrence's post-War behaviour".[8] Lawrence, they wrote, "never fully recovered from Salim Ahmed's death, and that later his strange employment of another youth was, in part, an attempt to recreate this relationship".

By general agreement, Dahoum is "the particular Arab" for whom Lawrence "thought that freedom for the race would be an acceptable present". As, according to Lawrence, Dahoum was "mixed Hittite and

Arab with possibly a strain of Armenian" one is tempted to enquire as to which particular "race" Lawrence may have had in mind. The Hittite suggestion is somewhat puzzling because there have been no Hittites for about three thousand years, so that the discovery of a Hittite strain in Dahoum must be attributed to Lawrence's archaeological perception: he ventured no alternative explanation. There could well have been both Arab and Armenian elements in Dahoum's background, for the place of his birth lay in the paths of conquering – and retreating – armies, from Egypt, from Syria and Babylon, Greece and Rome, and even from distant Mongolia: and the resulting populace formed a Levantine *melange*. All that is known of Lawrence's sympathies for the Armenians derives from an account by John Mack of an interview in which Lawrence suggested to Lincoln Steffens, the American journalist and reformer, that the United States should accept responsibility for the Armenian mandate. Mack reported: "He even lured him into suggesting that the Americans handle the Armenians as they handled the American Indians (by massacring them)".[9] If this is unacceptable as evidence of Lawrence's dedication to the thought of freedom for the Armenian race we are left only with the Arab element. But even here, as Lawrence himself demonstrates, there remains the problem of definition. "A first difficulty of the Arab movement was to say who the Arabs were. Being a manufactured people, their name had been changing in sense slowly year by year. Once it had meant an Arabian. There was a country called Arabia: but this was nothing to the point. There was a language called Arabic; and in it lay the test. It was the current tongue of Syria and Palestine, of Mesopotamia, and of the great peninsula called Arabia on the map."[10]

This was Lawrence's way of saying that the various peoples of Arabia were known as Arabs because they shared a common language. He might have added that the "language called Arabic" (and one is constrained to enquire as to what other name it could claim) had come to be used by non-Arab people because it was the language of the Koran. He made a further reference to the language element in Panarabism in a letter written in 1928: "The Arabic-speaking peoples are as diverse as the English-speaking and equally distinct . . . Our aim was to free from Turkey, and make self-governing, not the Bedouin, who have a secure unenvied freedom; but the settled peoples of Syria and Iraq . . . When people talk of Arab confederations or Empires, they talk fantastically. It will be generations, I expect, before any two Arabic states join voluntarily."[11]

In this statement he appears to make a distinction between the Bedouin and the mixed people of those areas of urban or rural character, as in Syria and Iraq. These two countries house a conglomeration of tribes and nationalities. Iraq has Kurds whose language is Indoaryan, Turcomans speaking a Turkish dialect, Yazidis, Sabaeans and Persians, together with a nomad Bedouin population who form a very small part of the total community. Syria also has Kurdish and Yazidad minorities, besides Druses and Circassians. Lawrence denied to the Syrians the affection he extended to the Bedouin. "The Syrians" he once told Wilfred Blunt "are monkeys and the Arabs lions"; while in *Seven Pillars* he describes them as "an ape-like people having much of the Japanese quickness, but shallow . . . They look outside for help, and expected freedom to come by entreaty, not by sacrifice".[12]

Thus Lawrence himself makes nonsense of the idea of a race for whom he would strive to obtain freedom. This is a good enough example of the "paradoxes and contradictions" which are considered by Mack to be related to "the complexities and ambiguities of his origins, family relationships and childhood development". Mack acknowledges that "Lawrence was a great creator of myths in the sense that his exploits and his own rich account of them – so vivid at times as to give the impression of fiction – served as the basis for the creation by others of the distorted legend which grew around him".[13] To those of Lawrence's "denigrators (who) have found Lawrence to be a charlatan and a liar" he replies "my own examination of the evidence has led me to different conclusions. Lawrence had a compelling need to tell stories, which grew in part out of his deep doubts about his self-worth. Profoundly uncertain about his value, he laid the foundation for the creation alongside of the actual Lawrence of a legendary personality built on the dramatizations and elaborations of his tales."

But Lawrence's *Seven Pillars of Wisdom* should not be regarded as a mere vehicle for myths and legends. Its pages reveal a great deal about the character of the author. Even though it may contain "dramatizations and elaborations" it remains the best record of Lawrence's involvement in the desert war. His "rich account" of his exploits does not fail to yield a great deal of truth to the attentive reader.

Chapter Four

Turkey plans war.
Storrs and McMahon consider the Sharif's
expectations and promises.

During his first year at the Military Intelligence Office in Cairo Lawrence displayed little evidence of any progress towards the fulfilment of his ambition to secure "freedom for the Arabs". He describes the work in which he was engaged in a letter to his brother Will which is dated 17.7.15.[1] "We live in offices and in railway trains: also interviewing Turkish prisoners, & supplying information on any subject that crops up. No civil work however and much map-drawing and geography, both of which please me."

But while he was absorbed in his office routine the cause of Arab freedom was being diligently pursued in other quarters. On the 14th July, 1915, a letter was sent to Sir Henry McMahon, British High Commissioner in Cairo. It was unsigned, but it came from the Sherif Hussein of Mecca; and it was enclosed in another letter, likewise unsigned, which was addressed to Ronald Storrs, the Oriental Secretary in Cairo. To Storrs must be credited the initiative which led to this letter and those others which then followed between Mecca and Cairo. Because of his close involvement with the events of the previous year which preceded the correspondence and his felicitous commitment to daily journals, diaries and copies of the official reports, it has been possible to record the pertinent history.

He has described the visit in April, 1914, of the Emir Abdullah, the second son of the Sherif, to Cairo as a guest of the Khedive. During the course of that visit Abdullah was received by Lord Kitchener. According to Storrs, he "appeared to have something to say, but did not reach the point of saying it. Meanwhile we were advised from Constantinople that such audiences were displeasing to the Sublime Porte, always suspicious of Arab intrigue in the Hejaz and in Syria. Lord Kitchener therefore received Abdallah no more, but before long Abdallah asked me to call".[2]

Abdullah's later account of this visit does not agree with Storrs' version, and the discrepancies between the two have been explained by the Arab writer George Antonius in his description of the Emir's version as "a fair summary of his recollections of the facts"[3]: a reference to Abdullah's reliance on his memory some twenty years after the event. However, Storrs' account receives support from a letter, preserved in the Grey MSS, from Lord Kitchener to Sir W. Tyrrell dated April 26th, 1914. It states that Abdullah "sent for Storrs who under my instructions told him that the Arabs of the Hejaz could expect no encouragement from us and that our only interest in Arabia was the safety and comfort of Indian pilgrims. The Sharif seemed to be disappointed with the result of his visit to Constantinople and with the determination of the Turkish Government to push the railway on to Mecca which he saw would mean the economic death of the camel-owning population of Arabia".

Kitchener's references to "the safety and comfort of India pilgrims", and Abdullah's concern with Turkish plans to extend the railway, call for further explanation. While the line from Damascus to Medina may have provided safer and more comfortable travel for the pilgrims proceeding to Mecca it at the same time possessed considerable strategic value: a value which would be substantially enhanced if the railway was extended, first to Mecca and then to the ports of Jedda and Yanbo. The prospect of these civilising improvements brought consternation to "the camel-owning population" because for centuries the tribes of the area had enjoyed the lucrative monopoly of escorting pilgrims to Mecca. "We sow no corn or *durra*: the *hajis* are our crops" is a saying of the Meccans; and possibly of those others who were able to exploit profitably the opportunities presented by the large numbers of visitors.

Kitchener's concern for the Indian pilgrims was prompted by the experiences of the tens of thousands who each year came to the Hejaz by the sea routes and were transferred to the care of their desert escorts. Many had suffered from the abuses which resulted from inter-tribal rivalries and warfare along the desert routes and which frequently called for armed action on the part of the Sharifian authorities. Abdullah describes an attempt to discipline a troublesome tribe: "the Mutari tribe near Hadhan, a mountain on the Hirrah, on the eastern road from Mecca to Medina, who were frightening the pilgrims and refusing to pay their tithes. Unfortunately they were in a strong position, and our forces were not able to inflict sufficient punishment on them".[4]

But however divided the tribes may have been by their rivalries they were strongly united in their opposition to the railway and its proposed extension, and accordingly prepared to support the Sharif in any struggle against Turkish "oppression", when this meant the development of the railway, and for "Arab independence", where this meant the freedom to control the desert routes and exact their traditional tolls from the pilgrims.

Storrs relates that during the meeting with Abdullah referred to in Kitchener's letter of April 26th the Emir asked "whether Great Britain would present the Grand Shariff with a dozen, or even half-dozen machine guns. When I enquired what could possibly be their purpose, he replied (like all re-armers) 'for defence'; and, pressed further, added that defence would be against attack from the Turks. I needed no special instructions to inform him that we could never entertain the idea of supplying arms to be used against a friendly power".[5] But before many more months had passed there developed doubts in the minds of the British in Cairo as to how much longer Turkey would remain "a friendly power", for after the outbreak of war between Britain and Germany apprehension grew that Turkey might choose to join the Central Powers. Storrs recorded "our constant preoccupation with the threat of Turkey on the Canal; less for its military effect than for the repercussion upon a Moslem Egypt". There could be no certainty that a Moslem Egypt would lend support to the infidel occupying forces if they came into conflict with a Moslem power.

It became clear that when Storrs penned this last comment he could not have been aware that a secret treaty of Turco-German alliance had already been signed (on August 2nd, in fact) and that the Dardenelles had been mined. A few weeks later it was reported that the Turks were massing large numbers of troops close to the frontier with Sinai, but it was October 29th before Turkish destroyers signalled the opening of hostilities against the Entente by the shelling of Russian Black Sea ports. In Cairo this news was preceded by the report that two thousand armed Bedouin had crossed the Sinai frontier and had occupied wells some twenty miles inside Egyptian territory.

The possibility of these last developments had been exercising the mind of Storrs for several weeks, and in the early part of September the emerging threat prompted him to give consideration to the prospects of reopening with Mecca the very approaches which in April, at the time of Abdullah's visit, he had felt obliged to reject. With the encouragement of Clayton (at that time the Agent in Cairo of the Sudan Government, whose Sirdar, Sir Reginald Wingate, controlled the Sinai Peninsula with its Palestinian frontier), he wrote to Kitchener in England suggesting the advantages of securing the neutrality, or even the alliance, of the Hejaz in the event of war between Britain and Turkey.

Kitchener's reply came back without delay. Dated September 24th, 1914, and addressed to H.M.'s Representative in Cairo, it carried the momentous message: "Tell Storrs to send secret and carefully chosen messengers from me to Sharif Abdallah to ascertain whether 'should present armed German influence in Constantinople coerce Sultan against his will, and Sublime Porte, to acts of aggression and war against Great Britain, he and his father and the Arabs of the Hejaz would be with us or against us'."[6]

Storrs' messenger left Cairo on October 5th, arriving back on the 30th, the day on which Britain declared war on Turkey. The reply he brought back from the Sherif was elaborately worded, invoking God at proper intervals: it could reasonably be construed as a declaration of pious willingness to help those who "stretch forth a helping hand" to Islam and Moslems, and it enabled Kitchener to send to Abdullah on the last day of the month a cable inviting the assistance of "the Arab nation" in the war against Turkey.[7] A further visit to the Hejaz was made by Storrs' messenger in November: he returned to Cairo on December 10th.

Storrs has chosen to remain silent on this period of protracted negotiations which preceded the opening stages of the McMahon-Hussein Correspondence, but the writer James Morris, who described Storrs as "the most brilliant of these diplomats" and a "man of exquisite sensibilities", has made his own contribution to our knowledge of Hussein's methods in playing his political hand. "The nearer war came . . . the more clearly the Grand Sharif foresaw in the tumult of conflict his opportunity for a decisive breach with Turkey . . . Backed by the agile and polite Abdullah, he was now determined to detach the Hejaz from Turkish sovereignty, and he was beginning to cherish the dream of an independent Hashemite Empire, uniting the whole of the Arab Middle East. If war came, he thought, some of those portentous ends might soon be attained: either by standing at Turkey's side, and earning the rewards of loyalty, or by seizing the chance to mount a proper full-scale rebellion, banners, armies and all. He understandably put his own interests first, and neither the Turks nor the British could be quite certain which way his fancies or judgements would fall."[8]

It is likely that until the arrival of the crucial moment the Sherif himself could not be sure. After the outbreak of hostilities he obeyed

Turkish orders to raise troops for the Ottoman armies, a task which he entrusted to his son Ali, but found it more difficult to respond satisfactorily to the Caliph's instructions to him to declare from Mecca the Holy War against the British and their allies. "To this", James Morris wrote, " he returned a series of sandy answers. Nothing could be nearer his heart, he said, than the holy war launched in righteousness by the Caliph. He was the servant of the Caliph, and prayed constantly for the success of his arms and the abasement of the infidels (may God lay them low!). All the same, he was sure the Caliph would realise that if he openly declared his endorsement of the *jihad*, the British Navy would instantly pounce upon the Hejaz shoreline, starving or bombarding the people into – if he might venture to use the word – rebellion. He would of course (added the Grand Sharif) raise recruits for the Turkish cause; and he prayed to God that all blessings would be bestowed upon the leaders of the holy war, and bring success to a cause so dear to the hearts of all true Moslems."[9]

Aided by his genius for circumspection the Grand Sherif was able to follow closely the ebb and flow of the opposing Powers until he reached the point, in the second week of July, 1915, when he decided to take the plunge and to write the first of his letters to McMahon, to which we have referred. This stated his conditions for accepting the support of Great Britain while at the same time affirming specific territorial demands on behalf (as he phrased it) of "the whole of the Arab nation", including, in his definition, the entire Arabian Peninsula from the Mediterranean to the borders of Persia, and from the 37° of latitude to the Red Sea and the Indian Ocean, "with the exception of the position of Aden to remain as it is". In return the "Arab Government of the Sherif" (an institution which at the time existed only in his mind) would generously grant to England "the preference in all economic enterprises in the Arab countries whenever conditions of enterprises are otherwise equal" (whatever that might mean). And, in addition, "both high contracting parties to offer mutual assistance, to the best ability of their military and naval forces, to face any foreign power which may attack either party".[10] The prospect of the Arab Navy offering assistance to British warships in an emergency would surely have been enhanced if the Sherif could have stretched his generosity by including the services of the equally mythical Arab Air Force.

McMahon's reply was dated August 30th, 1915, and observed the required polite formalities, being addressed "To the excellent and well-born Sayid, the descendant of Sharifs, the Crown of the Proud, Scion of Mohammed's Tree and Branch of the Kuraishite trunk, him of the Exalted Presence and of the Lofty Rank, Sayid son of Sayid, Sharif son of Sharif, the Venerable, Honoured Sayid, His Excellency the Sharif Hussein, Lord of the Many, Amir of Mecca the Blessed, the lodestar of the Faithful and the cynosure of all devout Believers, may his Blessing descend upon the people in their multitude". In a somewhat less exalted style, it proceeded sensibly to point out that "with regard to the question of limits and boundaries it would appear to be premature to consume our time in discussing such details in the heat of war, and while, in many portions of them, the Turk is now in effective occupation; especially as we have learned, with surprise and regret, that some of the Arabs in those very parts, far from assisting us, are neglecting this their supreme opportunity and are lending their arms to the German and the Turk, to the new spoiler and the old oppressor".[11]

The co-operation between the Arabs and the enemies of the Allies to which McMahon referred had become common knowledge, but the Sherif, although equally aware of the situation, preferred to regard reference to it as a rebuke, and complained in his September 9th reply to the High Commissioner of "the tone of coldness and hesitation with regard to our essential point (the limits and boundaries)." He offered the assurance that "the whole country, together with those who you say are submitting themselves to Turco-German orders, are all awaiting the result of these negotiations, which are dependent only on your refusal or acceptance of the question of the limits and on your declaration of safeguarding their religion first and then the rest of rights from any harm or danger". He then, with commendable piety, invoked a Third Party, writing: "In all cases it is only God's will which shall be executed, and it is God who is the real factor in everything";

explaining that "Up to the present moment I am myself with all my might carrying out in my country all things in conformity with the Islamic Law, all things which tend to benefit the rest of the Kingdom (?), and I shall continue to do so until it pleases God to order otherwise."[12]

To this letter McMahon replied on October 24th, offering comments on the "question of limits and boundaries" and reassurances concerning the areas which can "be said to be purely Arab", specifying other areas which should be "excluded from the limits demanded". He then raised the problem of "the interests of (Britain's) ally, France", and went on to ask for Arab recognition of Britain's own special interests in the "*vilayets* of Baghdad and Basra" which, he wrote, would "necessitate special administrative arrangements"[13] on the part of Britain.

In his November 5th reply the Sherif refused to renounce entirely the Arab claims to the Iraqi *vilayets*, but generously condescended that "in order to render an accord easy . . . we might agree to leave under British administration for a short time . . . those districts now occupied by the British troops . . . against a suitable sum paid as compensation to the Arab Kingdom for the period of occupation".[14] The close involvement by the Government of India, and its claims in that area were not taken into account.

McMahon replied on December 14th, avoiding further discussion on the Iraqi *vilayets*: carefully reminding the Sherif that the interests of Britain's ally, France, are involved in the Syrian *vilayets* of Aleppo and Beirut (which the Sharif claimed in his letter of November 5th to be "purely Arab *vilayets*): and concluding: "As an earnest of our intentions, and in order to aid you in your efforts in our just cause, I am sending you by your trustworthy messenger a sum of twenty thousand pounds".[15] For this generous gesture he was rewarded by the Sherif's response dated January 1st, 1916, referring to Iraq and conceding that "as to the matter of occupation we . . . leave the determination of the amount to the perception of

(Great Britain's) wisdom and justice".

"The amount", it was made clear in that letter, referred to "the matter of compensation for the period of occupation".[16] The audacity of this demand for cash payment in respect of territories to which the Sherif could have had no possible claim (and whose people were for the most part fiercely hostile towards him) could call for only one response. McMahon wrote that "concerning the *vilayet* of Baghdad (we) will take the question into careful consideration when the enemy has been defeated and the time for peaceful settlement arrives", and then followed this, perhaps with intention to soften what may have been regarded as a rebuke, with a reckless request to be informed "of any manner in which we can assist you" and an assurance that "your requests will always receive our immediate consideration".[17]

To this the Sherif lost no time in replying. With unrestrained enthusiasm his letter of February 18th told of the military moves he was planning: "forces, especially from the people of the country and the surrounding Arab regions at Aleppo and the south of Mosul, whose total is calculated at no less than 100,000": the despatch of his son Ali "to Medina with sufficient forces",[18] and so on. Needless to say, the 100,000 warriors never materialised, while it took four months for Ali to reach the outskirts of Medina, and then rather less than four weeks to retreat 200 miles to the distant refuge of Rabegh, safely out of the range of Turkish guns.

But the mere promises themselves smoothed the Sherif's path towards the more significant part of his letter: his response to McMahon's polite mention of possible assistance. Following the promise of military action he wrote:

"It remains for us to state what we need at present:-

Firstly. – The amount of £50,000 in gold for the monthly pay of the troops levied, and other things the necessity of which need no explanation. We beg you to send it with all possible haste.

Secondly. – 20,000 sacks of rice, 15,000 sacks of flour, 3,000 sacks of barley, 150 sacks of coffee, 150 sacks of sugar, 5,000 rifles of the modern pattern and the necessary ammunition, and 100 boxes of the two sample cartridges (enclosed) and of Martini-Henry cartridges and "Aza", that is those of the rifles of the factory of St. Etienne in France, for the use of those two kinds of rifles of our tribes; it will not be amiss to send 500 boxes of both kinds."

Storrs could not have been alone in his astonishment at the immediate response of the British authorities to these unreserved demands. In his capacity of Oriental Secretary he had been personally involved in the preparation and translation of these letters, and in his memoirs he recalled: "Our Arabic correspondence with Mecca was prepared by Ruhi, a fair though not a profound Arabist (and a better agent than scholar); and checked, often under high pressure, by myself. I had no Deputy, Staff or office; so that during my absence on mission the work was carried on better perhaps – by others, but the continuity was lost. Husain's letters on the other hand were written in an obscure and tortuous prose in which the purity of the Hejaz Arabic was overlaid and tainted with Turkish idioms and syntax . . . As I struggled through his difficult writing and even more difficult Arabic, I found myself murmuring

*'In matter of commerce the fault of the Dutch
Is offering too little and asking too much'*

for he demanded, with the exception of Aden, the whole of Arabic-speaking South-West Asia. The High Commissioner rightly refused to commit the government to precise areas, particularly in Western Syria and Lower Mesopotamia, and as time went on (for our communications were slow and risky) boundary questions became less, and the Hejaz revolt more, immediate.

"It was at that time and still is my opinion that the Sharif opened his mouth and the British Government their purse a great deal too wide. It seemed to me that having been little more than a sort of Erastian Administrator for the Turks, the Sharif and his people would be well treated and amply rewarded if they were gratuitously enabled to defeat and evict their traditional enemy, and were guaranteed immunity from external aggression in their permanent possession of the two Holy Cities, together with the independent sovereignty of their country of origin, the Hejaz. But Husain claimed to wield a general mandate as King of the Arabs for a Spiritual Pan-Araby, to which he knew better than we that he could lay no kind of genuine claim. Of the great Arab peoples of North Africa some must repudiate his Sunni claims to the Caliphate: others, like Egypt and the Sudan, vastly preferred their own superior civilization. The Christians of the Lebanon could never acknowledge him, Mesopotamia was mainly Shia; to the south the Imaam Yahya (Ruler of the Yemen) recognized him as nothing at all, whilst with Ibn Sa'ud on his immediate East he had long been on the terms which were to lead to his final ruin and exile. There was in a word not even as much prospect of Arab union then as there is now. When in addition we reflected that 90 per cent of the Moslem World must call Husain a renegade and traitor to the Vicar of God, we could not conceal from ourselves (and with difficulty from him) that his pretensions bordered on the tragicomic. Nevertheless, this partial sacrifice of his name before Islam, vital to our cause though also greatly to his interest, imposed upon us the real obligation of raising and maintaining his prestige to the limit of the possible so that for this and other reasons we were in the end committed far more deeply in bullion, in munitions of war, and in promises very hard to fulfil, than most of us had dreamed of in Sept. 1914".[19]

McMahon's final letter in the Correspondence was dated March 10th, 1916. It confirmed to the Sherif that the British Government had approved his requests and finally, perhaps to convey to the Sherif that the Moslems enjoyed no monopoly in the matter, it informed Hussein: "We ask God to prosper your endeavours and to further the work which you have taken in hand".[20] But according to Mousa, the Hashemite historian, the Sherif was not at that moment "in haste to declare the revolt",[21] which was originally set for August 1916, and was only prompted to make a move when he received, in April 1916, news of a Turkish force of 3,500 men accompanied by a German military mission led by Baron Von Stotzingen moving from Damascus towards Medina.

Cairo was first advised of the Sherif's alarm in a telegraphed message to McMahon on May 23rd: "Sharif's son Abdallah urgently requires Storrs to come to Arabian coast to meet him".[22] Accordingly Storrs set out from Cairo on the 28th, accompanied by Hogarth, Captain K. Cornwallis, and £10,000 in gold. Abdullah did not meet him on his arrival in the Hejaz, but left a signed note saying that he would be represented by his younger brother Zaid, and an unsigned note requesting "immediately 500 rifles of same pattern as those already sent us . . . also 4 machine guns, both with ammunition".[23] To these request Zaid, when he appeared, added a further list in which Storrs "observed the mention of £50,000 with an additional £20,000 making a total of £70,000". When Storrs explained "that the first sum would be forthcoming so soon as we had certain news that the rising had begun" Zaid announced "that it began yesterday at Medina", but on further questioning explained that by "began" he had meant "was timed to begin" or "doubtless began".[24] Of course it had not, and Storrs returned to Cairo in time to learn of the untimely death of his "dear old chief", Lord Kitchener.

CHAPTER FIVE

Lawrence's views of the Sharif's campaign:
His transfer to the Arab Bureau

"It is very difficult to assess Lawrence's role during his two years in Cairo" wrote Dr Mack;[1] but perhaps that difficulty arises only when it is first assumed that Lawrence *possessed* a "role" in that period other than the performance of routine duties. We have seen his description of these in the letter he wrote to his brother Will in July 1915, while in another letter, dated 28th February 1916, he complained "We do nothing here except sit and think our harassing schemes of Arabian policy". However, in the following month he was sent out to Mesopotamia on an ill-fated mission to persuade the Turks to raise the siege of General Townshend's forces on payment by the British of one million pounds, later raised to two millions. The other members of the mission were Aubrey Herbert, a Turkophile and a Member of Parliament, and Colonel Beach of the Mesopotamian Army, but curiously neither is mentioned in Mack's account, which states simply that "Lawrence was sent by the High Commissioner in Egypt, Henry McMahon, on a mission to negotiate with the Turkish commander",[2] and later, that "Lawrence's mission" was unsuccessful.

One could be forgiven for assuming from Mack's wording that Lawrence alone comprised the mission, though in truth while the qualifications of Herbert and Beach are obvious, Lawrence's role has been widely qustioned. McMahon wrote to Sir Percy Cox, the chief political officer in Iraq, that he was sending Lawrence because "he is one of the best of our very able intelligence staff here and has a thorough knowledge of the Arab question in all its bearings". It is very difficult to understand how "a thorough knowledge of the Arab question" could possibly assist in persuading Turks to forgo the capture of a British force in exchange for hard cash, and in the end the only tangible evidence of Lawrence's participation was the production of one of his celebrated reports.

According to Colonel Stirling, who worked closely with Lawrence in the later stages of the desert campaign, "he criticized the quality of the stones used for lithographing, the system of berthing barges alongside the quays, the inefficiency of the cranes for handling stores, the lack of system in shunting and entraining on the railways, the want of adequate medical stores, the blindness of the medical authorities and their want of imagination as to their probable requirements. And, horror of horrors, he criticized the Higher Command and the conduct of the campaign in general".[3] Nevertheless he failed to obtain the release of a single British prisoner.

On his return to Cairo he resumed his interest in the Sherif's campaign. In Chapter Seven of *Seven Pillars* he summarised the state of affairs in the Hejaz in the early autumn of 1916, pronouncing that they had gone "from bad to worse" and giving his reasons for this deplorable situation. According to him the Commander-in-Chief in Egypt, Sir Archibald Murray, "could not be entrusted with the Arabian affair; for neither he nor his staff had the ethnological competence needed to deal with so curious a problem. On the other hand, he could make the spectacle of the High Commission running a private war sufficiently ridiculous. His was a very nervous mind, fanciful and essentially competitive". Furthermore, he had failed to provide "proper liaison for the Arab forces in the field": a somewhat surprising criticism in the light of Lawrence's statement (in the first paragraph of the same chapter) that the Sherif's "eventual rebellion and opening of his coast to our ships and help took us and them (those who had not 'really believed that the Sherif would fight') by surprise"; which seems to suggest that any failure in communication was the fault of the Arabs rather than of the British.

But in any case Lawrence's criticisms – or excuses for the Arab failure – were completely unjustified and contrary to the facts of the case, for in June 1916 at the first news of the Sherifian actions against Medina the British sent from the Sudan "3,000 rifles, ammunition, and large supplies of barley, rice, flour and coffee", together with two mountain batteries and six machine-guns. The guns were accompanied by Egyptian Moslems, in deference to the Sherif's ban on the open admission into the holy territory of the Hejaz of infidels.

British warships went into action throughout the Red Sea. It was reported that by the end of July 1916 the Royal Navy had landed £528,000 in gold, 22,000 additional rifles and 14 guns. During the weeks which followed the total of rifles sent to the Hejaz by the British Government was near to 60,000, according to Storrs, to the considerable profit of the desert Arabs, who were known to be selling quantities of these arms to the Turks. While this last activity revealed a commendable spirit of enterprise on the part of the Arabs, it hardly fulfilled the purpose for which the rifles had been despatched, and Storrs in particular confessed to be uneasy with this situation, recording in his journal: "Though it is, as I trust you realise, infinitely more than half the battle to have lit this candle, the wick is as yet far from burning in that hard gem-like flame I could have desired. The Arabs, as you are doubtless aware, are naked, unarmed, and more esurient than the Greek himself: further they have not one *bobbo* to their name. We are therefore at present under the obligation to them, and the necessity for ourselves, of pouring into the yawning mouth of Jedda a ceaseless stream of corn, cash and cartridges, for the use of a people highly sensitive to any action (even for the maintenance of public health or security) which can be interpreted before the Arab world as an impingement upon their independence."

As the bulk of these supplies were being despatched from Egyptian or Sudanese ports it would have been impossible to conceal from common knowledge in those areas that the constant procession of merchant vessels down the Red Sea was engaged in bearing treasures for the Arabs of the Hejaz; and Storrs reported that there was in Egypt "a popular theory that the Sharif was playing with the English and that he had already extracted from them some three million pounds".[4]

Another of Lawrence's complaints about General Murray was that he wanted "no competing campaigns in his sphere": in other words, no "side-shows". But even if Murray was in fact failing to carry out his Middle East defence responsibilities in accordance with the ideas of the junior officer in the map department, he nevertheless did not fail to ensure the constant flow of supplies to the Hejaz, and when eventually an order was issued to stop the supplies it came from Whitehall and not from Egypt. If at the same time he was endeavouring to avoid diversions – "side-shows" – it could well have been due to his simultaneous involvement in the reconstitution of the Mediterranean Expeditionary Force (M.E.F.), newly evacuated from the disasters of Gallipoli, into a new fighting unit, the Egyptian Expeditionary Force (E.E.F.); the threat of the Senussi rising in the Western Desert: the need to reinforce the hard-pressed Anglo-Indian troops in Mesopotamia; and the strengthening of the Suez Canal defences against the menace of Kressenstein in the Sinai Peninsula.

Kressenstein had been appointed Chief of Staff to the Turkish Army VIII Corps, and was known to have assembled a force of 20,000 supported by nine batteries of field artillery and a battery of 5.9-inch howitzers.[9] Sir John Maxwell, responsible for the defence of the Canal and its approaches, saw these preparations as a threat by invasion to Egypt and asked Murray for twelve divisions to meet it. A further demand on Murray's resources came from the Western Front in Europe, where the battles of the Somme had taken a toll of 420,000 British lives, and reinforcements were sought from Egypt.

In the circumstances it could hardly be considered remarkable that Murray lacked the enthusiasm for yet another diversion, especially one which posed as many problems and uncertainties as did the Hejaz. His doubts were shared by others. Sir Edward Grey, the Foreign Secretary, expressed his disquiet to McMahon before the end of March, 1916, saying "We are giving arms and money and the sole question is whether the Arabs will do their part". Clayton, then Head of Military Intelligence, revealed to Mark Sykes in April his awareness of "a certain rapprochement" between some Arab groups and the Turks. Sir Arthur Nicholson, Permanent Under-Secretary of State for Foreign Affairs, made his protest: "As regards . . . the Sherif, I think we have gone far enough . . . we should wait for some action on his part. Hitherto, we have had plenty of promises from him – but nothing more – while we have given him, beyond assurances, arms and money".

There were other problems, too, of the sort which may have tested what Lawrence named Murray's "ethnological competence" in that they arose from the loyalty of the Arab troops in the Ottoman armies to their Moslem leaders in the service of the Turks. Wingate, regarded as a confirmed Arabist, at one point admitted that "the Moslems in general have hitherto regarded the Hejaz revolt, and our share in it, with suspicion and dislike", and as time went on it became increasingly evident that until the final collapse of the Turco-German forces the Grand Sherif and his rebellion had secured the involvement of a very small minority only of the desert tribes, and beyond the Hejaz virtually none of the town and village populations. Husein's promise to raise a force of 250,000 against the Turks never approached realisation.

Lawrence grew more and more eager for firsthand knowledge, and at last asked Storrs point blank to take him down on his next voyage to Jeddah. Nothing from Storrs' point of view could have pleased him more, and permission from his military superiors was granted with relief.

Why should his superiors have been so pleased to have the opportunity of getting rid of him? Some light is thrown on this in Brian Gardner's biography of Allenby. Writing of Lawrence's second-lieutenant period he reported: "In Egypt, his task was to interrogate prisoners, draw up manuals on Arab affairs for officers posted to the area, and other fairly routine intelligence tasks. He was not very good at the work and his superiors, who were probably better at it then he was, had a low opinion of his usefulness; he became more and more side-tracked into comparatively unimportant map-room tasks. He was not popular. Lawrence, unlike most of the staff in Cairo, had a good opinion of his own capabilities, and did not hesitate to make this plain going as far, on occasion, as rewriting official reports. He was inclined to provoke, procrastinate, and generally antagonize many people with whom he came into contact."[5]

Confirmation of this portrait comes from Lawrence himself when revealing the strategy he employed in his efforts to achieve his transfer to the Arab Bureau: "I decided that I must escape at once, if ever. A straight request was refused; so I took to stratagems. I became, on the telephone (G.H.Q. were at Ismailia, and I in Cairo) quite intolerable to the Staff on the Canal. I took every opportunity to rub into them their comparative ignorance and inefficiency in the department of intelligence (not difficult!) and irritated them yet further by literary airs, correcting Shavian split infinitives and tautologies in their reports. In a few days they were bubbling over on my account, and at last determined to endure me no longer."[6] The most sympathetic of his biographers could hardly ignore this evidence of his behaviour, but Mack seems to dismiss the subject by linking Lawrence's ambitions while a second lieutentant with "the frustration imposed by his junior status (which) may have caused him to react in ways that only accentuated his immaturity".

Clayton, in charge of the Arab Bureau, agreed in response to Lawrence's request to make the required application to the Foreign Office, giving Lawrence "this strategic opportunity to ask for ten days' leave, saying that Storrs was going down to Jedda on business with the Grand Sherif, and that I would like a holiday and joyride in the Red Sea with him". The journey to Jeddah which gave Lawrence his first opportunity to visit the Hejaz was Storrs' third. He records them all in his meticulous journals: his entry for "12.x.16. On the train from Cairo little Lawrence my super-cerebral companion". A later entry warns the reader that "Lawrence's account of the voyage, particularly of our conversations, is heightened by the use of what *The Thousand Nights and a Night* calls *Lisan-al-Hal*, the 'tongue of the state of the occasion': i.e., the language deemed appropriate to the characters and circumstances".

Chapter Six

Storr's account of October 1916.
Arab demands: gold and Hashemite rule.

The October 1916 journey to the Hejaz had not been planned by the High Commissioner or by Storrs, who had returned from the area at the end of the previous month. "I had hardly returned to Alexandria" he wrote "when we received a telegram from the Sharif Abdallah begging me to run back to Arabia and have a few words with him. (From time to time henceforth I would receive a cable from Mecca, through Jedda and Suakin; 'Please come as soon as possible and bring with you the same amount as you brought for me the first time'; expensive invitations, in which my *beaux yeux* were possibly not in the front plane of intention)."[1]

Despite his prompt response to Abdullah's request the Emir was not at the British Consulate to greet him when he arrived in Jeddah on the morning of the 16th. Storrs found the British Representative, Colonel Wilson, "in a rather defiant mood: uncertain whom he represented and from whom he was to take orders":[2] a state of affairs which could have reflected conditions in Cairo, from where he might have been called upon to report either to the Foreign Office representatives, or to the Commander-in-Chief, Egypt (who controlled supplies and war materials): or to the Sirdar, at that time Governor of the Sudan, later to succeed McMahon as High Commissioner. Furthermore, in naval matters he would have to refer to Admiral Wemyss, who in turn took his orders from Delhi although he operated from Ismailia.

Storrs' meeting with Abdullah, later in the day, was soured by a message conveyed in a telegram from the Sirdar, which had just arrived, giving notice "of H.M.G.'s final decision to send no British troops to Hejaz . . . that the Brigade, more than once promised by H.M.G., would not be sent; and that the flight of aeroplanes, promised and dispatched to Rabugh was being withdrawn on the very day that the appearance of Turkish planes had been announced".[3] Wilson read the telegram in English: Storrs had the privilege of translating it into Arabic for the benefit of Abdullah. Its contents were discussed until 7.15 in the evening, when Abdullah left, promising to return at ten the following morning.

On the morning of the 17th, Storrs was able to confer with Said Ali Pasha, the Sherifian Chief of Staff in direct charge of the Egyptian Artillery detachment which the Sherif had requested for use against the Turks, raising the delicate problem of the relations between his trained soldiers and the Hejaz tribes. "He says the Arabs are a cowardly and undisciplined rabble: and fears (not, it must be admitted, without reason) lest they should scamper off one day, leaving the gunners to suffer death, after nameless mutilations at the hands of the Turks. He complains moreover of their habit of occasionally discharging their pieces over the camp at night: and says that many, having received their rifles and ammunition from the Sherif, disappeared into the desert, to be seen no more. He adds that Abdallah is well aware of these little deficiencies, but that the Sharif is not, and that he will listen to no criticism of the Arab forces."[4]

When Abdullah arrived at ten o'clock, he produced a telegram from his brother Feisal "to the effect that two Turkish aeroplanes had begun to operate, to the dismay bordering upon panic of the Arabs. He said that unless these were driven off or in some way checked, the Arabs would disperse". The discussion which followed this was interrupted several times by telephone calls from the Sherif in Mecca "appealing for the Brigade and the Planes, till (Storrs) had to remind him that we had not, unfortunately, got the British Army drawn up in the Consulate back garden".⁵ This continued until lunch-time, when Abdullah departed, expressing the wish to see Storrs alone during the afternoon.

When he returned he expressed his deep disappointment that Storrs "had been unable to bring the £10,000 requested in his telegram". In response Storrs "explained to him without any *ménagement* that we had considered that the not illiberal subsidy we were supplying to his father should suffice for the operations of the sons also": a reference to the £125,000 monthly payments in gold which the British had been making to the Sherif.

Abdullah then raised the question of "the title of *Jalala* – Majesty and *Malek* – King of the 'Arab Nation'", upon which Storrs reminded Abdullah that such a move would provide "yet further food for the suspicions, and possibly hostility, of the Imam, Idrisi, Ibn Sa'ud and others. At least let them hold the country, before beginning to alter its status. He seemed to agree to these arguments, and said that he would use them, when he returned to his father".⁶ At the dinner which followed Storrs learned of the suspicions of Colonel Brémond, head of the French Mission in Jedda, "that the Sharif was considering peace terms from the Turks: so I took" (wrote Storrs) "occasion to ask Abdallah quietly whether any feelers had been put out. He said that several unofficial tentatives had been made, but that his father had always replied that the Arabs were now allies of Great Britain and could make no peace apart from her".⁷

On the following day, the 18th, they both left Jeddah: Abdullah to proceed to Mecca, Storrs to return to Cairo. He did not come to the Hejaz again until the following December, when he had his first meetings with the Grand Sherif and the Amir Faisal. This was his fourth and last visit, and Storrs used the occasion to point out to the the Sherif "that although H.M.G. had supplied close upon 60,000 rifles, with munitions and supplies corresponding, to the Hejaz, no sort of army appeared to be forthcoming or even in the process of creation".⁸

He had a further complaint. "Before leaving Jeddah after my previous visit I had taken occasion to repeat by telephone to Mecca my observations to Abdallah on the proposed assumption of the style of King. I warned him that such a step, the various objections to which he already knew, taken without consulting his principal Ally, must embarrass all concerned, reasoned with him and at last persuaded him to postpone the matter until His Majesty's Government should have had time to appreciate its full implications. Pleased with my success, I had telegraphed it to Cairo and taken the next boat north, to be greeted at Suez with the interesting news that the Sharif had three days previously proclaimed himself King. Considering the frankness and intimacy of our relations from the beginning of things, I was incensed by this treatment, and on this next visit to Jeddah told his Majesty so, without mincing words".[9]

On his way back to Cairo Storrs went ashore at Yanbo in order to meet Feisal. On the previous day "there had been a regular panic ashore, and many notables including Feisal had boarded H.M.S. *Hardinge*. The Turks moreover were reported closer still, some said within six miles, and in greater numbers than hitherto suspected. The Arabs had absolutely declined to hold the trench (which covered the plain across which the Turks must advance) and were hoping that the ship's guns would command the plain".[10]

At his meeting with Feisal ("whose mien generally is that of one chastened by failure") Storrs "took the opportunity of pointing out to him that, after the recent retreats, the courage of the Arab tribesmen stood in some need of vindication in the eyes of the world; even if they were for the moment unable to face their foes in the open field, their intimate knowledge of their own mountainous country should surely render them redoubtable enemies in guerilla warfare". But he was left with no illusions concerning the Arabs' ability to fulfil their expected role in the fighting, writing that "the incoherent and spasmodic nature of Arab organization and operations is an additional proof, if such were needed, of the necessity of one supreme and independent control of the campaign".[11]

Lawrence of Arabia with the Emir Feisal.

CHAPTER SEVEN

Abdullah's account.
The Hejaz becomes a Kingdom.

The account of the October meeting and conversations in the last chapter is derived largely from Storrs' reminiscences and journals. There are, however, two other versions on record: the three fail to agree. Lawrence wrote his version after the war: Abdullah's *Memoirs*, which include his account of these events, was written a quarter of a century later, being first published in the Jerusalem Arabic edition (*Muthakkarati*) in 1945 and in an English translation in 1950. Mousa acknowledges the problems of recall, confirming that "one finds some discrepancy in the writings of Abdullah, Storrs and Lawrence about these meetings" and suggesting that such discrepancies are "perhaps explained by the fact that, writing several years after the event, they were all influenced by the subsequent history of the revolt".[1]

While this might be said of the writings of Lawrence and Abdullah, Storrs has explained how he was able in his autobiography to provide detailed accounts of past events which might otherwise have had to depend on memory: "I had . . . the habit ever since leaving England in 1904 of writing weekly to my mother, and of enclosing briefly minuted items I thought might entertain her. All these documents she kept with my letters, including a few diaries of special missions or journeys during the War . . . These surviving records I have wherever possible quoted in original with, I hope, a gain in immediacy and actuality by recording not only historic facts, sometimes already known, but also my own feelings at the time; with stories and details, trifling in themselves yet constituting atmosphere – the hardest of all things to recapture after many years".[2]

Furthermore, he was able to call on official reports retained and available in the Public Records Office in London, so that there remain comparatively few gaps in his narrative. On occasion he is able to add an authenticating passage, such as his note on the September 1916 Hejaz journey: "Of this journey the journal survives",[3] enabling him to write without being "influenced by the subsequent history of the revolt".

But Abdullah's account is totally at variance with the others. He states that he received Storrs and *Lawrence* at his camp on his arrival at Jedda, while Storrs wrote that he was accompanied not by Lawrence but by Wilson. Lawrence, in the words of Mousa, "had no official capacity".[4] Storrs' diary records the timing of Abdullah's return call on that afternoon, but in Abdullah's version the Emir calls on Wilson the following morning, and "after the usual greetings Storrs said: 'My colleague, Captain Lawrence, and I came here to offer you the help of Great Britain in the Arab revolt, and we were glad and proud to do so, but unfortunately we have just received a telegram which has upset all our plans. It has been translated into Arabic and when you have heard it you will appreciate our embarrassment. It was a lengthy telegram, and the gist of it was that the news of the Arab revolt had been received in India with the greatest indignation and that agents or friends of the Germans and the Turks there had made capital out of it, maintaining that the Allies had occupied sacred Muslim areas. The British Government could not risk trouble in India and had therefore decided to withdraw all British and French military missions. Britain would continue to offer other forms of help such as arms, supplies and money but His Majesty's Government was of the opinion that it was better for the future of Arab liberty if foreign forces were not concerned in the revolt".[5]

There is hardly one word of truth in the entire account. One can understand Abdullah's reluctance to record the fact that this visit of Storrs was a response to the Emir's request for Storrs to return to the Hejaz to "have a few words" (and bring £10,000 in gold) but nothing could be more absurd than the statement that Storrs and Lawrence had come on an official mission to *offer* "the help of Great Britain in the Arab revolt", when that help had been so generously given over a period of several months. The telegram, as we shall show, was in no way concerned with Indian views on Allied participation in the Hejaz revolt, and, far from discouraging the employment of "foreign forces" it specifically stated that the British could not object to any military assistance which France was able to offer. But Abdullah continued: "This telegram was a heavy blow to me . . . So I said, 'Please read the telegram again so that I may appreciate it fully'. When he had finished reading, I said, 'I fully understand what you say', and gravely took my leave".

He then, he says, went "at once to the house of Colonel Brémond" who asked him what he proposed to do". 'It means concluding peace', I said. 'The Turks have offered to concede our demands with the guarantee of the German Emperor and we shall have to accept. I am going back now and our Government will resign and another Government will be formed which will conclude peace. We shall get what we want, and our allies will have no right to blame us in that, they have refused us the help we need".

There is no support anywhere for these statements, although they may reflect some echo of Brémond's suspicions, conveyed to Storrs at dinner on the 17th October, "that the Sharif was considering peace terms from the Turks", although any such rumours could hardly have been connected with Abdullah's subsequent reaction to the telegram. A possible explanation of Abdullah's story might be that after learning that the Sherif's secret correspondence with the Turks at that time had come to the knowledge of the British, he composed the fictitious terms of the telegram as some sort of justification for what might otherwise have been regarded as treachery.

The British Government's decision not to send troops to the Hejaz was confirmed in two telegrams, which have never before been published. The first is preserved in Foreign Office Records, under File No. F.O.371/6237. Page 72 of that file records:

Foreign Office Telegram No.744 dated 14th September 1916.

No.744. Your Telegram No.778.

On September 2nd War Committee considered proposal to send Sudanese troops to Hedjaz and replace them by British troops from Egypt and were decidedly of the opinion that latter could not be spared.

This decision would equally apply to sending British troops to Hedjaz. I cannot hold out any hope that objections of military authorities, which appear to me on military grounds to be well founded, can be overcome.

But this being so, we cannot object to, and must face assistance which French may be able to send if and when such is forthcoming.

The second telegram is from the C.I.G.S., War Office, London, to the Commander-in-Chief, and is dated 17th September, 1916.

21.B.206.

On the 2nd September War Committee considered a proposal to send a brigade of Soudanese and to replace latter by British brigade, and decided that latter could not be spared. No brigade can consequently now be spared for Rabegh, and moreover, proposal is open to objection indicated in last paragraph of your telegram.

Foreign Office is wiring to above effect to High Commissioner. Further, it is futile sending a brigade to give moral support, and equally futile to lay down that brigade would not go beyond Rabegh and would be absolute maximum.

Gallipoli and Mesopotamia should have given quite sufficient proof of such futility.

It will be seen that the wording of these telegrams confirms the substance of Storrs' account. The references to Rabegh are concerned with a controversy which arose when Wingate and McMahon proposed to send a brigade of Indian troops to Rabegh. This was strongly oppposed by Murray and the Arab Bureau who both, in Wavell's opinion, "rightly doubted both the wisdom and the effectiveness of the detachment".[6] The problem was further complicated by the Sherif's vacillating attitude. Whenever the threat of a Turkish advance from Medina against Mecca arose he was inclined to beg for the presence of British troops, but on other occasions he permitted himself to be influenced by the prejudices of the native population directed against the presence of any foreign troops, even Egyptian Moslems. Abdullah was of course fully aware of this situation, and produced the story of the "Indian difficulties" to protect his father from any blame for the British decision to forbid the transfer of forces to the area in question.

In this matter, as in all others his loyalty to his father was absolute. By the time he arrived back in Mecca, on the 19th October, it became clear that he had no intention of keeping his promise to Storrs. "By this time," he wrote, "I realize that there must be a declaration of our independence and that my father must be elected King of the Arabs, for the Turks were treating us as rebels and insurgents and it was necessary for us to have a recognized status. I consulted my colleagues in the Government and in the Army, and they all agreed with my proposal and urged its speedy execution. I went to my father and told him about it, but he was very much against the idea and strongly opposed it. Kissing his knee I pointed out that it was the desire of the Chiefs of the Hejaz and of the other Arab countries, and that they were most anxious that he should accept kingship. At first he was adamant in his refusal, but when I made it clear that my colleagues and I were not prepared to continue with the revolt unless he agreed, he saw that he would have to give in. 'Please ask them all to come in' he said. When they were all assembled he said to them: 'Is what my son says true?' 'Nobody would dare submit to your Highness anything that was not true' they answered. 'Are you resolved, then', he demanded, 'to withdraw your support if I do not accept your proposal?' 'We are resolved', they answered. 'Do what you like then,' he said. 'It is your own responsibility. In accepting your suggestion I am meeting your wishes without approving of them'. 'May God bless Your Majesty!' they all exclaimed. The proclamation took place on November 2nd, 1916".[7] Veritably a triumph of organisation: all organised and completed within fourteen days of Abdullah's October meeting with Storrs. But in the end it was, as Storrs later remarked, a triumph that would cost him dear.

CHAPTER EIGHT

Lawrence's account.
He is appointed Liaison Officer to Feisal.

"BOOK I" (comprising Chapters VIII to XVI) of *Seven Pillars*, subtitled "*My First Visit to Arabia*", contains Lawrence's fulsome account of that visit, compensating in some degree for Storrs' admitted failure to give him adequate mention in his own account. "Extracts from the journal of October 1916 containing his name" wrote Storrs, "occur with what must now seem a ludicrous infrequency and inadequacy". The implication appears to be that Lawrence's subsequent fame had entitled him to greater attention, however inadequate the records – or memories – of the other witnesses may have been.

Lawrence would have us believe that he had a most important role on that occasion. The "holiday and joyride" he wrote about becomes in the introductory note to "BOOK I" a momentous mission: " I had believed these misfortunes of the Revolt to be due mainly to faulty leadership, or rather the lack of leadership, Arab and English. So I went down to Arabia to see and consider its great men."[1]

He met Abdullah. "I was seeing him for the first time . . . I began to suspect him of a constant cheerfulness . . . On our part, I was playing for effect, watching, criticising him. The Sharif's rebellion had been unsatisfactory for the last few months (standing still, which, in an irregular war, was the prelude to disaster): and my suspicion was that its lack was leadership".[2] Having determined the cause of the problem it remained for him to discover the right man to solve it. Providentially the right man proved to be none other than Lawrence himself. "My visit was mainly to find the yet unknown master-spirit of the affair, and measure his capacity to carry the revolt to the goal I had conceived for it".

The memoirs of Storrs and Abdullah alike fail to prepare the reader for this newly-revealed role. Storrs does not mention the conversations at the Consulate in which Lawrence depicts himself as an important contributor. "We talked to him first about the state of Jedda . . . we contemplated the vision Abdullah drew for us . . . and then Storrs brought me into the discussion by asking Abdullah to give us his views on the state of the campaign for my benefit, and for communication to headquarters in Egypt. (And finally) I said that I would represent his views to Egypt . . . I would also like to see Feisal . . . Storrs then came in and supported me with all his might, urging the vital importance of full and early information from a trained observer for the British Commander-in-Chief in Egypt, and showing that his sending me, his best qualified and most indispensable staff officer, proved the serious consideration being given to Arabian affairs by Sir Archibald Murray".[3]

This account has brought forth a comment from Mousa, saying that it "raises several questions, for all other sources agree that the discussion was of the highest seriousness, and that Wilson and Storrs were officially informing the Emir of the views of the British Government. The telegram was produced as a document. How is one to believe that Lawrence played such a role in these discussions, when he had no official capacity? And how is one to believe Lawrence's claim to be a mover of the Revolt in the beginning? . . . Storrs could not possibly have said that the Commander-in-Chief in Egypt had sent Lawrence especially to visit the battlefield and report to him and that the serious consideration he gave the Arab Revolt had prompted him to send his 'best qualified officer' because we have already been told that for Lawrence this trip was to be a vacation. Surely Lawrence was not telling the whole truth?"[4]

Nevertheless Storrs at a later date did provide in the form of a droll note some confirmation of Lawrence's involvement, writing that "Abdallah was impressed by his extraordinary detailed knowledge of enemy dispositions which, being temporary Sub-Lieutenant in charge of 'maps and marking of Turkish Army distributions' he was able to use with masterly effect".[5] Abdullah would of course have had no means of judging the accuracy of this esoteric information; and it is difficult to escape the suspicion that Storrs' choice of words may have harboured at least an element of persiflage, for why, if he had heard Lawrence describe himself as staff officer, should he refer to him as a temporary Sub-Lieutenant? There does seem to have been a period of uncertainty about Lawrence's rank. When Liddell Hart asked him in 1932 "When did you become a captain?" Lawrence's answer was "I was Staff Captain. I lost it on going to Mespot, so Hedley arranged a local captaincy". How then could he have truthfully described himself in his conversation with Abdullah as "staff officer"?

The reader will recall that it was left to Clayton to arrange the transfer of Lawrence to the Arab Bureau after he had been granted leave of absence and permission to make the Hejaz trip. The transfer became effective during his holiday, and on the 17th October Lawrence despatched his first official telegram to Clayton. Later he wrote for Clayton what he described in *Seven Pillars* as "a violent memorandum" which apparently made such an impression that when he returned to Cairo at the beginning of November Clayton instructed him "to return to Arabia and Feisal. This being much against my grain" wrote Lawrence, "I urged my complete unfitness for the job . . . I was unlike a soldier: hated soldiering", but Clayton insisted that "Feisal must be linked to us, and his needs promptly notified to Egypt . . . So I had to go".[6]

The appointment of Lawrence to the post of liaison officer attached to Feisal was one of a series of moves on the part of G.H.Q. Egypt signalling a revision of their policy and reversing the October decisions which had so disappointed Abdullah. At about the same time McMahon was replaced ('somewhat brusquely – *e il modo ancor m'offende*' wrote Storrs) by Wingate, for whom, according to Lawrence, "the Arab Revolt had been his dream for years". Major Davenport and Colonel Joyce were sent out to command the Egyptian troops in the Hejaz and to assist in the organisation of an Arab Regular Force: Lawrence has described them as "the two Englishmen to whom the Arab cause owed the greater part of its gratitude".[7] Aeroplanes were again sent to Rabegh, and the French Mission assembled at Suez artillery, machine guns, and some cavalry and infantry, the latter consisting of Algerian Moslem rank and file (to ensure their acceptability in the Holy Hejaz) under French officers. And when Lawrence arrived at Yenbo on the 26th December he found Major Garland already established for the training of the Sherifians in the use of explosives.

These were some of the measures taken by the Allies in their vigorous attempt to revitalise the Sherif's revolt, and within the Hejaz the military situation remained stagnant. The Turkish garrison in Medina remained strongly entrenched, sustained by the regular supplies and reinforcements which reached them by way of the Hejaz Railway, from Damascus, and by land routes from the adjoining territories of Hail, whose Emir, Ibn Rashid, adhered to the Turkish cause throughout the duration of the war. The Medina troops posed a constant threat to those neighbouring tribesmen who may have been tempted to lend their support to the Sherif. Although these semi-nomads may have lacked comprehension of the political issues, or of the principles of "Arab independence", they were not averse to accepting the rifles and the gold which was being so generously distributed by the Sherifians, provided that their possession could be enjoyed without inviting retribution from the Turks, which could be quite severe. When occasionally some were drawn into actual fighting they applied their simple philosophy: after the battle they took their share of the spoils and returned to their homes.

Abdullah reported on this problem of Arab evanescence after the capture of Taif. "The Arab losses during the seige had not been heavy, but the tribal levies who played the major part in this operation had, as usual, dispersed to their homes, leaving their commander with a very small force".[8] This was a difficult situation for the British commanders to accept, and Wingate expressed his views on the subject without restraint, saying that "His (the Sherif's) army is practically a rabble and run on Dervish lines".[9]

In his Lawrence biography, Liddell Hart offers the following comment: "When the first enthusiasm waned, the maintenance of the Arab rising depended on the Sherif's power to feed his followers and also to compensate them for the loot they were now failing to secure from the Turks. Here Britain's help was the decisive factor. The supply ships that came into Jedda and Rabegh were the backbone of the revolt. Through them, and them alone, the Sherif was able to feed his forces and their families. With British money he was able to pay two pounds a month for a man and four for a camel. As Lawrence had remarked – 'Nothing else would have performed the miracle of keeping a tribal army in the field for five months on end'. Ali and Feisal found that only a trickle of supplies was reaching them. And no money . . . So Ali, exercising an elder brother's privilege, went down to Rabegh to find out why the British were not fulfilling their promises".[10]

Now Lawrence takes up the story, telling that on his arrival at Rabegh Ali "found that Hussein Mabeirig, the local chief, had made up his mind that the Turks would be victorious . . . and accordingly decided theirs was the best cause to follow. As the stores for the Sherif were landed by the British he appropriated them and stored them away secretly in his own houses . . . The two Sherifs (Ali and Zeid) took possession of his villages. In them they found great stores of arms, and food enough for their armies for a month. The temptation of a spell of leisured ease was too much for them: they settled down in Rabegh".[11]

Chapter Nine

The evanescent "revolt", and the picturesque procession to Wejh.

By the time that Lawrence arrived in the Hejaz at the end of December, 1916, the Sherif's revolt had reached the point of complete failure. Hussein had not only failed to enlist the support of the majority of the Hejaz tribes but had also to contend with the irresolution of the Anazeh and the Idrissi, the open hostility of Ibn Rashid and the inexorable coldness of Ibn Saud. His shrinking authority, together with any prospects of extended religious influence, were further threatened through the appointment by the Turks of a noble and respected descendant of the Prophet's family, the Sharif Ali Haidar (described by Storrs as "a gentleman of great charm"), as Sherif of Mecca (although his seat was in Medina) with the additional title of Vizier. Neither in Syria nor in Palestine was there any significant sign of support for the Sherif's revolt, while in Mesopotamia the greater part of the Arabs had thrown in their lot with the Turks, with unspeakably tragic consequences for the British who fell into their hands.

Lawrence's arrival at Yenbo coincided with the news that Ali, who had ventured forth from his safe retreat in Rabegh to attempt the occupation of Bir ibn Hassani, nearly seventy miles to the north, "had been shaken by false reports of disloyalty among the Subh, and had fallen back in rapid disorder to Rabegh".[1] The British found the situation intolerable. Garland, Joyce, Ross, Davenport, Lawrence and others had been sent into the area to promote positive military action, and the warships of the Red Sea Fleet effectively covered the Hejaz coastline, guarding the appproaches to the ports of Jedda, Rabegh and Yenbo, while their guns commanded the littoral routes from Turkish-held territories. The value of this naval support will be readily appreciated when it is recalled that when 4,000 Harb tribesmen failed to take Jedda in June the town surrendered two days after their departure to the Royal Navy.

"In this ominous pause," wrote Lawrence, "Colonel Wilson came up to Yenbo to persuade us of the necessity of an immediate operation against Wejh. An amended plan had been drawn up whereby Feisal would take the whole force of the Juheina, and his permanent battalions, against Wejh with the maximum of naval help." This decision to occupy Wejh, known to be held by a Turkish garrison of 200, initiated one of the most bizarre episodes in military history, besides inspiring literary flights which called for the employment of tens of thousands of words to describe the adventure. Lawrence himself devotes six whole chapters[2] to the description of the preparations and progress of what should have been "the attacking forces"; while his baroque prose is reflected in the paraphrased accounts of sympathetic biographers.

The underlying strategy was clear enough. Once Yenbo and Jedda were safely held under the protection afforded by the Red Sea Fleet the capture of Wejh would be the logical following objective. It lay roughly 200 miles north of Yenbo, which was about the same distance from Jedda to the south, so that its possession would ensure for the British a continuous stretch of Hejaz coast, and increase the threat to the railway running northwards from Medina, for the Red Sea coastline from Wejh to Yenbo ran roughly parallel with the railway, with an average distance between the two lines of rather more than one hundred miles. The country from the railway to the coast was for the most part hilly – even mountainous in some areas – so that the easy route for an army on the move would have to be coastal, hence the advantage of "the maximum of naval help" invoked by Lawrence, for the fleet could steam northwards in line with the land forces, and its powerful guns would protect them from the seaward side and from any inland threat within their range.

Descriptions of the capture and occupation of Wejh by the combined Arab land and the British naval forces on the 24th January, 1917, are to be found in the writings of Lawrence, Mousa, Major N.N.E. Bray and others. Mousa wrote that Feisal "began his march on 3rd January 1917 with an army that consisted of ten thousand warriors, most of whom were Bedouin including one thousand, two hundred Ageyl whom the Turks had conscripted at Kasim in Nejd and who later joined the Revolt. The army had a battery of Egyptian field guns, which the Arabs had been trained to operate in place of the Egyptians. It was at this point that Feisal began to make use of Lawrence's services. He was acting as liaison officer between Feisal and the British ships which were helping the Arabs in their march along the coast towards Wejh and transporting supplies to them. Feisal's army set out from Yenbo, while Lawrence boarded a ship for Um Lejj (*about half-way between Yenbo and Wejh*). The Commander of the British Fleet met Emir Feisal at a place close to Um Lejj and the two worked out their plans for the attack on Wejh. The ships carried five hundred Bedouin volunteers under Saleh Ibn Sehfia who intended to land them at the appointed time north of Wejh. The main attack was to be carried out at dawn on 23rd January . . . Feisal resumed his march from Um Lejj on 18th January, being soon overtaken by Colonel Newcombe, who had arrived from Egypt. Heavy rain, which fell at the time, delayed the Army, so that the Emir was not able to reach Wejh on the appointed day. As a result, the six British ships disembarked their load of Bedouin volunteers together with Major Vickery at a point close to Wejh, well before the main force arrived. The ships had also landed a detachment of British marines and proceeded to bombard the town. The Turkish garrison, which was made up of two hundred officers and men, surrendered after a short battle. Feisal reached Wejh the following day".[3]

Lawrence's account differs in detail from Mousa's but offers some explanation for Feisal's army taking three weeks to cover the 180 miles (by Mousa's reckoning) from Yenbo to Wejh. "The march became rather splendid and barbaric. First rode Feisal in white, then Sharraf at his right in red headcloth and henna-dyed tunic and cloak, myself on his left in white and scarlet, behind us three banners of faded crimson silk with gilt spikes, behind them the drummers playing a march, and behind them again the wild mass of twelve hundred bouncing camels the bodyguard packed as closely as they could move, the men in every variety of coloured clothes and the camels nearly as brilliant in their trappings. We filled the valley to its banks with our flashing stream".[4]

A most impressive and colourful cavalcade: assuredly too extravagant a muster for the ultimate subjugation of two hundred miserable Turks. But despite the artistic arrangement of the colourful costumes this spectacular procession failed to make the opening night, for when the *Hardinge* "exact to the rendezvous, arrived off Wejh at dawn on the appointed day" they found "no Feisal and no Lawrence and no supporting tribesmen". Anxious to ensure that the Turkish garrison did not escape, Vickery and Bray decided to attack without the help of the dilatory main force. The 400 Arabs, landed at a cove about two miles from Wejh, provided the two regular officers with some shocks. The first was that 200 tribesmen refused to fight and took cover under a cliff. About 100 of the remainder made direct for the town and rushed for the nearest house.

"Having entered it", recorded Bray, "and slain all whom they found there they proceeded to loot it. Later I saw the result. In the street, before its entrance, lay three dead Arabs, and a pool of congealed blood covered the grey flat stone . . . The interior was in a state of indescribable confusion. Everything was smashed, even the legs of the chairs. The whole place was littered knee deep in kapok. Mattresses, pillows and cushions had been torn to shreds in the frantic search for the gold the Bedouins hoped might be concealed within".[5]

Bray went on to report that the main body of looters "proceeded to reduce the place by attrition, going from house to house, eating their way into the bowels of the town". Next morning a shell from *Fox* hit the mosque, where a small crowd of fanatics had been holding out and preventing the others from surrendering. "A huge gaping hole was blown in the wall and fifteen very bewildered and begrimed men staggered out without their weapons, in token of surrender".[6] That was how Wejh was captured by the Arabs.

Lawrence's account succeeded in evading these unpleasantnesses. He describes how (on the 20th January) "we slept late the following day, to brace ourselves for the necessary hours of talk"[7] (could this be an example of ironic humour?). "We were already two days behind our promise to the Navy, and Newcombe decided to ride ahead this night to Habban. There he would meet Boyle and explain that we must fail the *Hardinge* at the rendezvous, but would be glad if she could return there on the evening of the twenty-fourth, when we should arrive much in need of water. He would also see if the naval attack could not be delayed till the twenty-fifth to preserve the joint scheme".[8]

The navy did not of course agree to this preposterous suggestion, and while Vickery's Arabs were murdering and looting in the doomed town, Feisal's Juheina, some twenty miles or so to the south, were endeavouring to employ their leisure less dangerously but not without promise of profit.

At Kurna the tribesmen had observed camels pasturing "away to the east". They streamed out, captured them, and drove them in. But it happened that they belonged to the Billi Arabs, who were quite capable of exacting redress and, in order to avoid the danger of having a real war on his hands, Feisal was obliged to impound the stolen beasts until they could be returned to their rightful owners. "Our success" Lawrence commented "lay in bond to such trifles".[9]

It was these beguiling delays which prevented Feisal's army from reaching Wejh until the 25th. "So we knew the work had been finished for us . . . Vickery, who had directed the battle, was satisfied, but I could not share his satisfaction . . . Even from the military point of view the assault seemed to me a blunder. The two hundred Turks in

Wejh had no transport and no food, and if left alone a few days must have surrendered. Had they escaped, it would not have mattered the value of an Arab life. We wanted Wejh as a base against the railway and to extend our front; the smashing and killing in it had been wanton. The place was inconveniently smashed. Its townspeople had been warned by Feisal of the coming attack, and advised either to forestall it by revolt or to clear out; but they were mostly Egyptians from Kosseir, who preferred the Turks to us, and decided to wait the issue; so the Sherfia men and the Biasha found the houses packed with fair booty and made a sweep of it. They robbed the shops, broke open doors, searched every room, smashed chests and cupboards, tore down all fixed fittings, and slit each mattress and pillow for hidden treasure; while the fire of the fleet punched large holes in every prominent wall or building".[10] This was Lawrence's report.

Chapter Ten

A leisurely excursion with Aqaba in mind, and an unexplained diversion.

With the loss of Wejh the only Red Sea port to the north of Jedda in Turkish hands was Aqaba. Because of its position – it marked the point where the frontiers of Sinai, Palestine and Arabia came together – the War Committee in London had on July 6th, 1916, decided on its capture. But Wejh had to be taken first. While the assault on Wejh was being prepared Wingate, George Lloyd and Brémond met at Khartoum to discuss the implementation of the War Committee's instructions.[1]

The Turkish garrison in Aqaba was known to number no more than 300 men, so that an attack from the sea would have presented few serious problems: Aqaba had in fact twice been taken by small landing parties without casualties. Lawrence's view was that an invasion from the sea would merely result in the garrison abandoning its forward positions and establishing itself in the difficult mountainous country beyond. This is precisely what happened on April 20th, 1917, when a unit of British marines landed and inflicted casualties on the Turkish garrison, which then promptly withdrew. Less than three weeks later a small force left Wejh, with the aim of descending on Aqaba from the North. It was led by the Sherif Nasir, and included, in addition to an escort of Ageyl, a celebrated sheikh, Auda abu Tayi, chief of the Howeitat, and Lawrence, carrying what he described as an "inconvenient load of four hundred pounds of gold".[2]

Lawrence, taken at Akaba.

Although Aqaba lies north-west of Wejh – about 250 miles in a straight line – a route denied by the mountainous character of the hinterland – the party set off in a north-easterly direction, travelling some three hundred miles to reach the Hejaz railway where it crossed the Wadi Diraa (some 200 miles south-east of Aqaba) and then making their way to Arfaja, roughly 250 miles due east of Aqaba. From Arfaja, which they had reached on the 24th May, they turned towards the north-west, and three days later reached the camps of the Howeitat. Lawrence described the welcome they received.

"Our march was prosperously over. We had found the Howeitat: our men were in excellent fettle: we had our gold and our explosives still intact. So we drew happily together in the morning to a solemn council on action. There was agreement that first we should present six thousand pounds to Nuri Shaalan, by whose sufferance we were in Sirhan . . . Auda would explain to Nuri what we hoped to do, and Feisal's desire that he make a public demonstration of adherence to Turkey. Only so could he cover us, while still pleasing the Turks".[3]

They continued their journey on May 30th and made their way to Ageila, where they received "fusillades of honour, deputations ,and gifts of ostrich eggs, or Damascus dainties . . . and we set three men to make coffee for the visitors . . . Besides their formal presents, each new party deposited on our carpet their privy, accidental gift of lice; and long before sunset Nasir and I were in a fever,with relay after relay of irritation. Auda had a stiff arm, the effect of an old wound in the elbow joint, and so could not scratch all of himself; but experience had taught him a way of thrusting a cross-headed camel-stick up his left sleeve and turning round and round inside against his ribs, which method seemed to relieve his itch more than our claws did ours".[4]

By the third of June they had reached Nebk, where, Lawrence wrote, they "sat down for days, to consider enrolling the men, and to prepare the road along which we could march, by approaching the tribes and the sheikhs who lived near. Leisure remained for Nesib, Zeki and myself".[5] It was by this time almost four full weeks since they had set out from Wejh, and they were still hundreds of miles from their destination. The brief account in these pages of their progress is a sensible summary of the sixteen chapters of *Seven Pillars*[6] which Lawrence devotes to the journey from Wejh to Aqaba. There may be little in them to interest the military historian, but they do conform to Lawrence's prescription of "a personal narrative pieced out of memory" and at the same time provide scope for his literary indulgences, which at least describe the way in which the time was spent. "Maulad had musicians in his unit; and bashful soldiers were brought up each evening to play guitars and sing café songs of Damascus or the love verses of their villages. In Abdullah's tent, where I lodged, distance, the ripple of the fragrant outpouring water, and the tree-leaves softened the music, so that it became dully pleasant to the ear".[7]

This blissful note brought to an end the first of those sixteen chapters. Those which followed describe the countryside, the weather and the local customs. Chapter XLVI is titled – and completely devoted to – "Feasting", and the descriptions of the food and the eating and the drinking fill every page, until in the final paragraph the "second and third sittings by the dish were having their turn, and . . . when our backs were turned the children would run in disorder upon the ravaged dish, tear our gnawed bones from one another, and escape into the open with valuable fragments to be devoured in security behind some distant bush".[8]

The following chapter continues in the same vein. "We feasted on the first day once, on the second day twice, on the third day twice . . ."[9] The reader will not be surprised to learn that its caption is "Gradual Progress". But Chapter XLVIII covers, in an unheralded leap, the first eighteen days of June; and the central twelve days of that period are shrouded in a mystery which has not been resolved. Lawrence refers to them in *Seven Pillars* as "this long, dangerous ride",[10] but in his report to Clayton he described it as a lone 14-day trip, from the 4th to the 18th June, which is inconsistent with his statement in *Seven Pillars* that: "When I returned it was June the sixteenth".[11] He claimed that during this journey he met the Turkish G.O.C., Damascus, on June 13th at Ghuta, three miles from Damascus.[12]

Mousa's verdict on this mysterious trip is that "it never happened at all. We can assert here that this story was entirely fabricated by Lawrence".[13] In the course of his investigations, endeavouring to establish the facts, Mousa obtained a statement from Naseeb al-Bekri, who had been named by Lawrence in his secret report, and published it in his Lawrence biography. "As for Lawrence's claim", wrote Naseeb, "that he went in disguise to Damascus, Ba'albek and Tudmore, it strikes me as very strange indeed, because it is far from the truth. I am certain that Lawrence did not leave us for a single day, and we were not separated until after he left for Aqaba . . . I must also mention the fact that Lawrence was inclined to double dealing, slander and dissemination of discord and that he urged Auda and Nassir to take the 7,000 pounds which Feisal had allotted to me to spend in Syria and Jebel Druze. They actually asked for the money on the grounds that their own allotment had run out; in spite of much argument I insisted on keeping the money. Sherif Nassir informed me confidentially that Lawrence was the instigator. Nassir said that to prevent a misunderstanding, he would inform Auda and Lawrence that I had passed the money on to him. I belive that until he died Lawrence thought that I had actually surrendered the money".[14] Mousa continues: "Lawrence came near to confessing that the story of his alleged trip was pure fiction in the note he sent on 22nd July 1927 to Robert Graves who was at the time engaged in writing his biography".[15]

The notes to which Mousa refers are to be found on pages 88-90 of *T.E. Lawrence to his Biographers, Part I*, and include the following extracts: "In my report to Clayton after Aqaba I gave a short account of my excursion from Nebk north-ward. It was part of the truth. During it some things happened, and I do not want the whole story to be made traceable. So on this point I have since darkened counsel. You'll have to say something but you'll not be able to be right in what you say. So hedge yourself, and me, if you can, by cautionary phrases.

Some such thing as the following: 'From Nebk during the Aqaba expedition's halt there, 'L' went off on a solitary excursion northward. On this ride he was said to have been convoyed by relays of local tribesmen, beginning with the Rualla and changing them at each tribal boundary. Apparently none of his own, nor of Sherif Nasser's men completed the journey with him. He is said to have been franked by private letters of Emir Faisal, but nothing certain is known of his purpose, his route, and the results of his journey'. You may make public if you like the fact that my reticence upon this northward raid is deliberate, and based on private reasons: and record your opinion that I have found mystification, and perhaps statements deliberately misleading or contradictory, the best way to hide the truth of what really occurred, *if anything did occur*".

Hence Mousa's accusation that Lawrence's secret report to Clayton "contained a startling conglomeration of lies and fabrications".[16] It is unlikely that we shall ever have the true story. Knightley and Simpson agree that "The issue must remain unsolved", but nevertheless reveal that "We came to the conclusion that during the secret trip Lawrence claimed to have made to Damascus he had come across Dahoum, whom he found dead, or dying of typhus".[17] Could this be the explanation for Lawrence extending the Wejh-Aqaba odyssey into a thousand-mile journey occupying two whole months?

If we refer to the wording of his report to Clayton we will find that he claimed that while he was away on the alleged Damascus trip, "Sherif Nassir stayed in Kaf" (near Nebk) "to enrol Rualla, Shererat and Huweitat for the Aqaba expedition", and then, on his return, that the whole party set its course for Aqaba. Mousa gives the number of volunteers whom Nassir and Auda "succeeded in recruiting" as five hundred,[18] and states that en route for Jefer (rather less than one hundred miles north-east of Aqaba) they received promises of support from the Dumaniyeh, Darawsheh, Dhiabat, and Huweitat clans.[19] Jefer was reached on June 30th, and after a clash with Turkish troops near Aba el Lissan the Arabs surrounded the 120-strong garrison at Guweira and obtained its surrender. This was on July 4th, and on the following evening they reached Khadra, the fortress covering Aqaba. By this time, Mousa reports, "the number of Arab warriors had multiplied, owing to the arrival of some neighbouring clans"[20] and, realising their hopeless position, the garrison of 300 then surrendered. The town itself was empty: its inhabitants had long abandoned it; and Sherif Nasser was able to establish his headquarters there.

The fighting – if one could so describe it – was now over, leaving other problems to emerge. There was neither food nor fodder in the town, and the twenty thousand golden sovereigns with which Nassir had commenced his journey had by now been distributed: the coffers which held the sinews of war were now empty. Although there was no civilian population to feed the town was crowded with swarms of Arabs demanding food, supplies and gold, and Lawrence was ordered to make his way to Cairo with the least possible delay to explain these pressing needs. Cairo responded immediately, and the *Dufferin*, fully loaded with required provisions, reached Aqaba on the thirteenth of July.

CHAPTER ELEVEN

The price of Arab co-operation: backstairs dealings with the Turks.

Lawrence's participation in the Aqaba expedition afforded him the opportunity to compose a report which would invite the commendation of his superiors. "Upon Clayton I opened myself completely" he wrote. "Aqaba had been taken on my plan by my effort. The cost of it had fallen on my brain and on my nerves. There was much more I felt inclined to do, and capable of doing – if he thought I had earned the right to be my own master".[1]

This extravagant claim caused the Arab historian George Antonius to write: "His (Lawrence's) summing up that 'Akaba had been taken on my plan by my effort' is a claim that will perplex the historian . . . The Arab evidence is that the plan was first suggested to Feisal by Auda at their first meeting at Wejh: that Lawrence was not made privy to it until Feisal had given his consent; and that it was carried into execution by Auda and his Howeitat tribesmen independently of all outside help".[2] Apart, of course, from that "inconvenient load of four hundred pounds of gold".

Whatever Clayton may have thought of Lawrence's modest claim he was not able to recommend him for the command that he was seeking, for in both rank and service he was junior to the other officers serving in the Hejaz and could hardly have been promoted over their heads. He was, however, promoted to Major, and confirmed in his position of Feisal's Liaison Officer, while Colonel P.C. Joyce was appointed to command at Aqaba. Clayton also responded to Lawrence's urgent demand for gold to satisfy the expectations of the two thousand tribesmen impatiently awaiting its distribution in Aqaba. He drew sixteen thousand pounds, and the gold was sent immediately to Suez.

By the 17th Lawrence was back in Wejh, but had to return to Aqaba when telegrams from Egypt revealed that the Howeitat "were in treasonable contact" with the Turks. It seems that Auda himself was personally implicated. Lawrence made the journey from Aqaba to Guweira by camel: "and at dawn" (he wrote) "we found Auda and Mohammed and Zaal all in a tent. They were confused when I dropped in on them, unheralded, but protested that all was well. We fed together as friends".[3] During the morning others of the Howeitat came in, and Lawrence distributed "the King's presents". What followed reveals, in any interpretation of his telling, the conspirators' concept of loyalty. "After lunch, by pretence of sleep, I got rid of the visitors; and then abruptly asked Auda and Mohammed to walk with me . . . When we were alone I touched on their present correspondence with Turks. Auda began to laugh; Mohammed to look disgusted. At last they explained elaborately that Mohammed had taken Auda's seal and written to the (Turkish) Governor of Maan, offering to desert the Sherif's cause. The Turk replied gladly, promising great rewards.

Mohammed asked for something on account. Auda then heard of it, waited till the messenger with presents was on his way, caught him, robbed him to the skin: and was denying Mohammed a share of the spoils. A farcical story, and we laughed rightly over it: but there was more behind.

"They were angry that no guns or troops had yet come to their support; and that no rewards had been given them for taking Akaba. They were anxious to know how I had learnt of their secret dealings, and how much more I knew . . . I played on their fear by my unnecessary amusement, quoting in careless laughter as if they were my own words, actual phrases of the letters they had exchanged. This created the impression desired . . . Finally I suggested that Auda's present expenses in hospitality must be great; would it help if I advanced something of the great gift Feisal would make him, personally, when he arrived? Auda saw that the immediate moment would not be unprofitable; that Feisal would be highly profitable; and that the Turks would always be with him if other resources failed. So he agreed, in a very good temper, to accept my advance; and with it to keep the Howeitat well-fed and cheerful. Afterward I remounted, with Mufaddih (to draw Auda's allowance) and abd el Rahman, a servant of Mohammed's who, so he whispered me, would receive any little thing I wished to send him separately . . .

"We rang up Cairo and announced that the situation at Guweira was thoroughly good, and no treachery abroad. This may have been hardly true; but since Egypt kept us alive by stinting herself, we must reduce impolitic truth to keep her confident and ourselves a legend. The crowd wanted book-heroes, and would not understand how more human Auda was because, after battle and murder, his heart yearned towards the defeated enemy now subject, at his free choice, to be spared or killed: and therefore never so lovely".[4] In this cynical report Lawrence made no attempt to conceal his own deceit in his message to Egypt. That the Arab Bureau was not deceived by this duplicity is clear from the *Arab Bulletin* article of 5th August 1917 which stated that "there is no doubt that the Turks are making great efforts to win over the tribes around Ma'an and induce them to assist in an attack on Akaba, and are spending considerable sums of money with this object. The G.O.C. Eighth Army Corps is reported to have sent a messenger to Auda Abu Tayeh with the object of inducing the latter to join the Turks".

It is clear that the Hejaz tribes were in the enviable position of being able to collect rewards from both sides in the conflict and that some of their leaders accumulated substantial wealth by exploiting the opportunities afforded by the war. Some sheikhs may have possessed riches even before the war. Speculating on the loyalties of Nuri Shaalan, Lawrence ventured that Nuri "hesitated to declare himself only because of his wealth in Syria, and the possible hurt to his tribesmen if they were deprived of their natural market".[5] But none could have been more avaricious than Auda Abu Tayi, if one adds to Lawrence's evidence the later experiences of Peake Pasha. Lieutenant Colonel F.G. Peake, C.M.G., C.B.E., to give him his full title, raised and commanded the Arab Legion after the war, and for twenty years was adviser to the Emir Abdullah and his close friend. In September 1918, when he was in charge of the Egyptian Army Camel Corps, he was ordered to move towards Deraa, together with three hundred Arab regular troops supported by armoured cars and aeroplanes. Major C.C. Jarvis, Peake's biographer (and former Governor of Sinai) recounts: "The Arab regular army announced suddenly that it would not undertake any further operations unless the arrears of pay due to it were settled, and, as the usual monthly subsidy had not then arrived, it became an urgent matter to obtain it . . . The situation became critical as it was uncertain if the monthly subsidy would arrive in time for the regular army to take part in the operations. The result of this was that the Camel Corps, Gurkhas, and armoured cars were sent off to the wells at Jafar, whilst Colonel Joyce and various other officers were to follow with the Arab regulars later. At Jafar was Audah Abu Tayi, the famous paramount sheikh of the Howietat Arabs, a man of great local eminence. To him Peake on his arrival paid his respects, with a request that the rations which were waiting there for him be handed over and permission given for the watering of his camels. To his amazement both requests were indignantly refused. Something at a loss, he endeavoured to placate the irate chieftain, but the man was adamant, asserting that he had been grossly insulted by a British officer the day before and that Peake and his party would only water at his well over his dead body . . .

"No amount of talk or persuasion could overcome the determination of Abu Tayi to obstruct the advance of the Camel Corps, and Peake was forced to fix up his heliograph and send a message through to H.Q. at Abu Lissal. Shortly afterwards an aeroplane arrived carrying Lawrence himself with a letter from Feisal and a supply of gold. After this everything went smoothly – the men of the Camel Corps received their rations, and the camels went down to water. It is believed that the sum necessary to placate Abu Tayi was £10,000 and, if this was the case, the water for each camel worked out at about £66 per head".[6]

That was not the only occasion when Peake ran into trouble with the tribes. In the opening paragraphs of Chapter CVIII of *Seven Pillars* Lawrence reports a failure by Peake to carry out a railway demolition on the Hejaz line at Mafrak station, but it was left to Jarvis to give the reasons for the aborted mission, telling of the interception of Peake's column by a group of Beni Sakhur tribesmen. "They were friends of the Emir Feisal, but on the other hand they had come to an agreement with the Turks to guard the railway line in return for being allowed to water their animals at the station. This being the case they did not attend to allow Peake or anyone else to interfere with the railway, and, incidentally, with their water supply".[7]

CHAPTER TWELVE

Mudowwara; Lawrence announces his design, and his failure.

We have now accompanied Lawrence through sixteen chapters of his book recounting his adventures in the desert areas to the east of the River Jordan. To the west of the river a very different sort of war was being fought. On the 30th March a telegram had been sent to General Murray "indicating Jerusalem as an immediate objective of his army".[1] The main obstacles to the achievement of this objective were first Gaza and then Beersheba. At Gaza the preparations for an assault on its defences had occupied the leaders on both sides, with the Turks bringing in their 16th and 17th Infantry Divisions together with the 3rd Cavalry Division to add to Kressenstein's garrison forces. The three battles for the possession of Gaza proved to be for the British very costly affairs. The first was defeated on March 27th with nearly 4,000 British casualties. Storrs wrote of this action: "The 27th Arab Division (of the Turkish Army) distinguished itself against the British in the first successful defence of Gaza, 1917".

The second effort was even more disastrous. The Turks had assembled in the front line of their defences (nearly four thousand yards of sandhills running to the sea's edge) a force of over 18,000 rifles supported by 101 guns and 86 machine guns. According to Wavell, the British forces mustered against them possessed "at least a 50 per cent advantage in infantry and guns, besides their overwhelming superiority in mounted troops; and their fighting capacity was, according to their commander's account of the late battle, greatly superior to that of their adversaries".[2] Despite this superiority the attack failed, with British casualties close on 6,500. The Turkish losses were reported at a little over 2,000. They captured six officers and 266 men.

It was this defeat of March 20th which resulted in the recall of General Murray and his replacement by Allenby, who arrived in Egypt on June 27th to command the Egyptian Expeditionary Force. Before his departure to Egypt he was told by Lloyd George, the Prime Minister, that "he wanted Jerusalem as a Christmas present for the British nation".[3] Within three weeks of his arrival he was able to telegraph home an outline of his proposals and his requirements for the successful outcome of his planned objective, and in the weeks which followed he was able to complete his plans and his dispositions in preparation for what proved to be the final battle for Gaza.

During all this martial activity Lawrence, no more than one hundred miles distant, was happily rusticating in Guweira. Writing under the date 9.ix.17. he records: "Guweira was thronged with life, and a mart for the Howeitat of both hills and highlands. As far as the eye reached the plain was softly moving with herded camels, whose multitude drained the near waterholes each morning before dawn so that late risers must travel many miles to drink. This was little matter, for the Arabs had nothing to do but wait for the morning aeroplane; and after its passing, nothing but talk to kill time till night was full enough for sleep . . . Auda was ambitious to take advantage of our dependence on his help to assort the tribes. He drew the bulk-wages for the Howeitat; and, by the money, sought to compel the smaller free-sections to his leadership.

"They resented it, and were threatening to retire into their hills or to re-open touch with the Turks. Feisal sent up Sherif Mastur as mediator. The thousands of Howeitat, in hundreds of sections, were uncompromising, hard-headed, greedy land-lawyers . . . The three southern clans on whom we had been counting for our raid were among the dissidents . . . One day, going along before noon under the rock, Mastur met me with news that the southerners were mounting to desert our camp and movement. Full of vexation I swung round into Auda's tent".[4] At this point the reader will tense himself in preparation for the expected explosion: a Lawrence "full of vexation" must surely pose a terrifying retribution. But let him continue the story: it cannot be paraphrased:

"When I suddenly burst in, the little woman whisked away through the backflap like a rabbit. To gain ground with him, I began to jeer at the old man for being so old and yet so foolish like the rest of his race, who regarded our comic reproductive processes not as an unhygienic pleasure, but as a main business of life . . . The upshot of our talk was that I should go off to a clean spot, to wait events. We hired twenty camels to carry the explosives; and the morrow, two hours after the aeroplane, was fixed for our start".[5] which, somehow, goes to show how tough Lawrence could become when he was filled with vexation. He disclosed that the "clean spot" would be the railway line at Mudowwara.

Mudowwara station lay about fifty miles east of Aqaba, and Lawrence reached the appointed place on September 16th. There he had to contend with further problems. "There were groups of Zuweida, Derausha, Togataga, and Zelebani . . . No one group would ride or speak with another, and I passed back and forth all day like a shuttle, talking first to one lowering sheikh, and then to another, striving to draw them together, so that before a cry to action came there might be solidarity. As yet they agreed only in not hearing any word from Zaal as to the order of our march; though he was admitted the most intelligent warrior, and the most experienced. For my private part he was the only one to be trusted further than eyesight. Of the others, it seemed to me that neither their words nor their counsels, perhaps not their rifles, were sure".[6]

Three more days passed before this motley force, supported by "Stokes" and "Lewis", two Royal Field Artillery sergeants on loan with their guns from the Ten-Pounder Talbot Battery, mined and ambushed a Turkish train. Lawrence described the scene. "The valley was a weird sight. The Arabs, gone raving mad, were rushing about at top speed bareheaded and half-naked, screaming, shooting into the air, clawing one another nail and fist, while they burst open trucks and staggered back and forward with immense bales, which they ripped by the railside, and tossed through, smashing what they did not want . . . To one side stood thirty or forty hysterical women, unveiled, tearing their clothes and hair; shrieking themselves distracted. The Arabs without regard to them went on wrecking the household goods; looting their absolute full. Camels had become common property. Each man frantically loaded the nearest with what it could carry and shooed it westward into the void, while he turned to his next fancy. Lewis and Stokes had come down to help me. I was a little anxious about them; for the Arabs, having lost their wits, were as ready to assault friend and foe. Three times I had to defend myself when they pretended not to know me and snatched at my things".[7]

Finally, "we broke up into little parties and struggled north. Victory always undid an Arab force, so we were no longer a raiding party, but a stumbling baggage caravan, loaded to breaking point with enough household goods to make rich an Arab tribe for years . . . Two days later we were at Akaba; entering glory, laden with precious things, and boasting that the trains were at our mercy".[8]

These "precious things" together with his sly boasting served to conceal his failure, for he had been preparing a special raid for weeks, collecting detonators and explosives from H.M.S. *Humber* and enlisting the services of the two sergeant-instructors from the Army school at Zeitun. Mudowwara was chosen as the target because it was, he wrote, "the most promising and easiest-reached . . . As we worked on the organization of the raid, our appetites rose. Mudowwara station sounded vulnerable. Three hundred men might rush it suddenly. That would be an achievement, for its deep water well was the only one in the dry sector below Maan. Without its water, the train service across the gap would become uneconomic in load".[9]

The raiding party had arrived at Mudowwara on the 17th, and after dusk Lawrence and the two sergeants were able to view the garrison quarters from a concealed position on a crest. "We moved back to our hill and consulted in whispers. The station was very long, of stone buildings, so solid that they might be proof against our time-fused shell. The garrison seemed about two hundred. We were one hundred and sixteen rifles and not a happy family. Surprise was the only benefit we could be sure of. So, in the end, I voted that we leave it, unalarmed, for a future occasion, which might be soon. But, actually, one accident after another saved Mudowwara; and it was not until August, 1918, that Buxton's Camel Corps at last measured to it the fate long overdue".

Clearly Mudowwara proved to be less vulnerable than it "sounded", and the only profit of the enterprise lay in the "glory" and the piles of booty from the Turkish train. One hundred and sixteen rifles seemed to be inadequate: but what about the ten-pounder guns, manned by "Stokes and Lewis"? Were they not be to be counted? And could not the weeks of preparation have included the furtive survey which finally convinced Lawrence that the attempt should be abandoned and which might have avoided the elaborate and costly exercise? G.H.Q. may have been asking the same questions.

Chapter Thirteen

The River Yarmuk Bridge survives Lawrence's plan for its destruction.

Within two or three weeks of the abortive Mudowwara adventure Allenby summoned Lawrence to Cairo, where, wrote Lawrence, "He asked what our railway efforts meant; or rather if they meant anything beyond the melodramatic advertisement they gave Feisal's cause".[1] Lawrence's reply to this significant question was couched in his characteristic prose. "I explained my hope to leave the line just working, but only just, to Medina; where Fakhri's corps fed itself at less cost than if in prison in Cairo. The surest way to limit the line without killing it was by attacking trains. The Arabs put into mining a zest absent from their pure demolitions. We could not yet break the line, since railhead was the strongest point of a railway, and we preferred weaknesses in the nearest enemy neighbour till our regular army was trained and equipped and numerous enough to invest Maan".[2]

We have no means of learning Allenby's response to this instructive discourse, or of confirming that Lawrence actually addressed his Commander-in-Chief in this style, for he is relating the conversation some years after it allegedly took place, and one may question whether he prepared his speech in writing or just made notes at the time. But there is reason to believe that behind this persiflage Lawrence recognised that his Chief was demanding some useful action and that it was necessary for him to make some response. One may perceive some acknowledgement of this in the opening paragraph of Chapter LXX of *Seven Pillars,* in characteristic Lawrence prose: "However, the Arab Movement lived on Allenby's good pleasure, so that it was needful to undertake some operation, less than a general revolt, in the enemy rear: an operation which could be achieved by a raiding party without involving the settled peoples; and yet one which would please him by being of material help to the British pursuit of the enemy. These conditions and qualifications pointed, upon consideration, to the attempted cutting of one of the great bridges of the Yarmuk valley.

Lawrence drives a Talbot car in the desert.

"It was by the narrow and precipitous gorge of the River Yarmuk that the railway from Palestine climbed to Hauran, on its way to Damascus. The depth of the Jordan depression, and the abruptness of the eastern plateau-face made this section of the line most difficult to build. The engineers had to lay it in the very course of the winding river-valley; and to gain its development the line had to cross and recross the stream continually by a series of bridges, the farthest west and the farthest east of which were hardest to replace.

"To cut either of these bridges would isolate the Turkish army in Palestine, for one fortnight, from its base in Damascus, and destroy its power of escaping from Allenby's advance. To reach the Yarmuk we should need to ride from Akaba, by way of Azrak, some four hundred and twenty miles. The Turks thought the danger from us so remote that they guarded the bridges insufficiently. Accordingly we suggested the scheme to Allenby, who asked that it be done on November the fifth, or one of the three following days".[3]

The fifth of November, 1917, was the day when the British striking wings, the Desert Mounted and the XX Corps, were poised for what proved to be the final attack on Beersheba; and the destruction of a bridge at Tell el Shehab on the same day, or during the ensuing battle which would follow a British attack, would most certainly have been a most acceptable diversion, but in the event "the specious operation of cutting the Yarmuk Valley Railway", as Lawrence described it, resulted only in a literary triumph, accompanied by a military failure. Its telling filled six complete chapters of *Seven Pillars*.

The first chapter commences: "Starting was as difficult as ever. For my bodyguard I took six recruits. Of these Mahmud was a native of the Yarmuk. He was an alert and hot-tempered lad of nineteen, with the petulance often accompanying curly hair. Another was Aziz . . . A third was Mustafa, a gentle boy from Deraa". There was also "Rahail, the lusty, conceited Hourani lad", and Matar, whose "fat peasant's buttocks filled his camel-saddle", while "Farraj and Daud, with Khuidr and Mijbil, two Biasha, completed the party". Thus fortified,

Lawrence's momentous expedition was ready for action with every promise of a successful outcome. No time was lost in imposing the necessary discipline, and on the first day Farraj and Daud received their ritual flogging, with the promise of more to come.

"This business had delayed us", wrote Lawrence. "So we had an immense final meal in the luxury of camp, and started in the evening".[4] Of the next day there is little more to report than the newly-acquired "saddle-soreness" of Farraj and Daud, "which made them walk mile after mile". But in the evening they lit "great fires", and feasted on rice and bully beef and Army biscuits; and at the end of the next day's travel they found a green valley "sheltered from the wind, and warmed by the faint sunshine . . . Someone began to talk again about food".

The caravan continued on its leisurely way: perhaps the way in which all campaigns should ideally be fought. On the 30th October, within a few days of the agreed assignment, Lawrence was able to write: "So far for us each day was an easy movement, without effort, quite free from bodily strain. A golden weather of misty dawns, mild sunlight, and an evening chill added a strange peacefulness of nature to the peacefulness of our march. This week was a St. Martin's summer, which passed like a remembered dream. I felt only that it was very gentle, very comfortable, that the air was happy, and my friends content. Conditions so perfect must needs presage the ending of our time: but this certainty, because of its being unchallenged by any rebellious hope, served only to deepen the quiet of the autumnal present. There was no thought or care at all. My mind was as near stilled those days as ever in my life".[5]

This bucolic blissfulness did not extend across the River Jordan, where the British were massing for their attack against Beersheba, planned for the following day. Their preparations had galvanised the Turks into counter-activity, and on the 27th they virtually wiped out a post held by the London Yeomanry of the 8th Mounted Brigade: only three of the garrison survived. While Lawrence was basking in "the quiet of the autumnal present" 40,000 British troops were moving into their allotted positions, some 2,000 to 2,500 yards from the enemy's defence works. By 3a.m. on the 31st all these troops had reached their stations. They emerged from the battle as victors, but at heavy cost, for Allenby's XX.Corps lost nearly 1,200 men in the Beersheba fighting, and on the following day his XXI.Corps suffered 350 killed and a similar number missing, together with 2,000 wounded in their attack on Gaza.

On the other side of the Jordan Lawrence celebrated the last day of October in a very different fashion. There had been bickering among the tribes which had been followed by a reconciliation which took the form of "a great supper . . . Howeitat feasts had been wet with butter: the Beni Sakhr were overflowing. Our clothes were splashed, our mouths running over, the tips of our fingers scalded with its heat . . . Meanwhile, Abd el Kader sat spitting and belching and picking his teeth". And when this delighful feast was ended the guests "sat in the tent-mouth . . . and heard again the quiet, steady thudding of the heavy guns preparing assault in Palestine".[6]

But in the final paragraphs of this chapter Lawrence is able to revert to a more familiar and agreeable theme, introducing yet another Arab youth. "This lad, Turki by name, was an old love of Ali ibn el Hussein; the animal in each called to the other, and they wandered about inseparably, taking pleasure in a touch and silence. He was a fair, open-faced boy of perhaps seventeen; not tall, but broad and powerful, with a round freckled face, upturned nose, and very short upper lip, showing his strong teeth, but giving his full mouth rather a sulky look, belied by the happy eyes . . . Turki's great anxiety was to be sure that he was reckoned a man among the men, and he was always looking to do something bold and wonderful which would let him flaunt his courage before the girls of his tribe. He rejoiced exceedingly in a new silk robe which I gave him at dinner and walked, to display it, twice through the tent-village without his cloak, railing at those who seemed laggard from our meet".[7]

No wonder that Mousa complained after reading Lawrence's

account of this raiding expedition that it not only occupied sixty-seven pages ("or close to thirty thousand words") but included "many details which have no direct connexion with the Revolt".[8] It really does seem that Lawrence felt the need to expand his narrative with all manner of bonne bouche without regard to the relevance of the anecdote to the main subject.

The next day was November 3rd, leaving them only two days to spare before Allenby's first requested date. By chance they came across a party of the fighting men of the Serahin tribe, prepared to give their allegiance to Feisal but unwilling to participate in the attempt on the bridge. This reluctance appeared to present Lawrence with a serious and apparently unanticipated problem. "We were now in deep trouble. The Serahin were our last resource, and if they refused to come with us we should be unable to carry out Allenby's project by the appointed time".[9]

But this does not agree with his previous account of his prior arrangements for this important mission, when he listed his potential: his possible allies in the venture. "Ali (the Harith Serif) would bring us the Beni Sakhr. We had good hopes of the Serahin, the tribe at Azrak. I was in touch with the Beni Hassan."[10] The reader is left to assume that the Beni Hassan were not available to him, and that the Beni Sakhr would be inadequate for the task, although he had written that "Only half a dozen sentries were stationed actually on the girders and abutments", and that he proposed to deal with these with only "a handful" of men.

But now everything seemed to depend on the willingness of the Serahin to go with him, and in desperation he resorted, in his efforts to persuade them, to extraordinary flights of oratory. "We began to combat in words this crude presence of the Serahin, which seemed all the more shameful to us after our long sojourn in the clarifying wilderness". (Could this possibly mean "after all the time we have already dissipated"?) "We put it to them, not abstractedly, but concretely, for their case, how life in mass was sensual only, to be lived and loved in its extremity. There could be no rest-houses for revolt, no dividend for joy paid out. Its spirit was accretive, to endure as far as the sense would endure, and to use each such advance as base for further adventure, deeper privation, sharper pain. Sense could not reach back or forward. A felt emotion was a conquered emotion, an experience gone dead, which we buried by expressing it.

"To be of the desert was, as they knew, a doom to wage unending battle with an enemy who was not of the world, nor life, nor anything, but hope itself; and failure seemed God's freedom to mankind. We might only exercise this our freedom by not doing what it lay within our power to do, for then life would belong to us, and we should have mastered it by holding it cheap. Death would seem the best of all our works, the last free loyalty within our grasp, our final leisure: and of these two poles, death and life, or less finally, leisure and subsistence, we should shun subsistence (which was the stuff of life) in all save its faintest degree, and cling close to leisure. Thereby we would serve to promote the not-doing rather than the doing. Some men, there might be, uncreative; whose leisure was barren; but the activity of these would have been material only . . . We must believe, through and through, that there was no victory except to go down into death fighting and crying for failure itself, calling in excess of despair to Omnipotence to strike harder, that by his very striking He might temper our tortured selves into the weapon of His own ruin".[11]

The reader has been spared the greater part of this incredible peroration, which Lawrence would have us believe that he inflicted on a tribal gathering. Many questions about this performance must leap to the enquiring mind, but for the main part they are destined to remain unanswered. What language could he have used to natives who probably had no English, for not even the most enthusiastic of Lawrence's admirers could suggest that he was capable of delivering this profound homily in Arabic? Had he prepared a script, or did he just take written notes at the time to enable him later to incorporate the sermon in those pages of *Seven Pillars* which Mousa complained were filled with "details which have no connexion with the Revolt"?

Its ostentatious fluency is denied by its perpetrator in his final paragraph of Chapter LXXIV. "This was halting, half-coherent speech, struck out desperately, moment by moment, in our extreme need, upon the anvil of those white minds round the dying fire; and hardly its sense remained with me afterwards; for once my picture-making memory forgot its trade and only felt the slow humbling of the Serahin, the night quiet in which their worldliness faded, and at last their flashing eagerness to ride with us whatever the bourne".[12] These last words signal Lawrence's success, but the outcome showed that his interests would have been better served if his oratory had failed to win over the Serahin.

Too late to achieve Allenby's preferred date of November 5th, it was the 7th (by which time Gaza had been taken by Allenby) before he was able to complete the final arrangements for his striking force. And then, at that late hour, he had misgivings concerning his new recruits: "The Beni Sakhr were fighting men; but we distrusted the Serahin. So Ali and I decided to make the Beni Sakhr, under Fahad, our storming party. We would leave some Serahin to guard the camels while the others carried the blasting gelatine in our dismounted charge upon the bridge . . . My bodyguard had to be carefully distributed . . . Ali ibn el Hussein took six of his servants, and the party was completed by twenty Ben Sakhr and forty Serahin".[13]

Thus organised, the party reached the bridge on the evening of the 8th. Lawrence observed how "the rising moon slowly made beautiful the gorge" – but one of his warriors dropped a rifle, and the clatter alerted the Turkish sentries, who started firing. The Serahin had not bargained for such misbehaviour, and, remembering (wrote Lawrence) "that gelatine would go off if hit"[14] promptly dumped the sacks containing the explosive over the edge of the ravine, and as promptly departed. They were closely followed by the rest of their party, who found them scrambling on their camels. Thus ended the raid which failed to destroy the Yarmuk bridge but inspired nearly thirty thousand words for 67 pages of *Seven Pillars*.

However, the raiders did not go home entirely empty-handed, because in the flight from the Yarmuk gorge, wrote Lawrence, "our rush over-ran a party of peasants returning for Deraa. The Serahin, sore at the part they had played (or at what I said in the heat of running away) were looking for trouble, and robbed them bare . . . We left the Serahin offenders with their encumbering loot, and drove on in grim silence. Allenby's guns, still shaking the air away there on our right, were bitter recorders of the failure we had been . . . We were fools, all of us equal fools, and so our rage was aimless. Ahmed and Awad had another fight, young Mustafa refused to cook rice; Ferraj and Daud knocked him about until he cried; Ali had two of his servants beaten; and none of us or of them cared a little bit".[15] By the 12th they were safely back in Azrak, and a month later Lawrence was ordered to report to Allenby at the new headquarters, now beyond Gaza. Apprehensive at the prospect of explaining the Yarmuk failure, he was relieved to find Allenby apparently unconcerned.

During the three weeks of Lawrence's fruitless expedition the British forces had fought their way to Jaffa and occupied it, so that they were now in possession of over sixty miles of Palestinian coastline, while Jaffa itself gave Allenby a port for the landing of supplies and reinforcements for his advancing army. When Lawrence arrived in Palestine Jerusalem too had fallen to Allenby, and neither the success nor the failure of an attack on a railway bridge in the north was of any great consequence. It was more important to secure the areas of Jaffa and of Jerusalem where the Turks were regrouping and preparing for counter-attacking. The River Auja, four miles north of Jaffa, had to be crossed, and this was accomplished by the morning of the 21st December.

Lawrence had no place in these urgent areas of military activity, and after he had taken a week's holiday in Cairo, Allenby was content to encourage his return to Aqaba, which Lawrence reached on Christmas Day, 1917. There he learned that Maulud, Feisal's A.D.C., who had at one time served as a regular officer in the Turkish Army, had been successfully leading raids against the Turkish position around Aba el

Lissan, some fifty miles NNE of Aqaba. By January 7th, on the eve of the British capture of Jerusalem, the Turks retreated from Aba el Lissan, falling back on the outpost lines three miles west of Maan. This agreeable situation encouraged Lawrence to extend his leave for a further period. "Prosperity" he wrote "gave us ten day's leisure";[16] in celebration of which he joined Joyce in a car-trip, writing later that, "For me it was a holiday, with not an Arab near, before whom I must play out my tedious part".[17]

Chapter Fourteen

*Tafileh: a farcical battle, a parodied report,
and a serious embezzlement.*

CHAPTER LXXXIII of *Seven Pillars*, heralding the opening weeks of the final year of the war, commences with a reference to "the bodyguard which I formed for private protection", a topic which occupies much of the remaining part of the chapter. Its first page introduces a new recruit: "an Ageyly, thin, dark, and short, but most gorgeously dressed. He carried on his shoulder the richest Hasa saddle-bag I have ever seen. Its woollen tapestry of green and scarlet, white, orange and blue, had tassels woven over its sides in five rows, and from the middle and bottom hung five-foot streamers of geometric pattern, tasselled and fringed".[1]

But after depositing all this treasure Abdulla disappeared suddenly, and "on the third day reappeared empty-handed, in a poor cotton shirt . . . He looked odd without his silk robes; for his face, shrivelled and torn with smallpox, and hairless, might have been of any age; while he had a lad's supple body, and something of a lad's recklessness in his carriage. His long black hair was carefully braided into three shining plaits down each cheek. His eyes were weak, closed up to slits. His mouth was sensual, loose, wet; and gave him a good-humoured, half-cynical expression".[2]

Assuredly a close and detailed description, but apparently incomplete, because Lawrence devotes two more pages to this portrayal, until finally the reader is informed: "In fact, he was the perfect retainer and I engaged him instantly".[3] Lawrence was sufficiently impressed with him that he appointed him to "rule" over his bodyguard, seemingly an important position. "Fellows were very proud of being in my bodyguard, which developed a professionalism almost flamboyant. They dressed like a bed of tulips, in every colour but white; for that was my constant wear, and they did not wish to presume . . . we had but one resignation. The others, though adolescents full of carnal passion, tempted by this irregular life, well-fed, exercised, rich, seemed to satisfy their risk, to be fascinated by their suffering . . . These lads took pleasure in subordination; in degrading the body; so as to throw into greater relief their freedom in equality of mind . . ."[4] There are pages more of the same, with speculation on "the relation of master and man in Arabia", finally arriving at a definition of "our bodies . . . not as vehicles of the spirit, but, when dissolved, their elements served to manure a field".[5]

Mousa, regarding all this from "*An Arab View*", offers some acid comments. "Undoubtedly, Lawrence greatly exaggerated the merits of his bodyguard whom he enlisted to vie with the leaders of the Revolt. How could he – the lover of flashy appearances – let an opportunity like this go by, when he had enough money to indulge his tastes? Al-Ajluni has described his men as 'servants, followers, and Bedouin mercenaries'. Lawrence endowed them with heroic characteristics like Alexander Dumas's Three Musketeers. Evidence of Lawrence's lack of precision is to be found in the photograph published by Robert Graves in *Lawrence and the Arabs*, with the caption "Lawrence and his bodyguard at Aqaba – Summer, 1918", which included only fourteen men wearing different sets of clothes . . .

"In a letter to Robert Graves he mentioned that he learned Arabic from his *servants*. There has been unanimous agreement among all those I have talked to who knew him, that his followers were in fact servants and mercenaries and that their number never exceeded 15 from various tribes. Their main task was to work with him as guides and informers . . . It appears from Lawrence's records and writing that he did nothing during the twenty days between his return to Aqaba and his arrival at Tafileh on 20 January, five days after it was captured".[6]

This last imputation proves to be of greater significance than might at first appear, because, as we shall see, Lawrence's claim to have effected the capture of Tafileh had some very far-reaching effects. Tafileh had been discussed with Allenby at the meeting which Lawrence attended before he left for his December Cairo holiday. Allenby's interest was obvious, for with Jaffa, Ramleh and Jerusalem in British hands the next logical objective would be Turkish-held Jericho, astride the road from Jerusalem to the Jordan. Its possession would permit the completion of an Allied front extending from the Mediterranean to the Jordan close to the point where the river enters the northern end of the Dead Sea. Jericho was in fact captured by the British on the morning of February 21st, with the result that the entire western shore of the Dead Sea was then in British hands.

From the southern tip of the Dead Sea, the Wadi Arava ran down to the northern shores of the Gulf of Aqaba, marking the division between British-held territory up to roughly the latitude of 32° (at which stood Jaffa on the Mediterranean coastline) and Turkish-held areas from Medina (approximately at latitude 27°) northwards, from which there was the constant threat of Turkish attacks on Allenby's right flank from their garrisons east of the river. It was estimated that there were from ten to twelve thousand Turks in Medina, and over 5,000 rifles and 15 guns at Amman (just below latitude 32°). Maan, between these two last-named places, was held by the Ottoman II Corps, while at each intermediate station as well as in the blockhouses along the railway line were garrisons which had proved on so many occasions able to repel the attacks of regular as well as the irregular Arab forces.

The capture of Tafileh would therefore have assisted the conjunction at the southern end of the Dead Sea of British troops from the western areas and Arabs from the east, thus aiding the defence of the British right flank. This was all that Allenby had asked for at the December meeting, but Lawrence, seemingly undismayed by his failures at Mudowwara and the Yarmuk bridge, felt that he could go one better, and boldly suggested that a more effective link would be secured "at the north end of the Dead Sea".[7] Manifestly an excellent idea, which in the event proved to be completely beyond the capability of either Lawrence or Feisal, and the two forces – the British in Palestine and the Arabs to the east of the Jordan – were not brought together until the final days of the Turkish collapse, immediately prior to the Armistice.

But Tafileh did not present the same problems: in fact the place was occupied by the Howeitat under Abu Tayi on the evening of January 19th, (if we accept this date from Lawrence, for Mousa makes it the 15th.) In Lawrence's account Feisal's young half-brother Zeid rode into the town on January 20th, together with Jaafar Pasha, commander of the Arab regulars. Lawrence wrote that they "thanked and paid Auda and sent him back to his desert . . . By Zeid's plenty of gold the economic situation improved. We appointed an officer-governor and organized our five villages for further attack".[8]

A further attack proved to be more than a mere possibility, the Turks having decided to regain Ottoman control of the town. The news of the Turkish return created a panic. "The peasants thought we were running away (I think we were)" wrote Lawrence, "and rushed to save their goods and their lives. In the blistering dark the confusion and crying through the narrow streets were terrible . . . The housewives bundled their goods pell-mell out of doors and windows, though no men were waiting to receive them. Children were trampled on, and yelled, while their mothers were yelling anyhow".[9]

According to his own version, hotly disputed by Mousa and others, Lawrence took charge of the defence and organised a counter-attack. His (varied) descriptions of the resultant battle have appeared in a number of publications. In his article for the *Arab Bulletin* he described how he launched "a frontal attack of 18 men, 2 Vickers and 2 large Hotchkiss", a strategy which led to the defeat of an enemy force numbering 600 men. This despatch was dated "Tafila, January 26th" and gave the date of the battle as the 25th.[10] It brought him the reward of the Distinguished Service Order, an unexpected honour which stirred the glimmerings of an unsuspected conscience on the part of its recipient. In *Seven Pillars* he wrote of the battle: ". . . nothing came of all the loss and effort, except a report which I sent over to the British headquarters in Palestine for the Staff's consumption. It was meanly written for effect, full of quaint smiles" (was this meant to read *'similes'*?) "and mock simplicities . . . Like the battle, it was nearly-proof parody of regulation use. Headquarters loved it, and innocently, to crown the jest, offered me a decoration on the strength of it. We should have more bright breasts in the Army if each man was able, without witnesses, to write out his own despatch".[11]

Robert Graves also describes the report as "a parody, like the battle itself"; and Liddell Hart wrote that Lawrence "made the report a fuller parody of orthodoxy than the battle . . . His jest was crowned by the award of the Distinguished Service Order". But Mousa uses sterner language. He avers that it was Zeid who directed the cavalry unit which, supported by a mountain gun and two machine guns, successfully engaged the Turks on the morning of the 25th, and that Lawrence did not arrive on the scene until the afternoon. One of Mousa's informants "remembered Lawrence sitting in the presence of Emir Zeid, silent most of the time, with his head in his hands". Mousa continues: "None of the people I spoke to recalled Lawrence give an order or direct anybody to do anything. None of them believed that Lawrence was in any position of power, nor did they think that any of the people of Tafileh were prepared to be influenced by him. The developments of the battle were not the result of predetermined planning, but grew out of natural impromptu circumstances . . . We must, however, look at Lawrence's version of the battle of Tafileh, for his biographers consider that this was the only regular battle he supervised and conducted, and they take it as evidence of his rare military genius and superior leadership. This is to be expected, for these writers have based their views on Lawrence's own statements.

"Lawrence managed to catch up with the leaders of the Revolt who had preceded him to Tafileh . . . We might say, therefore, that it was sheer coincidence that enabled Lawrence to witness the battle of Tafileh, the death of Hamid Fakhri and the defeat of the Turks. It was reasonable, however, that Lawrence should write a report about this important battle in which the Arabs were so successful, but it was not at all reasonable that he should claim for himself credit which he did not merit, secure in his knowledge that he was writing in English to his own English Command".[12] Mousa follows this with a reference to Lawrence's "exceptional promotion to the rank of Colonel" and then exposes what he describes as "several contradictions" in Lawrence's account of the battle, concluding: "There is no doubt of Lawrence's sense of humour. He was at pains to admit his own pranks, but his biographers were prone to take them seriously".[13]

Although not everyone will agree with all that Mousa has said about this incident, it is nevertheless interesting to recall some passages from the *Introduction* which Lawrence wrote for the 1922 (Oxford) printing of *Seven Pillars*, in which he confesses: "My proper share was a minor one, but because of a fluent pen, a free speech, and a certain adroitness of brain, I took upon myself as I describe it, a mock primacy. By the accidental judgement of a publicist who visited us in the field, this mock primacy was published abroad as truth. In reality I held a subordinate official place. I never held any office among the Arabs; was never in charge of the British mission with them".

The "sense of humour" which Mousa recognised in Lawrence was destined to be sorely tested during the days which followed the battle. The weather worsened, and it snowed heavily towards the end of the month. Barley ran short in Tafileh, and the camels were cut off by the weather from natural grazing. "We were penned in verminous houses of cold stone", wrote Lawrence; "lacking fuel, lacking food; stormbound in streets like sewers, amid blizzards of sleet and an icy wind".[14] In these unhappy conditions quarrels broke out among his followers: there was bloodshed, and consequent punishment; and Lawrence decided to go off "in search of the extra money we should need when fine weather came",[15] for Zeid had already spent the first part of the sum set aside for Tafileh and the projected Dead Sea adventure.

He set off on this mission, with four followers, on the morning of the fourth of February, and after a painful journey arived at Guweira, which had become a station for the armoured cars. There he learned of Feisal's failure to "overwhelm" Mudowwara, the station from which, in the previous September, Lawrence had withdrawn after discovering that the Turks had artfully constructed their garrison buildings of stone, rendering them difficult targets for rifles. At that time the Turkish garrison had been estimated to consist of "about two hundred" men, but it could later have been augmented, for Feisal had the support of both Alan Dawnay and Joyce, in addition to both regular and irregular Arab forces, but still had failed. Lawrence reported "Lazy nights, three of them, in the armoured car tents at Guweira . . . pleasant . . . and Tafileh to boast about",[16] vaunting his great success against his friends' recent failure.

On the eighth of February thirty thousand pounds of gold came up from Aqaba, conveyed in thirty bags each containing one thousand pounds. He gave two bags each to fourteen members of his escort, and took the last two himself. The weight of each bag was twenty-two pounds, and thus laden they commenced their return journey, or shelter for the night.

They parted company, and Lawrence rode into Shobek, where he spent the night of February 10th in the house of a Sherif whose name he gives, within the space of a single page, as Abd el Main, Abd el Mayein, Abd el Muein, Abd el Mayin and abd el Muyein. (When *Seven Pillars* was being prepared for publication this inconsistency was brought to his notice by the puzzled proof-reader. Lawrence replied: "Good egg. I call this really ingenious.") His host served him with supper, claiming it to be his last reserve of food and that he had no money for his two hundred followers, and Lawrence promptly responded, "commanding my saddle-bags, and presented him with five hundred pounds on account, till his subsidy came. This was good payment for the food, and we were very merry over the oddness of riding alone, in winter, with a hundredweight and more of gold for baggage".[17]

The next day he rode into Tafileh, where he gave Zeid his letters and some money, and then gladly went to bed. On the following morning he "asked Zeid to take from Motlog the coming twenty-four thousand pounds, and spent what was necessary for current expenses until my return . . . Zeid heard me coldly. I saw Motlog next to him, and greeted him sarcastically, asking what was his tally of the gold: then I began to repeat my programme of what we might fairly do. Zeid stopped me: 'But that will need a lot of money'. I said, 'Not at all': our funds in hand would cover it, and more. Zeid replied that he had nothing; and when I gaped at him, muttered rather shame-facedly that he had spent all I brought. I thought he was joking: but he went on to say that so much had been due to Dhiab, sheikh of Tafileh; so much to the villagers; so much to the Jazi Howeitat; so much to the Beni Sakhr".[18]

In short, Motlog had handed over the twenty thousand pounds in gold, and Zeid had generously distributed it. "I was aghast", Lawrence wrote, "for this meant the complete ruins of my plans and hopes, the collapse of our effort to keep faith with Allenby. Zeid stuck to his word that all the money had gone. Afterwards I went off to learn the truth from Nasir, who was in bed with fever. He despondently said that everything was wrong – Zeid too young and shy to counter his dishonest, cowardly counsellors".[19]

On the following morning he told Zeid that if he would not return the money he would leave him. Of course there was not the slightest hope of recovering the gold from the tribesmen, and Lawrence left for Beersheba, which he reached on the 21st of February, to learn that Allenby's troops had just taken Jericho. When in the previous December he had travelled disconsolately to Allenby's headquarters to report the Yarmuk failure, he had arrived there in time to join Allenby in celebrating the capture of Jerusalem: now he brought the news of his misfortunes at Tafileh at the very moment of another Allied success.

Sadly he ends this chapter of his misadventure with a mournful threnody: "My will had gone and I feared to be alone, lest the wind of circumstance, or power, or lust, blow my empty soul away".[20]

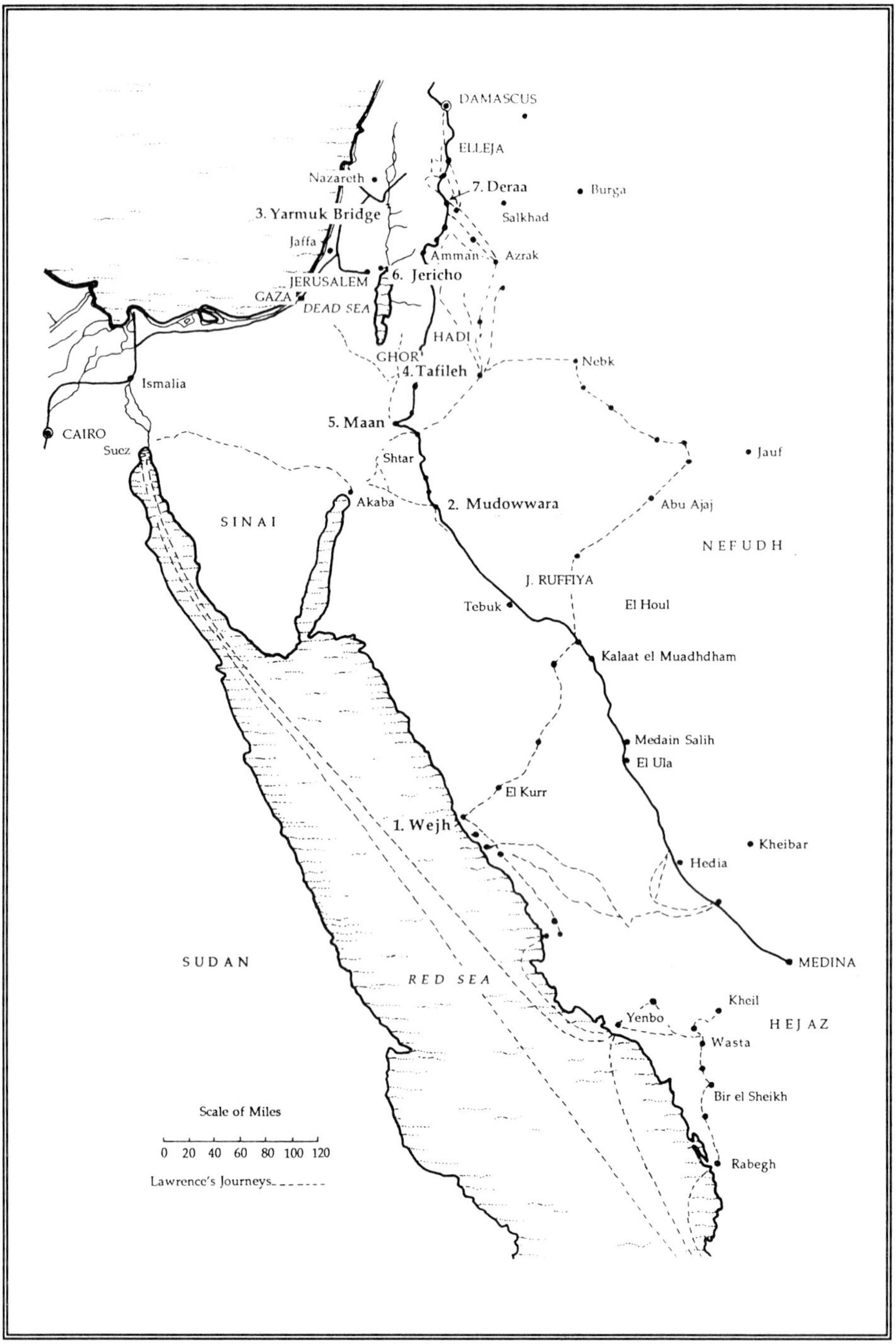
DAMASCUS
ELLEJA
7. Deraa
Burga
Nazareth
3. Yarmuk Bridge
Salkhad
Jaffa
Amman
Azrak
JERUSALEM
6. Jericho
GAZA
DEAD SEA
HADI
GHOR
4. Tafileh
Nebk
Ismalia
5. Maan
CAIRO
Suez
Shtar
Jauf
Akaba
2. Mudowwara
Abu Ajaj
SINAI
NEFUDH
J. RUFFIYA
Tebuk
El Houl
Kalaat el Muadhdham
Medain Salih
El Ula
El Kurr
1. Wejh
Kheibar
Hedia
SUDAN
MEDINA
RED SEA
Kheil
Yenbo
HEJAZ
Wasta
Scale of Miles
Bir el Sheikh
0 20 40 60 80 100 120
Rabegh
Lawrence's Journeys

Seven Pillars of Folly

T.E. Lawrence's Failures in the Desert Campaigns.

1. WEJH, 25th January, 1917. "At dawn we rallied the various contingents twelve miles south of the town, and advanced on it in order . . . covering the ground at nearly six miles an hour, dead silent, and reached and climbed the ridge without a shot fired. So we knew the work had been finished for us . . . "

2. MUDOWWARA, October 17, 1917. "The station was very long, of stone buildings . . . so in the end I voted we leave it unalarmed, for a future occasion. But it was not until August, 1918, that Buxton's Camel Corps at last measured to it the fate long over-due."

3. THE YARMUK BRIDGE, (to be demolished by Lawrence on November 5th, 1917). Cutting it "would isolate the Turkish army in Palestine from its base in Damascus, and destroy its power of escaping from Allenby's advance" (p.103), but when the demolition party arrived at the target on November 8th one of Lawrence's warriors dropped a rifle, and the clatter alerted the Turkish sentries. The raiders dumped the explosive and rapidly decamped.

4. TAFILEH, (25th January, 1918), where "a frontal attack of 18 men,

2 Vickers and 2 large Hotchkiss" was reported by Lawrence to have defeated, under his direction, a Turkish force numbering 600. But Tafileh was back in Turkish hands five weeks later.

5.MAAN, "In conjunction with Allenby we laid a triple plan to join hands across Jordan, to capture Maan, and to cut off Medina, in one operation . . . neither of us fulfilled his part".

6.JERICHO, At the end of December Lawrence suggested to Allenby that "we might join him at the north end of the Dead Sea. If he could put Feisal's fifty tons a day of supplies, stores and ammunition into Jericho, we would abandon Akaba and transfer our headquarters to the Jordan Valley . . .We began well; but when we reached the Dead Sea, bad weather, bad temper and division of purpose blunted our offensive spirit and broke up our force."

7.DERAA, On May 5, 1918, Lawrence asked Allenby to give him 2,000 riding camels "to put a thousand men in Deraa any day you please". Lawrence got the camels but never reached Deraa until after its capture by Allenby's troops.

Chapter Fifteen

Maan; more mountains of gold.
Allenby suffers defeat at Es Salt.

The reader will be relieved to learn from the opening paragraphs of the following chapters of *Seven Pillars* that Lawrence's "empty soul" had not after all been blown away. Instead he has breakfast with Clayton, to whom his friend and mentor Hogarth had taken him, and from whom he learns that Allenby was planning a final assault on the Turks. "Turkey was to be put out of the war once and for all" but Allenby's great problem "lay with his eastern flank, the right, which to-day rested on the Jordan".

Never at a loss to produce at a moment's notice the ultimate plan for victory, Lawrence offered to "deal" with Maan, which, he promised, would be reduced by "units of the Arab Regular Army", and this would enable the British to cross the Jordan and occupy Salt, opening the way to Damascus. All that Lawrence needed for this was "seven hundred baggage camels, more guns and machine-guns, and lastly, assurance against flank attack from Amman, while we dealt with Maan".[1]

Within the week the preparations were agreed, and by the first of March Lawrence was in Cairo, where he stayed for two days before returning to Feisal at Aqaba. There Feisal was overjoyed to learn that Allenby had put three hundred thousand pounds into Lawrence's independent credit, and given the Arabs a train of seven hundred pack-camels complete with personnel and equipment; but saddened, a few days later, by the news that the Turks had retaken Tafileh. After all those eloquent despatches, all that lavish distribution of the British taxpayers' gold – and all to no avail: the Turks were back again in Tafileh.

BOOK VIII of *Seven Pillars* carries the ominous heading: The Ruin of High Hope. It would seem that the reckless obstinacy of the Turks was depriving Lawrence of one carefully-planned victory after another: Mudowwara, the Yarmuk bridge, Tafileh, and now Maan. West of the Jordan, there was stiff fighting from the 9th to the 12th as the Turks endeavoured to contain the Allied forces as these moved northwards from the front which now extended from beyond Jaffa to Jericho; and in the last week of the month the British succeeded in crossing the Jordan for an attack on Amman. This should have received the support of Lawrence's simultaneous assault on Maan, but, as he himself wrote, it proved to be "impregnable"[2]. As usual, Lawrence fills the void left by unsuccessful military action with lengthy philosophical discourse.

From March the 27th to the 30th the British – the 60th Division, the Anzac Mounted Division, and the Imperial Camel Brigade, under General Shea – strove to capture Amman, but were forced to withdraw on the night of the 30th. Their losses amounted to 1,350, and as they were pulling back their troops from the town the Turks mounted an attack from the north against Es Salt, which had been occupied by the British on the evening of the 25th.[3] Lawrence had been at Atara when the news – false, as it proved to be – came to him that the English had taken Amman, but as in response to that news he moved towards Themed – about thirty miles south of Amman – new messages came to say that the British were falling back. Later they were told that the Turks were "chasing Allenby far down the Jordan valley", and that "it was thought that Jerusalem would be recovered".[4]

It was particularly unfortunate that these reverses were being suffered at a time when Allenby had been warned that troops were needed urgently for France, where the Germans had launched their great offensive on the very day that Allenby had sent his own forces across the Jordan for the ill-fated Amman attack. Wavell reported that: "During the first half of April two complete divisions, the 52nd and 74th, embarked for the Western Front. Nine Yeomanry regiments, five-and-a-half siege batteries, nine British battalions, and five machine-gun companies were also withdrawn from the (Palestine) front for embarkation. Fourteen more British battalions were sent in May".[5] Yet despite this heavy drain on his resources, Allenby was determined to maintain the offensive action against the Turk, and on the first day of April ordered Peake to bring his Egyptian Army Camel Corps to Aqaba.

His arrival there and his subsequent participation in the desert war has been described in Jarvis's biography. Peake reported that Aqaba at that time had "a normal population of about four hundred and two dug-out canoes": an unimpressive description of the seat of the headquarters of the leaders of the Arab Revolt. On arrival he found "ships lying in the anchorage and unloading stores, including boxes of golden sovereigns . . . He was then taken to a small cement and stone building behind the main office, and handed a sealed canvas bag complete with leather holster in which to carry it. Then a document was produced, a receipt form, and he was asked to sign for £1,000 in gold, which he was informed was in the bag. Peake protested that he did not want gold, that he had no place to carry it, and that it would be of no use to him as he would not know how to spend it, but it was in vain. The order was that not less than £1,000 was to be carried by every British Officer in charge of a column. After this interesting and unusual financial transaction had been completed Peake had a look into the small room and saw, stacked up to the ceiling, dozens of sealed ammunition boxes, and, on the floor near the door, an array of canvas bags similar to the one he had just received. Each of the boxes, he learned, contained five canvas bags, and to quote Peake's own words: 'Never have I seen, no do I expect to see again, the sinews of war so blatantly exposed'.

On his way up the Wadi Ithm two Model T Fords passed him,

loaded up and well down on the back axles with these sealed boxes such as Peake had seen in the store at Aqaba, and each vehicle with its solitary escort was carrying upwards of £30,000 in gold. This struck him as being so unsafe, that he mentioned it to the Emir Feisal when he met him some days later, but the Emir replied that there was not the slightest necessity to be anxious about it as every Bedouin knew that the boxes contained gold, which was shortly to be distributed to them".[6]

Small wonder that Lawrence (quoted by Storrs) had written that "the coast towns are glutted with gold and the Rupee is only 10-12 to the sovereign".[7]

The llth of April, 1918, proved to be a sad day in the annals of all the fighting fronts. In the foothills of Judea the 75th Division, after battling for three days with the German units posted at Berukin, suffered defeat. On the Western Front in Europe the British 50th and 51st Divisions were being pushed back by the German LV. and XIX. Corps, while the Bavarian II. Corps advanced through Nieppe to Steenwerck. The German gains south of Ypres cost the British the staggering total of 40,000 casualties. And at Raraifra, on the road from Azrak, Lawrence witnessed the death of Farraj.

"We tried to move him", wrote Lawrence, "for he was helpless, though he showed no pain. We tried to stop the wide, slow bleeding, which made poppysplashes in the grass; but it seemed impossible, and after a while he told us to let him alone, as he was dying, and happy to die, since he had no care of life. Indeed, for long he had been so, and men very tired and sorry fell in love with death, with that triumphal weakness coming home after strength has been vanquished in a last battle".[8]

On the following day (the 12th) he joined Dawnay, who, with a mixed force of British, Egyptian, and Bedouin troops was preparing a series of raids on the railway. These were intended to be no hit-and-run raids of the sort which had provoked Allenby's sarcasm, but concerted efforts involving Peake's Egyptian Army Camel Corps and a section of the British Armoured Cars, together with a special detachment of Bedouin under Sheikh Haza. The whole force set out on the dawn of the 19th. Hornby descended on the first target, a railway bridge, with two Rolls tenders and a hundredweight of gun-cotton, and blew it up without further ado. Other targets succumbed in quick succession until the time came for an assault on the major target, the station at Tell Shahm. This was softened up by a preliminary bombing from the air: then the armoured cars went in and the Turks at once surrendered. The British forces having effectively destroyed the enemies' defences and taken the garrison prisoners it was time for the Arabs to play their part. Their performance was described by Lawrence: "A minute later, with a howl, the Bedouin were upon the maddest looting of their history. Two hundred rifles, eighty thousand rounds of ammunition, many bombs, much food and clothing were in the station, and everybody smashed and profited. In the pause the Egyptian officer found an unbroken storehouse, and put a guard of soldiers over it, because they were very short of food. Haza's wolves, not yet sated, did not recognize the Egyptians' right to share equally. Shooting began: but by mediation we obtained that the Egyptians pick first what rations they needed: afterwards there followed a general scramble, which burst the store-room walls.

"The profit of Sham was so great that eight out of every ten of the Arabs were contented with it. In the morning only Haza and a handful of men remained with us for further operations"[9] Peake reported that Bedouin "moved off during the night with no intention of fighting again until their store of foodstuffs was exhausted".[10] As they had apparently played no part in fighting the Turks one may wonder whether "fighting again" meant a renewal of their battle with the Egyptians.

The next objectives in Dawnay's programme were the stations at Ramleh and Mudowwara. At Ramleh the armoured cars went in first, and found the station closed up and "empty of men, though full enough of desirable goods to make Haza and the faithful remnant prize their virtue aloud"; while Peake in more prosaic language adds that when the station "was taken . . . it was amusing to see the deserter Bedouin rushing in from the hills for more loot". Of the attack on Mudowwara, Peake reported that it was cancelled by Lawrence after the Turkish garrison there brought their four mountain guns into action: "for the information of a defeat accompanied by considerable casualties – and news travels fast in the desert – would have a most serious effect on the Bedouins farther north, who were sitting on the fence and watching events before they came in openly with Feisal".[11]

Had Allenby at that time shared the awareness of Peake that the policy of the tribes was always to await the outcome of events so that they could be sure of finishing up on the winning side he might have averted the failure of the attack on Es Salt which he had planned for the middle of May. His hand was prematurely forced when before the end of April a deputation arrived from the Beni Sakhr tribe to say that their fighting men were assembled about Madeba, some twenty miles south of Es Salt, and prepared to go into action together with the British, but that their stock of supplies did not permit them to wait later than 4th May.

In his history of the Palestine Campaigns Wavell makes a number of comments on this unfortunate and costly venture. "It was a bold plan that promised well had it not been based on faulty intelligence of the enemy and misplaced trust in the unstable Arabs. The Beni Sakhr made no effort to fill the role they had undertaken, while the Turks reacted with unexpected swiftness and strength . . General Allenby had no experience of the instability of the Arabs, nor of their inaptitude for regular warfare and prolonged operations. Their offer fitted in so well with the plan he was maturing that it seemed worth while to hasten on the date in order to secure their assistance . . .If, while our mounted troops seized Es Salt, the Beni Sakhr, coming up from the south, barred the Ais Sir track, which they professed themselves well able to do, the Turkish force at Nimrin would be completely isolated and might be destroyed".[12]

The cost of this perfidy was withdrawal and defeat with a toll of over fifteen hundred casualties. It has nowhere been suggested that the defeat might have been the consequence of deliberate treachery and conspiracy with the Turks on the part of the Beni Sakhr, but if such an accusation was in fact justified the consequences would have been those that the British suffered. Lawrence commented on the failure in characteristic equivocatory style: "The check taught the British to be more patient with Feisal's difficulties: convinced the Turks that the Amman sector was their danger point; and made the Beni Sakhr feel that the English were past understanding: not great fighting men, perhaps, but ready on the spur of the moment to be odd. So, in part, it redeemed the Amman failure by its deliberate repetition of what had looked accidental. At the same time it ruined the hopes which Feisal had entertained of acting independently with the Beni Sakhr. This cautious and wealthy tribe asked for dependable allies".[13]

Some may find this statement preposterous, suggesting as it clearly does that the Beni Sakhr did not regard the British as dependable allies: not great fighting men and ready to be odd! One can only imagine from this extraordinary comment that the British had in some way betrayed the Beni Sakhr. Wavell lets Lawrence down lightly on this passage, merely writing that he "makes some pungent comments on the folly of initiating an operation on the unverified promises of unknown sheikhs; but it was difficult for G.H.Q. at the time to realise the complete irresponsibility of Arab warfare".[14]

Lawrence of Arabia

Chapter Sixteen

Deraa, another Lawrence miscarriage. A disputed massacre at Tafas. Flagellation, sadism and masochism.

Allenby's reverses in the Jordan valley, together with the reduction of the manpower available to him for renewed action in the Palestine campaigns through his contributions to the needs of the Western Front in Europe, influenced his decision to abolish the Imperial Camel Brigade so that its men could be employed as mounted reinforcements for other units. Lawrence happened to be present at the meeting on May the fifth and immediately asked whether he could have two thousand of the riding-camels which would become available. "He looked at me with a twinkle", wrote Lawrence, " 'And what do you want them for?' I replied hotly,' To put a thousand men in Deraa any day you please' ".[1]

Allenby agreed to let him have the camels, and Lawrence brought the good news to Feisal. "It is nearly finished," he told him. "Soon you can let me go . . . we have been made victorious". The ecstasy of the anticipated victory fills the following pages in his book: but there is little else for him to report for the following two months except some light relief on the last day of May, when a Beni Sakhr leader, Fawaz, conspired to ensnare Lawrence and sell him to the Turks. The trap was cunningly laid and attractively baited.

"He received me with fair words and hospitality, fed us richly, and brought out, after we had talked, his richest bed-quilts". During the night Lawrence was warned by Nawaf el Faiz that Fawaz had sent horsemen to Ziza, and that soon the Turks would come to take him; he escaped by crawling out through the tent-curtain to reach the camels and disappear into the night. "A few days later Sheikh Fawaz was dead,"[2] was the dramatic ending to this adventure.

Then follows Lawrence's account of his efforts to persuade King Hussein to sanction the transfer to Aqaba of the units under Ali and Abdullah, of whose activities there had been nothing to report for some time. Wingate also wrote letters to Hussein advising this reinforcement for Feisal and his approval of the proposed transfer. But it came to nothing, for, wrote Lawrence, "the old man was little inclined to take Feisal's advice, out of green-eyed hatred for this son who was doing too well and was being disproportionately helped by the British".[3] This division among the Arab leaders, extending even into the ranks of the chief Hashemite family, together with the (not isolated) example of the Sheikh Fawaz treachery, serve to make a mockery of Lowell Thomas's extravagant exultation of "the young Oxford graduate" who united the Arabs against their Turkish oppressors.

In a final effort to obtain "Ali's and Abdullah's khaki-clad contingents" for Feisal, Lawrence travelled to G.H.Q. to enlist Allenby's support. This was readily obtained, but proved to be of no avail: the King would not agree to the reinforcement of this hated son, and Lawrence was obliged to abandon the idea. But while at G.H.Q. he learned of Allenby's decision to open "a general and sustained offensive in September", prompting him to announce "Our role would be as laid down in the spring; we must make the Deraa raid on the two thousand new camels".[4]

This firm declaration was followed by weeks of preparation and discussions: by the 16th July "they had figured out the food, ammunition, forage and transport for two thousand men of all ranks, from Aba el Lissan to Deraa. They had taken into consideration all our resources and worked out schedules by which dumps would be completed and the attack begun in November . . . But Allenby meant to attack on September the nineteenth, and wanted us to lead off not more than four nor less than two days before he did. His words to me were that three men and a boy with pistols in front of Deraa on September the sixteenth would fill his conception; would be better than thousands a week before or a week after. The truth was, he cared nothing for our fighting power, and did not reckon us part of his tactical strength. Our purpose, to him, was moral, psychological, diathetic; to keep the enemy command intent upon the trans-Jordan front. In my English capacity I shared this view, but on my Arab side both agitation and battle seemed equally important, the one to serve the joint success, the other to establish Arab self-respect, without which victory would not be wholesome".[5]

It must be clear from this last that Allenby had been freed from his earlier illusions concerning the value of Lawrence's plans and of Arab cooperation, yet twelve days later Lawrence was talking about his "new proposal . . . an intricate dovetailing in the next crowded month and a half, of a 'spoiling' raid by the British Camel Corps and the main road to surprise the Turks by Deraa".[6] He would concentrate a camel column of a thousand men in Azrak by September the 13th, and on the sixteenth would envelop Deraa, and cut its railways. On the 18th he would fall back east of the railway and "wait events with Allenby".[7] Nuri Pasha would command the Deraa expedition.

These planned dates would certainly have suited Allenby's timetable, for at 4.30 a.m. on September 19th every available gun on his fronts opened up in a sustained and concentrated bombardment of the Turkish positions. Seven Allied divisions, including a French one at the extreme right, swept across the Turkish lines, and by midday the Eighth Turkish Army had collapsed into hopeless confusion. Haifa was captured on the 23rd, and the following day witnessed the complete annihilation of the remnants of the Turkish Seventh and Eighth Armies.

On that 23rd day of September, a week later than Allenby's chosen date for the mustering of "three men and a boy with pistols in front of

Deraa," – Lawrence had reached Umtaiye, about seventy-five miles to the south of Damascus and some miles to the south of Deraa. It was not until the 27th – the day on which the Australian Mounted Division began its victorious march on Damascus, which it entered four days later – that Lawrence and his Arabs came within sight of Deraa. Heavy smoke hung over the town: the Germans there had set fire to aeroplanes and storehouses in their preparations for its evacuation, for they had received the news that Barrow's troops were near Remtha, ten miles away.

But while the Germans were still in possession of the town Lawrence's party would not venture within range of their guns. Instead, he gave the place a wide berth and made his way towards Tafas, north-east of Deraa. There his men came across gruesome evidence, from Lawrence's account, of a massacre, and atrocities at the hands of the retreating Turks. Although Lawrence's story is in part supported by the evidence of Nuri as-Said it is contradicted by Sayyid Nasir el Fawwaz el Barkat, whose father was chief of Remtha (about half-way between Tafas and Deraa) and of the surrounding villages.

The manner of Lawrence's telling of the scenes he claimed to have witnessed deeply exercised the mind of John Mack, who commented: "I have dwelt at length upon the Tafas episode, and have taken particular pains to establish Lawrence's role in it, because it not only, I believe, is pertinent to the evaluation of his character, but raises at the same time issues pertinent to assessing the actions. and personality of any public figure".[8] Lawrence had written a number of descriptions of the Tafas atrocities, the earliest of which was included in the Arab Bulletin No.106. This consisted of no more than twenty-nine words (three lines of print), but in Seven Pillars he devoted three entire paragraphs – nearly twenty-five lines – to the story. The first two paragraphs describe the appalling wounds inflicted on a little girl . . . "a child, three or four years old, whose dirty smock was stained red over one shoulder and side, with blood from a large half-fibrous wound, perhaps a lance-thrust, just where neck and body joined . . . I looked close and saw the body of a woman . . . bottom upwards, nailed there by a saw bayonet whose haft stuck hideously into the air from between her naked legs. She had been pregnant, and about her lay others, perhaps twenty in all, variously killed, but set out in accord with an obscene taste."[9]

This frightfulness becomes the cue, in Lawrence's account, for the wanton killing of the Turkish prisoners and wounded. "In a madness born of the horror of Tafas we killed and killed, even blowing in the heads of the fallen and of animals; as though their death and running blood could slake our agony".[10] The loss of control depicted in this account is attributed by Mack to an "identification with the Arabs in revenge connected with his own desire for revenge for what had been done to him by the Turks at Der'a ten months before and, combined with the other stresses of the campaigns he had undergone, accounts for his loss of control".[11]

Mack, a medical psychiatrist, bases this diagnosis on his acceptance of Lawrence's reports, but these have been flatly contradicted by accounts from Arab sources. Both Nuri as-Said and Nasir el Fawwaz confirm that there was fighting between the villagers of Tafas and the Turks in which Talal, described by Lawrence as Sheikh of Tafas and chief of Hauran, was killed by a Turkish hand-grenade. Nuri as-Said's report that his Arabs took a considerable number of prisoners and wounded men after the fighting and dispersal of the Turks[12] contradicts Lawrence's assertion that "By my orders we took no prisoners, for the only time in our war."[13] It must be asked whether a Liaison Officer would in fact possess the authority to give such an order in the presence of the Arab army's Chief of Staff.

Nasir el Fawwaz's version is that after spending a night unmolested at the nearby village of Turra, a column of Turkish soldiers was next day at dawn attacked in the rear, while in the course of withdrawing from the area. The troops retaliated, and in the course of the fighting Talal and some of the villagers were killed. "With regard to the murder of women and children," writes Mousa, "this source says that there is no truth in this report: nothing of the sort happened, either at Turra or at Tafas".

Returning to Mack's analysis we find that he expresses the view that: "A man who, with little provocation orders, takes part in, and even enjoys, killing helpless prisoners, while experiencing no guilt, is a sadist who invites little sympathy or interest. The film *Lawrence of Arabia* would lead us to believe this true of Lawrence . . . The Der'a and Tafas experiences are, in my opinion, of special importance because of their link with the substance of unconscious conflicts and with areas of psychic vulnerability which, until these events occurred, had remained merely potential areas of emotional disorder without overt indication of unusual distress . . . But Der'a and Tafas touched off in Lawrence – there seem to be no right words – or brought into his consciousness in an abrupt and devastating way, forbidden or unacceptable sexual, aggressive and vengeful impulses . . . In addition, he was left with a compulsive wish to be whipped, attributable to the Der'a experience, which was the source of much later misery".[14]

Mack returns later in his book to the theme of "the precipitation in Lawrence of a flagellation disorder. His powerful identification with his guilt-ridden mother; the childhood experience of being beaten repeatedly by her in a manner to break his will; the lifetime fascination with, dread of, and need to master pain; the absence of any offsetting heterosexual adaptation; the guilt and shame which resulted from the war experience; and conceivably, a biologically rooted masochistic predisposition – all of these combined to make Lawrence vulnerable to this disorder . . . "[15]

Mack twice refers to the "Deraa experience"; this relates to a much debated incident described by Lawrence in the eightieth chapter of his epic, when he claimed to have suffered a brutal flogging and violation at the hands of his Turkish captors. The date of this outrage is given in the book as the 20th November, 1917, between the times of Lawrence's return to Azrak after the Yarmuk bridge failure and his December visit to Cairo. It was deliberately passed over in this present account for the very good reason that it could not sensibly be related to the course of the fighting. It was, if it actually happened, a personal experience, without any place, in a formal war history. But the importance which Mack attaches to it in his examination of Lawrence's behaviour places us under the obligation of returning to Lawrence's story, or rather to one of the versions in which he described what happened.

As a punishment for rejecting the sexual advances of an officer who is described as the "Bey, the Governor" he is delivered over to the guards. One, armed with "a thong of supple black hide . . . began to lash me"(he recounted) madly and madly across with all his might . . . To keep my mind in control I numbered the blows, but after twenty lost count, and could feel only the shapeless weight of pain, not tearing claws, for which I had been prepared, but a gradual cracking apart of my whole being by some too great force whose waves rolled up my spine till they were pent within my brain, to clash terribly together . . . [16] I remembered the corporal kicking with his nailed boot to get me up; and this was true, for the next day my right side was dark and lacerated, and a damaged rib made each breath stab me sharply. I remembered smiling idly at him, for a delicious warmth, probably sexual, was swelling through me; and then that he flung up his arm and hacked with the full length of his whip into my groin".[17]

In the final words of that chapter he tells of "the burden, whose certainty the passing days confirmed: how in Deraa that night the citadel of my integrity had been irrevocably lost".[18] On the following morning he recalled an earlier experience, "where something, less staining, of the sort had happened". This, it seems, was at a place called Khalfati, between Aintub and Urfa, when in the September of 1909 he "was attacked by Kurds who beat him and left him for dead."[19] Of this alleged incident there are a number of different accounts ("not quite reconcilable", commented Garnett) and some confusion as to the actual date: even the actual year.

Mack does not refer to the Khalfati incident, but again broaches the connection, in his diagnosis, between the beatings Lawrence endured at Deraa and those he suffered at the hands of his own mother in childhood, writing that: "The emphasis upon the overwhelming of his 'bodily integrity', or in Seven Pillars, upon 'the loss of the citadel of my integrity', is very similar, to the way in which Lawrence viewed the threat of intimacy with his mother. 'I think I'm afraid of letting her get, ever so little, inside the circle of my integrity', he wrote in 1928, 'and she is always hammering and sapping to get it'; and, three months later, 'I always felt that she was laying siege to me and would conquer, if I left a chink unguarded'."[20]

Mack appears to attribute the most extraordinary significance to these childhood chastisements, writing of Lawrence and his mother: "His psychological vulnerabilities may be traced in large part to their relationship. 'The strongest impression: I have', his younger brother Arnold once wrote, 'is that his (T.E.'s) life has been injured by his mother'. Lawrence's resistance as a child to his parent's authority often took familiar forms of naughtiness. Discipline, according to Arnold, was administered in the form of severe whippings on the buttocks and was delivered by his mother because his father was 'too gentle, too imaginative – couldn't bring himself to'. Arnold remembered receiving only one such beating himself. His mother once told him, 'I never had to do it to Bob, once to Frank, and frequently to T.E.'."[21]

Continuing his hypothesis Mack proceeds: "Now let us examine what happened to Lawrence. As far as I can tell, intimacy with the mother was present in his early childhood, although he received physical affection more continuously from nurses. Religious and intellectual values and devotion of the members of the family to each other were exaggerated as a result of parental guilt and self-imposed social isolation". This leads Mack to suggest that the Deraa episode "aroused or revived earlier conflicts in Lawrence's relationship with his mother, a need to avoid surrendering to her desires and demands which, in view of the childhood beatings at her hands, may also have had the meaning of self-surrender".

But what if Lawrence's account of the Deraa episode was proved to be an invention? Mousa reproduces part of this account, following an introduction which reads: "Here is a summary of this alleged adventure, which I give at this point, although I am convinced that it never happened at all,"[22] and concludes: "This is the account as Lawrence gave it and as it was taken over by his biographers as the truth. I find the whole story highly implausible . . . Faiz el Ghussein has always assured me that he is fully convinced the episode never happened at all, and is purely imaginary. He attributes it to Lawrence's literary inclinations . . . I have not found one person in Transjordan and Syria who had heard of this story or knew anything about it."[23]

Knightley and Simpson discuss the evidence both for and against the veracity of the story and give consideration to the element of masochism which, they maintain, "involves going back to Lawrence's childhood". They do not agree that "the facts show Mrs. Lawrence to have been as great a tyrant as has been suggested", adding, not unreasonably, that: "It is not unknown for parents to beat their children's bottoms without turning them into heroes or neurotics".[24] But, as we have seen, Mack and Arnold Lawrence agree in their belief that the childhood-spanking sessions may have played some part in Lawrence's neurotic disorders.

The three writers just quoted all find some association between the alleged Deraa experience and the Bruce floggings[25] which were revealed in 1968, and similarly invoke the childhood chastisements when discussing this question. But it is surprising that they fail to cite the element of "just retribution" which Lawrence employed in the elaborate fictions surroundings the flogging sessions with Bruce. The beatings inflicted by Bruce were represented by Lawrence, as ordeals to be suffered as a form of merited punishment for an (invented) misdemeanor, though Mack reveals that Lawrence "required the beatings to be severe enough to produce a seminal emission".[26] In the final analysis it may be said that Mrs. Lawrence spanked "Ted" for being naughty: Daud and Farraj were also spanked for being naughty; and Lawrence had to invent a naughtiness to justify to Bruce the spanking he received from him.

He may have been flogged at Khalfati, and also at Deraa for all that anyone now can tell, but the whole sorry business appears to suggest a long-standing masochism, compelling him towards continued falsehood and deceit. His biographers have diligently investigated and discussed the problem of his behaviour and its influence on his "motivation" for his participation in the desert war. While it is important to consider their views, however varied and conflicting these may prove to be, if we may now return to Lawrence's own writings we will find that he makes his own generous contribution to the debate, with little attempt to conceal his own attitudes, however unacceptable these may prove to be in a conventional society. We will find that there is more than a hint of an indulgence on his part which is more closely related to sadism rather than to the masochism to which his biographers have devoted so much space.

Chapter Seventeen

*Lawrence's views on the love-life of the desert warriors.
Castigation and obscenity.*

In his life of Lawrence, Mack acknowledges that he is treating *Seven Pillars* as a "psychological document rather than a literary work:[1] as a book which reveals Lawrence as "the mythic heroic character he could not help creating" and also his "insight into his own limitations, his awareness of the distortions of truth in the legend he helped to create".[2] That Mack should deal with the subject in this way is understandable in the light of his professional interest, yet it is surprising that he has dealt so briefly with a significant motif which continues throughout the book and which even the most casual reader must recognise.

Aldington writes of "the affair of Farraj and Daud, two members of Lawrence's bodyguard to whose behaviour he devotes a disproportionately large space, especially for a book supposedly occupied with great historical events and the unfolding of profoundly original views on warfare – as if the Emperor in the memorial of St. Helena had dwelt long and affectionately on the jeunes ébats of two drummer-boys in the Young Guard',[3] while Mack comments that "Lawrence's older brother spoke with me about Lawrence's affection for individual Arabs and of his distress over the deaths of his young friends Daud and Farraj, and the pain he experienced over the atrocities, other deaths and various hardship suffered by Arabs in the desert".[4]

In his book Lawrence writes about Daud on eleven pages and about Farraj on sixteen. Aldington comments on Lawrence's peculiar and repeated use of the word "clean" when describing the young men he met in Arabia, complaining that "Lawrence used the appeal to Puritan prejudices of the word "clean" in the most unscrupulous way. Thus he warmly recommends Farraj and Daud (who, on his own showing, were a couple of unwashed desert homosexuals) as 'so clean'." In *Seven Pillars* Lawrence lost little time in expressing his sexual empathy, for he writes on the second page of text: "The men were young and sturdy: and hot flesh and blood unconsciously claimed a right in them and tormented their bellies with strange longings. Man in all things lived candidly with man. The Arab was by nature continent; and the use of universal marriage had nearly abolished irregular courses in his tribes. The public women of the rare settlements we encountered in our months of wandering would have been nothing to our numbers, even had their raddled meat been palatable to a man of healthy parts. In horror of such sordid commerce our youths began to slake one another's few needs in their own clean bodies – a cold convenience that, by comparison, seemed sexless and even pure. Later, some began to justify this sterile process, and swore that friends quivering in the yielding sand with intimate hot limbs in supreme embrace, found there hidden in the darkness a sensual coefficient of the mental passion which was welding our souls and spirits in one flaming effort. Several, thirsting to punish appetites they could not wholly prevent, took a savage pride in degrading the body, and offered themselves fiercely in any habit which promised physical pain or filth".

Daud and Farraj make their first appearance on the scene on the 15th May, 1917, a few days after the commencement of the leisurely nine-week journey from Wejh which ended with the fall of Aqaba. Lawrence is enjoying the peace of the countryside: a tranquillity which is about to suffer a romantic interruption. "The valley was instinct with peace, and the wind's continuing noise made even it seem patient. My eyes were shut and I was dreaming, when a youthful voice made me see an anxious Ageyli, a stranger, Daud, squatting by me. He appealed for my compassion. His friend Farraj had burned their tent in a frolic, and Saad, captain of Sharrif's Ageyl was going to beat him in punishment. At my intercession he would be released . . . Saad, laughing, told me stories of the famous pair. They were an instance of the eastern boy and boy affection which the segregation of women made inevitable. Such friendships often led to many loves of a depth and force beyond our flesh-steeped conceit. When innocent they were hot and unashamed. If sexuality entered, they passed into a give and take unspiritual relation, like marriage. Next day . . . two bent figures, with pain in their eyes, but crooked smiles upon their lips, hobbled up and saluted. These were Daud the hasty and his fellowlove Farraj, a beautiful, soft-framed, girlish creature, with innocent smooth face and swimming eyes. They said that they were here for my service. I said I was a simple man who dislikes servants about him. Daud turned away, defeated and angry; but Farraj pleaded that we must have men, and they would follow me for company and out of gratitude. While the harder Daud revolted, he went over to Nasir and knelt in appeal, all the woman of him evident in his longing. At the end, on Nasir's advice, I took them both, mainly because they looked so young and clean."[5]

The chastisement which Daud and Farraj were made to endure becomes a recurrent theme in the pages of *Seven Pillars*. On the day before the fall of Aqaba, when one would imagine that the men would have been fully occupied with their military needs, the two youths were made to suffer punishment for some misdemeanour in a most curious fashion: they had been "for correction . . . set on scorching rocks till they should beg pardon".[6] Some time later they received further punishment, on this occasion by "Sheikh Yusuf, who, after doing his best with a palm-rib to hurt their feelings, put them in irons for a slow week's meditation . . . Then," wrote Lawrence, "I explained our instant need of the sinners, and promised another dose of his treatment for them when their skins were fit: so he ordered their release".[7]

Lawrence succeeds in providing further examples of incidents involving accounts of young Arabs being beaten or tortured by their fellows. A typical one is related under the date-heading of 26.vi.17, concerning a young Circassian cowherd "captured" by Lawrence's band of warriors at the wateringplace of Khau. "The lad was in a head-and-tail flux of terror offending our sense of respect. To kill him seemed unimaginative: not worthy of a hundred men. At last the Sherari boy . . . . looped his wrist to the saddle and trotted him off with us for the first hour, till he was dragging breathlessly . . . then he was stripped of his presentable clothes, which fell, by point of honour (!), to his owner. The Sherari threw him on his face, picked up his feet, drew a dagger, and chopped him with it deeply across the soles. The Circassian howled with pain and terror, as if he thought he was being killed. Odd as was the performance, it seemed effective, and more merciful than death. The cuts would make him travel to the railway on hands and knees, a journey of an hour; and his nakedness would keep him in the shadow of the rocks, till the sun was low. His gratitude was not coherent; but we rode away, across undulations very rich in grazing."[8]

In several respects this nauseating anecdote repeats the theme of an earlier happening, where Lawrence relates the "capture" of "a little ragged boy" who had been tending his sheep and goats in the neighbourhood of Aba el Naam. This wretched lad also offended the "sense of respect" of his captors, crying continuously. "In the end," wrote Lawrence, "the men lost patience and tied him up roughly, when he screamed for terror that they would kill him . . . the tears made edged and crooked tracks down his dirty face."[9] If these two accounts appear to suggest some distaste on the part of Lawrence for shepherds and cowherds there is some explanation for this prejudice in the paragraph which commences, "Shepherds were a class apart" . . . and concludes: "With manhood they become sullen, while a few turned dangerously savage, more animal than man, haunting the flocks, and finding the satisfaction of their adult appetites in them, to the exclusion of more licit affections".[10]

Could this have represented some sort of Lawrence campaign against the sexual perversion of bestiality, combined with a protest on behalf of those who were thereby being deprived of their licit affections'? This might have been deemed a demonstration of his sense of virtue by those who could ignore his failure to intervene on behalf of the terrified victims. What evidence is there in these accounts of "the pain he experienced over the atrocities and various hardship suffered by Arabs in the desert" reported by his brother? The odd detachment, not unmixed with relish, in the narration of both stories must surely be found offensive to any taste, and their inclusion in what Winston Churchill described as one of "the greatest books ever written in the English language" can only be explained by suggesting that they provide additional evidence of Lawrence's obsession with chastisement and retribution.

To return to the events of the 23rd September, 1918, when, it will be remembered, Lawrence was making his way towards Deraa, he relates an anecdote telling how he spent the evening of that day. "At Um el Surab we found that Nasir wished to fix camp once more at Umtaiye. It was a first stage of our journey to Damascus, so his wish delighted me, and we moved; winning thereby good excuse for doing nothing this night to the line. Instead, we sat and told stories of experience and waited for midnight, when the Handley-Page was to bomb Mafrak station . . . We slept, having given first prize of the night to a tale of Enver Pasha, after the Turks retook Sharkeui. He went to see it, in a penny steamer, with Prince Jemil and a gorgeous staff. The Bulgars, when they came, had massacred the Turks; as they retired the Bulgar peasants went too. So the Turks found hardly any one to kill. A greybeard was led on board for the Commander-in-Chief to bait. At last Enver tired of this. He signed to two of his bravo aides, and throwing open the furnace door, said, 'Push him in'. The old man screamed, but the officers were stronger and the door was slammed-to on his jerking body. 'We turned, feeling sick to go away, but Enver, his head on one side, listening, halted us. So we listened, till there came a crash within the furnace. He smiled and nodded, saying, 'Their heads always pop, like that'."[11]

It will be remembered. that the night of this story-telling came before the Tafas atrocities, so that one cannot invoke that "shattering of the integrity of the self" which Mack relates to the Tafas experiences, nor can its gratuitous inclusion be attributed to "the guilt and shame which resulted from the war experience". Mack may come nearer to the point when he writes that "pleasures, especially sexual ones, are often associated with aggression and violence which, in their admixture with pain, are categorized as "sado-masochism'." Lawrence may be said to have shown evidence of both.

Chapter Eighteen

Lawrence and the "Arab Revolt."
Major Jarvis and the Generals offer their views.

On the 27th September word came to Lawrence that the enemy had evacuated Deraa, and early the next morning he mounted his camel and rode into the town. General Barrow reached Deraa with his Desert Mounted Corps that same morning, and Lawrence rode out to meet him. Their meeting became a confrontation: each has left his own version of what happened. Lawrence had apparently nurtured a grievance against the General, writing: "I had studied Barrow and was ready for him. Years before, he had published his confession of faith in Fear as the common people's main incentive to action in war and peace . . . I could have no alliance with his pedant belief of scaring men into heaven: better that Barrow and I part at once. My instinct with the inevitable was to provoke it."[1]

It appears that Barrow enquired about shooting that he had heard as he approached Deraa. Lawrence told him that he and his Arabs "had spent the night in the town, and the shooting he heard was joy-firing", explaining the reasons for the "joy-firing" in an earlier paragraph. "With local help the Rualla plundered the camp, especially finding booty in the fiercely burning storehouses whose flaming roofs imperilled their lives; but this was one of the nights in which mankind went crazy, when death seemed impossible, however many died to the left and right, and when others' lives became toys to break and throw away".[2]

Barrow, Lawrence wrote, was "short" with him, and told him "to ride beside him: but his horses hated my camel, so the General Staff bucked along the ditch, while I soberly paced the crown of the road . . . He had no orders as to the status of the Arabs. Clayton did us this service, thinking we should deserve what we could assert: so Barrow, who had come in thinking of them as a conquered people, though dazed at my calm assumption that he was my guest, had no option but to follow the lead of such assurance. My head was working full speed in these minutes, on our joint behalf, to prevent the fatal first steps by which the unimaginative British, with the best will in the world, usually deprived the acquiescent native of the discipline of responsibility, and created a situation which called for years of agitation and successive reforms and riotings, to mend".

In a letter which was published in *The Daily Telegraph*, Barrow has written "Finding after the publication of the book" *(Seven Pillars of Wisdom)* "that I took no notice of its sour references to me, friends who had been present on the occasions when I had met Lawrence and who knew the facts, urged me to make some comment. If I did not do so, it seemed to them, it would be assumed that I had no good answer to give. Here, then, is my belated reply.

"My first meeting with Lawrence was after crossing the Jordan with the foremost troops of the Desert Mounted Corps heading for Deraa. Damascus was the final objective given me by Allenby. Lawrence hastened to meet me. The road was straight and guidance unnecessary. He took the middle of the road, and I and a staff officer were jockeyed off it into the ditches on either side by Lawrence on his camel. It was one of the acts of discourtesy on which he seemed to pride himself. He retailed it in his book and spoke of our "bucking" horses in the ditches. As we had just done a 100-mile trek on short commons there was not a single buck in the whole crowd.

"Lawrence says: 'Barrow had come thinking that we were a

conquered people'. It was a very stupid remark. He was not a thought reader, but had he been able to penetrate my thoughts he would have found how foolish his own thoughts were. A train full of wounded Turks was standing in Deraa station when we got there. The Arabs were cutting the throats of these wounded men and pulling the clothes off broken arms and legs. I asked Lawrence to turn the Arabs off the train, but he refused. So I ordered a guard of Indians to do so. After this Lawrence lost no opportunity of casting slurs and gibes at me.

"We continued the march towards Damascus. Lawrence overtook me on the road. He said I was surprised, being a cavalryman, and ignorant of what camels could do. I was not surprised because I had ridden camels almost before he was born. Lawrence stated that he and his Arabs captured Damascus, but Australian cavalry were in possession of the city at dawn, and he arrived at 7 a.m. It was General Chauvel and the Australians who led the triumphant march through it. A few years later when I was talking to Allenby I asked him whether Lawrence and his Arabs had been as useful on his flank as they claimed. 'They were of nuisance value in annoying the Turks', he declared, 'but of very little help to me'. I then inquired: 'Could anyone else have played the part in command and leadership like Lawrence?' 'I had several officers who would have done as well,' he replied, and some who would have done much better.' "

The Indians who had carried out Barrow's orders at Deraa station likewise became objects of Lawrence's rancour. He wrote of them " . . . the station stood at the limit of the open country, and the Indians round it had angered me by their out-of-placeness . . . My mind felt in the Indian rank and file something puny and confined; an air of thinking themselves mean; almost a careful, esteemed subservience, unlike the abrupt wholesomeness of Bedouin. The manner of the British officers towards their men struck horror into my bodyguard, who had never seen inequality before."[3]

Lawrence's uninhibited hostility to officers, so often vented in his writings, was not necessarily extended to lower ranks. He told Liddell

Hart: "I weighed the English army in my mind, and could not honestly assure myself of them. The men were often gallant fighters, but their generals as often gave away in stupidity what they had gained in ignorance." But not all senior officers were content to maintain a dignified silence in the face of his jibes. Major-General George Rankin, D.S.O., who had commanded the Australian Light Horse on the Palestine-Arabia front during the war, wrote in the Melbourne Argus in March, 1955: "Lawrence was without doubt one of the great impostors of the 1914-1918 war. But for Lowell Thomas he would never have been heard of. The contribution made by the Arab forces under Lawrence in the desert campaign were negligible. Ask any Light Horse men who served in the desert. The Arabs were craven in the face of any real opposition, preferring to skulk behind the battle, waiting to lay waste towns captured by our organised armed forces. Their barbaric slaughter of wounded and helpless prisoners and senseless pillage and destruction were sickening to any civilised man. If Lawrence was not a sadist, at least he made no attempt to control the primitive savagery of the Arab rabble at his heels, bought by Foreign Office gold. On one occasion I threatened to shoot Lawrence for this very reason. Shortly after the entrance into Damascus by the 4th Light Horse Regiment (the Arabs afterwards claimed it as theirs) my regiment was called out to prevent the looting and slaughter in which Lawrence's Arabs were indulging. I had my Sergt.Major Robertson set up a Hotchkiss machine-gun covering Jemal Pasha Avenue, where some of the worst incidents were happening, with orders to shoot any Arab who refused to desist. Lawrence, theatrically garbed in the silken garments and gold-threaded head-dress of an Arab Shareef, haughtily complained that my troops were shooting his Arabs. I threatened to shoot him if he didn't attempt to control them. When I think of what the Sherifians did in Damascus and other towns, I am sometimes sorry I did not shoot. The men who really did something towards organizing the Arabs were Col. Newcombe and Major Joyce, two fine British Army officers, who were in the Hejaz long before Lawrence ever appeared. I once asked Newcombe, why do you stand this little tinpot fake swaggering around, taking whatever kudos is going?"

Some of Rankin's views are reflected in the reminiscences of Major Jarvis. He wrote: "As an Arab administrator who has lived on the borders of the Hejaz for some fourteen years, I am supposed by those who have not taken the trouble to estimate the size of the Arabian Peninsula to be an expert on all Arab affairs from the Persian border in the east to Italian Tripoli in the west, and this is too much for any man. Another question I am also asked constantly is, 'And what is your opinion of Lawrence and the Arab campaign?', and this is very difficult to answer as I only met Lawrence once for five minutes during the War and I did not take part in the Arab campaign at all, having served on the Palestine side till the Armistice. I do, however, know something of the men and the tribes that fought with him and I have seen much of the country through which Lawrence operated.

"There are two schools of thought about the Arab campaign – if 'thought' is not too flattering a word for what can best be described as fleeting impression gleaned from magazine articles and hearsay. One is that the war was entirely won by Lawrence's levies, and the other that the Arabs did nothing that could not have been accomplished by a few companies of British Camel Corps.

"The criticism that one hears levelled against the Arab campaign is that though it was a nation in arms fighting for its independence against the oppressor, they accomplished nothing in the way of a spectacular battle or capture of big towns with their garrisons. The truth of the matter is that the national desire for independence was confined solely to the few educated Arabs in the cause, such as Feisal, and that among the fighting men and the sheikhs of the tribes who led them this feeling was conspicuous by its absence. The Bedouin Arab of the Hedjaz who fought the campaign disliked the Turk and wished to be rid of him – a feeling that he entertains for everybody who is not of true Bedouin stock – but it was quite beyond his understanding to envisage the campaign as a whole or to think as a nation. His petty jealousies and his blood feuds against other tribes were always of far greater importance to him than striking a blow against a common enemy. Moreover, the Turk having been cleared out of his own particular area he took no further interest in the War – it was no concern of his if the enemy was still occupying the country of an adjoining tribe: that was entirely their affair. His old tribal hatreds caused him to resent the passage of other Arabs through his country and his outlook from the beginning of the campaign was definitely parochial as opposed to national; and moreover there was always the suspicion and more than the suspicion of treachery. These may be hard words, but the evidence in support of them is to be found in Lawrence's own book, *The Seven Pillars of Wisdom*, and Lawrence was wholly pro-Arab.

"In action they were entirely without discipline, and the first hint of loot meant that the greater part of the attacking force broke off the engagement before it was completed to rifle the enemy's captured baggage. After a successful raid when the Arabs were loaded with looted corn and rations nothing would keep them in the field, and they trickled back to their tents and their womenfolk so that a striking force on which their commander was relying for another attack on the railway would scatter into the desert in a night. The only method of keeping these patriots in the field was by payment in gold, and when the Arab sees gold his natural avarice causes him to lose all control of himself so that squabbles as to the respective donations to various tribes were of daily occurrence. They resented the presence in their midst of the Egyptian artillery and other units sent by the Allies to strengthen their forces and in every possible way did their Arab utmost to stultify the efforts of the commanders. And on top of it all there was constant jealousy on the part of King Hussein towards his son Feisal; and Hussein from his throne in Mecca out of sheer pique issued orders that from time to time jeopardised the cause . . . The Arabs might have thought that they were fighting for the independence of their race, but their actions from the beginning to the end proved that they were only interested in the revolution for three objects in the following order of importance . . . gold, loot and the satisfactory clearing up of their own daraks or areas.

"Great Britain is held responsible for 'letting the Arabs down' because at the Treaty of Versailles they were not given all that they were promised, i.e. to hold all the territory they captured, but looking at the matter from an unbiased standpoint I cannot see, considering all things, that we failed to honour our bond to any great extent. The Iraqians who took no part in the War have their independence, and the Hedjaz or Saudi Arabia has it also. Trans-Jordan has a very modified form of British Mandate which practically amounts to independence. Syria is a French Mandate, and the difference between a French Mandate and a French Colony may not be very easy to define, but it must be remembered that the Syrians as a people did nothing whatsoever towards assisting the Arab cause except for the isolated action of some eastern Bedouin in the last stages of the campaign and the services of a few Syrian officers who deserted from the Turkish Army. The great mass of the Syrian people did absolutely nothing beyond hold secret meetings and talk. The inhabitants of Palestine did rather less than this, and yet it is from the educated *effendiyah* of the Syrian and Palestinian towns that one hears all this talk of Arab independence and Great Britain's perfidy. In the first place these people took no part whatsoever in assisting the Allies to drive out the Turks, from their country, and secondly they are not Arabs. An Arab must of necessity be of Arabian birth, and neither Palestine nor Syria is Arabia proper. Both these countries are inhabited by a race of cultivators and townsfolk who are undoubtedly descended from the ancient Syrians, Jebusites, Canaanite, Philistines or others that occupied these lands before the days of Christ. True, they were conquered by the Arabs of Arabia in the seventh century, but that does not make the inhabitant of that country to-day an Arab any more than the conquest of Great Britain in A.D.43 makes the Englishman an Italian. I frequently hear fat and juicy Syrians and equally fat and juicy Palestinians – men who could not sit on a camel for five minutes – talk proudly of their Arab birth. I have lived and worked with Arabs for eighteen years and know the race, and no amount of oily food and cloying sweetmeats could turn this hardy stock into the effete and languid creatures that now claim kinship with the nomads of Arabia and talk so loudly of the Arab independence for which they fought."[4]

Chapter Nineteen

Damascus surrenders: The allies enter.
Lawrence's loyalty called into question.

The last day of September, 1918, was also the last day of Turkish rule in Damascus. Bulgaria, another of the Central Powers, surrendered to the Allies on the same day. The Great War was coming to an end. On October 4th the Germans sent proposals for an armistice to President Wilson. The capture of Aleppo was followed by announcement of an armistice with Turkey on October 31st, and on November 11th the Germans laid down their arms. In London Lloyd George and the "Easterners" celebrated the success of their policies: they were satisfied that events had proved that the shortest way to complete victory lay first in the subjugation of the weaker enemies, Bulgaria and Turkey.

When ultimately the figures were published they revealed that even Allenby's 'three men and a boy with a pistol at Deraa' may well have been superfluous to his needs, for on his fifteen-mile front he had been able to concentrate on September 19th 35,000 infantry with 9,000 cavalry and 383 guns against 8,000 Turkish infantry with 130 guns.[1] As Wavell later wrote: "The battle was practically won before a shot was fired". His map of the positions of the forces surrounding Damascus on September 30th[2] shows the western approaches to the city held by three Australian Light Horse brigades, and another on the line of the railway, flanked by two more A.L.H. brigades to the west and north-west respectively. Forward units of the 5th Cavalry Division lay astride the railway line to the south of the city, while others contained the remnants of the Fourth Turkish Army which had been trapped between the Deraa-Damascus road and the Fourth Cavalry Division to the south. In their wake Arab groups reached the Nahr el Awaj, six or seven miles south of Damascus, on the evening of the 30th, while others flanked the line at Kiswe, a few miles further south.

Wavell then describes the "official" entry into Damascus: "At dawn the next morning, October 1st, the 3rd A.L.H.Brigade, which had now received permission to enter the city, passed through on its way to the Homs Road. These were the first of the British forces to enter Damascus. Soon afterwards Lawrence and his Arabs arrived . . . "³ There is a special significance in the wording of Wavell's account, suggesting that the Brigade had been held back from entering the city until the permission had been granted, and, indeed, Mack states "that there is evidence to indicate that British forces were given orders to *avoid* (added italics) entering Damascus, when they might have captured the city hours or days earlier than they did, in order to enable the Arab forces to claim that they, not the British armies, liberated the city".⁴

It is interesting to read the varied accounts of this entry. Mousa, giving *An Arab View*, forbears to mention any British brigade, saying simply that "In the morning, Sherif Nassir, at the head of his forces, entered the city in the name of its Arab Government", and that "The city gave the Arab Army an unparalleled welcome".⁵ Chauvel sent a telegram to Allenby confirming that

> **THE AUSTRALIAN MOUNTED DIVISION ENTERED OUTSKIRTS OF DAMASCUS FROM THE NORTH-WEST LAST NIGHT. AT 6 A.M. TODAY THE TOWN WAS OCCUPIED BY THE DESERT MOUNTED CORPS AND THE ARAB ARMY.**

"Today" was of course October 1st. Edmund Dane, whose *British Campaigns in the Nearer East 1914-1918*, published in 1919, ranks among the earliest accounts, confirms the essentials of Chauvel's telegram, writing: "At six in the morning of October 1st the Allied forces came in, the 10th Australian Light Horse from the north, the Hedjaz Arabs from the south."[6] He makes no mention of Lawrence. In fact Lawrence's name appears nowhere in his book, a comprehensive work in two volumes, with thirty maps and plans, which was extensively reviewed in the *Times Literary Supplement* of November 27, 1919. It is safe to assume that Lawrence arrived some hours later.

Feisal arrived in Damascus on October 3rd, travelling by train from Deraa, (for the Hejaz Railway was still operating in this sector) having reached Deraa on September 29th from Azrak in his Vauxhall car. Almost immediately on his arrival he went with Lawrence to meet Allenby: his first meeting with his Commander-in-Chief, and his farewell of Lawrence.

Lawrence's brief account of that meeting is limited to the simple statement that Allenby gave him a telegram from the Foreign Office, recognizing to the Arabs the status of belligerents, and asking him to translate it to the Emir.[7] Lawrence does not mention in his book that Chauvel and Wavell were present at this meeting, an omission on his part which will be readily understood when reference is made to the accounts which both generals have left of the occasion. They are in agreement that Allenby there informed Feisal of the terms of the Sykes-Picot Agreement, explaining that France would now be the Protecting Power in Syria and that Lebanon would come under direct French administration. Feisal would be permitted to set up a military administration in the occupied enemy territory east of the Jordan.

Both Chauvel and Wavell report that Feisal objected very strongly, saying that he had understood from the 'Advisor' (meaning Lawrence) that the Arabs were to have the whole of Syria, including the Lebanon but excluding Palestine, and that he declined to have a French Liaison Officer or to recognize French guidance in any way. At this, Allenby, according to Chauvel, turned to Lawrence and said: "But did you not tell him that the French were to have the Protectorate over Syria?"

Lawrence replied: "No Sir, I know nothing about it", and Allenby then said to him: "But you knew definitely that he, Feisal, was to have nothing to do with the Lebanon?" Lawrence replied: "No Sir, I did not."[8] From the manner of Allenby's questioning of Lawrence it would seem that he may have been aware of Lawrence's self-confessed "earlier betrayal of the (Sykes-Picot) treaty's existence to Feisal"[9] and that he knew that Lawrence was lying to him. However, he refused further discussion of Feisal's claims reminding Feisal that the Emir was a Lieutenant-General under his command and that he, Allenby, was the Commander-in-Chief, and that Feisal would have to obey orders. According to Chauvel, "Feisal accepted this decision" and left, without Lawrence. "After Feisal had gone, Lawrence told the Chief that he would not work with a French Liaison Officer and that he was due for leave and thought he had better take it now and go off to England. The Chief said: 'Yes. I think you had!' and Lawrence left the room".

Lawrence's motives for omitting from his book any mention of this exchange are perfectly understandable; in earlier pages he had described the discussions he had with Feisal on the conditions of the Sykes-Picot Agreement, and it would hardly have been possible for him to include at the end the denials reported by Chauvel. How could he have said to Allenby that he knew "nothing" about the Franco-British agreement on the status of Syria and Lebanon after writing in *Seven Pillars* "Fortunately, I had early betrayed the treaty's existence to Feisal, and had convinced him that his escape was to help the British so much after peace that they would not be able, for shame, to shoot him down in its fulfilment . . . I begged him to trust not in our promises . . . "?

He revealed also that he was aware that after Allenby's failures at Es Salt Feisal had been in treacherous correspondence with the Turks, who, in that moment of British reverses, decided that the changed military situation might be exploited by means of a personal emissary from Jemal Pasha. This emissary, the Emir Mohammed Said, was, according to Lawrence, favourably received by Feisal. "Feisal told him that he was come at an opportune moment. He could offer Jemal the loyal behaviour of the Arab Army, if Turkey evacuated Amman, and handed over its province to Arab keeping".

Not surprisingly, Lawrence "feared that the British might be shaken at Feisal's thus entertaining separate relations". Nevertheless he could see good reasons, from the Arab point of view, why it could be in their best interests to establish "avenues of accommodation with Turkey. If the European war failed, it was their only way out . . . " And if the British were keeping silent about their contacts with "not the Nationalist, but with the Conservative Turks" this was "at once an example, a spur and a silence to me to do the like".[10]

The reader will doubtless recall Lawrence's reactions to the similar treachery of Auda after the capture of Aqaba, which he denied to Egypt, "to keep her confidence and ourselves a legend". And yet we are still repeatedly told that Lawrence was guilty of deceiving the Arabs by pretending that he was devoting himself to their interests when in reality he was working against them. Knightley and Simpson wrote "that there is evidence that Lawrence never intended the Arabs to have freedom as we understand the word to-day. He had no *schwarmerei* for the Arabs. He dressed and behaved as an Arab in order – in the typical colonial idiom – to be able to 'handle' them better".

Mack saw Lawrence from the opposite viewpoint, writing that: "As he had taken it upon himself to represent Britain's plans and promises to the Arabs, so he would try to see to it that these promises were honoured".[11] And certainly he lost no time once he left Damascus behind him in launching himself into a vigorous prosecution of the Arab claims which Allenby had rejected at the meeting with Feisal. By the 14th of October he was in Cairo, and seems to have arrived in England before the end of the month, for a report which he wrote for the British Cabinet is dated the 4th November.

David Garnett has described it as a "secret document' but it is nevertheless included in the published *Letters* under the heading of

Reconstruction of Arabia.[12] An enthusiastic plea for the ideal of Arab independence, it is not free from significant inaccuracy, such as his statement that the British Government gave discretion to McMahon to conclude "an agreement" with the Sherif of Mecca. "An agreement" could well be understood to signify a formal instrument of the nature of a treaty, whereas McMahon was merely authorized to reach agreement with the Sherif on a number of specific issues: a very different matter. That Lawrence himself recognised this is clear from his Draft Preface (to *Seven Pillars*) written in November 1922, when he states that the "McMahon undertaking" was "called a treaty by some who have not seen it". And it was dishonest of him to describe the Sherif throughout the correspondence as "the mandatory of the Arabs", because no one more than Lawrence was aware that the Sherif possessed no such mandate, and that any claims that he may have made during the course of the negotiations to such authority had been promptly, vehemently and even derisively rejected by Arab leaders.

It was flagrantly untruthful of Lawrence to write that the Sherif "was able eventually to carry all Western Arabia with him from Mecca northwards" when he later made it quite clear in his book that the Sherif had failed signally to accomplish that very thing. It was misleading to state that "Feisal undertook for his father the liberation of Syria" when Feisal was morally pledged to serve the Allied interest in return for the financial and military support they afforded him, and Allied aims were clearly stated to include the liberation from Turkish control of all the subject territories including Syria in the Ottoman Empire, to ensure the rights of the native populations. And in the light of the history we have seen recorded it was frankly absurd to suggest that Allenby's carefully planned and brilliantly-executed offensive, which achieved the final victory, was in any way dependent on an "Arab alliance", when all he asked for on that occasion was the symbolic appearance of "three men and a boy with pistols" on a specified date: and failed to receive even that.

In the Garnett-edited *Letters* this November 4th report is followed by the text of a telegram from "Secretary of State for India to Foreign,

Delhi, repeated Baghdad (Dated 19th and received 19th November, 1918)". It commences: "*Foreign Secret.* Colonel Lawrence, now home on leave from Syria, has submitted proposal to H.M.G. for dealing comprehensively with Arab question. He advocated formation of three Councils of Arab States outside Hedjaz and its dependencies, viz.: (1) Lower Mesopotamia, (2) Upper Mesopotamia and (3) Syria, to be placed respectively under Abdullah, Zeid and Feisal, sons of King Hussein. Hussein himself would remain King of Hedjaz and would ultimately be succeeded by his eldest son Ali."[13]

The adoption of this proposal would have resulted in the division of the greater part of the Arabian Peninsula, together with Syria and Mesopotamia, between the members of King Hussein's family. Although the telegram proceeded: "It is of course understood that both (Mesopotamian) states would be in the British sphere and Lower Mesopotamia under effective British control," it was clear that here Lawrence was advocating the appointment by the Allies or with Allied agreement of Hashemite rule over Syria and the whole of Mesopotamia. There is no suggestion that the native populations in these areas would be consulted as to their own choice of rule, nor comment on the probability that a Hashemite would in Syria be regarded as a foreigner, and in Mesopotamia with even stronger feelings; or that the Shia and Druse and other divisions of Islam would readily submit themselves to a Sunni ruler.

Neither was there any mention in this necessarily brief telegram of the French or other Allied interests in these area, nor of the existing agreements between France and Britain on the division of their separate zones; nor was there mention of Palestine or the Lebanon, or the dominating and already menacing presence of Ibn Saud in the vast areas which stretched from Mesopotamia to the Hejaz. What does clearly emerge from these last two documents is the completely unequivocalness of Lawrence's advocacy of the Hashemite interest above all others, so clearly stated that one is moved to ask how it was possible that the genuineness of his motivations could reasonably be questioned. Yet Knightly and Simpson have found it possible to write of him that: "The tortuous double dealing and deceit that this role involved made Lawrence, like all agents playing a double game, doubtful at times where his loyalties lay . . . But there is also evidence that his real motives were not so much concern for promises made to the Arabs as his super-patriotic concern for Britain's position in the Middle East; his stubborn determination to see his plan for Syria – which he no doubt believed to be in the Arabs' best interests – triumph over that of his rivals in Whitehall; and his fanatical determination to make certain that the French were not allowed even a toehold in the area."[14]

Yet when he attended the Peace Conference in Paris, which opened on the 18th January, 1919, officially a member of the British delegation, he cooperated so openly with Feisal, whose position as delegate for the Hejaz had been secured through British insistence, that Lawrence could truly have been regarded as an additional representative for the Hejaz, especially as he wore Arab head-dress or full Arab costume and acted as Feisal's interpreter.

At the Conference Arab affairs did not come under official discussion until February 6th, when Feisal announced his claims for Arab – but preferably Hashemite – rule in Syria and was immediately opposed by the Chairman of a group identified as the National Syrian Committee who strongly attacked the suggestion of "the inclusion of Syria in an Arab state" and was fiercely contemptuous of the idea of a 'highly civilised people' like the Syrians being governed by the Hejaz. In the event it would have gone better for Feisal had he accepted the Committee's views, for however strong was his antagonism towards French control of Syria there was little hope that the French could be persuaded to relinquish their claims to the country.

Their forces took over the control of Syria in September, 1919, when the British troops there withdrew. The country was in a turmoil. Protests against French rule complemented the unconcealed animus of the Syrian Nationalists directed at a Hejazi ruling clique which had assembled in the capital. In the eyes of both sections the French could only be regarded as foreign intruders, while to the Nationalists King Hussein was an alien pretender. There were other divisions also: Alawites, Kurds, Druses, Ismailis, Mutawalis and innumerable Christian sects in a constant froth of turbulence. From this seething confusion Feisal emerged as a somewhat bewildered "king", having been elected to this dignity by a meeting in Damascus anxious for him to occupy a non-existent throne, while at the same time they conferred on his brother Abdullah a chimerical crown of Iraq.

Throughout these happenings Lawrence continued diligently to present the Arab case through the columns of the British Press. On September 11th, *The Times* printed part of his letter – suppressing the rest – which claimed that the Sykes-Picot Agreement was unworkable, yet "in a sense" he wrote, the "charter of the Arabs, giving them Damascus, Homs, Hama, Aleppo and Mosul for their own, with such advisers as they themselves judge they need". But here again Lawrence had added to the reality his own little touches, for the Agreement provided only that those named towns would be included in the so-called 'A' Zone which comprised the French sphere of influence and in which semi-independent Arab states (or a confederation of such states) might be established under French advisers, and with the French receiving economic privileges. This was by no means the same as having these places "for their own" or allowing the Arabs to choose their advisers.

Ten years later Lawrence was brought back to this question through a letter from a New Hampshire Professor of History which reached him through Robert Graves. His reply mentions "the fatuous proclamation of King Hussein in Damascus", explaining that "these things were as much anti-Feisal as anything. The Damascenes hoped to avoid the near activities of Feisal by appealing to the distant Hussein, who hated Feisal. I had no intention of proclaiming any king in Damascus. Feisal governed it as an Army commander of Allenby's, an unassailable position. King Hussein was a nuisance to me, only . . . Your remark that 'British political officers were working to create a situation in Syria which would make impossible . . . the Sykes-

Picot treaty' amazes me. The S-P treaty was the Arab sheet-anchor. The French saw that, and worked frantically for the alternative of the mandate. By a disgraceful bargain the British supported them, to gain Mesopotamia. Under the S-P treaty the French only got the coast: and the Arabs (native administration) were to have Aleppo, Hamma, Homs, Damascus and Trans-Jordan. By the mandate swindle England and France got the lot. The S-P treaty was absurd, in its boundaries, but it did recognize the claims of Syrians to self-government, and it was ten thousand times better than the eventual settlement.

"In justice to England I must add that financial pressure, the Mesopotamian rebellion of 1920, and perhaps conscience aroused by my agitation in London, did finally persuade England to abrogate, de facto, her mandates in Iraq and Trans-Jordan, though she still holds them, de jure, to exclude third parties. It is my deliberate opinion that the Winston Churchill settlement of 1921-1922 (in which I shared) honourably fulfils the whole of the promises we made to the Arabs, in so far as the so-called British spheres are concerned. If we had done this in 1919 we could have been proud of ourselves."[15]

Chapter Twenty

The letters Lawrence "hated" to write.
Lawrence abandons his Arabian identity.

In the Garnett-edited collection of Lawrence's *Letters* the reply to Yale just quoted is numbered 397. The entire collection comprises 583 items, covering a period of 28½ years and affording some guide to his political and emotional evolution. The letter to Yale does not derive from any initiative on Lawrence's part to re-enter the debate: indeed, he goes on to inform Yale: "I have not been to the Middle East, or read a book or article about it, or written or received a letter thither or thence, since 1922 when I joined the R.A.F."

When, in the summer of 1922, he resigned from his post in the Middle East Department of the Colonial Office, he wrote that he "must put on record my conviction that England is out of the Arab affair with clean hands. Some Arab advocates (the most vociferous joined our ranks after the Armistice) have rejected my judgment on this point. Like a tedious Pensioner I showed them my wounds (over sixty I have, each scar evidence of a pain incurred in Arab service) as proof I had worked sincerely on their side. They found me out of-date: and I was happy to withdraw from a political milieu which had never been congenial".[1]

In the letter to Yale, written seven years later, he states that "Winston's settlement so pleased me that I withdrew wholly from politics, with clean hands, I think, and enlisted in the Air Force, where

I have the happiness to be still. It is not glorious, but very free of cares, healthy and interesting." How different is this plain statement from the portrayal offered by others. Knightley and Simpson inform us that "Lawrence, writing *Seven Pillars of Wisdom*, is in a deeply disturbed emotional state as he relives the Revolt in the desert and faces the question: was it all a fraud? . . . Lawrence is physically, emotionally, and financially exhausted when he finally receives Trenchard's permission to join the R.A.F., which he does under the pseudonym of John Hume Ross".[2]

Reading on, we are informed that Lawrence's condition when he "returned to England from Jordan and his 'settling' of the Middle East" was "near to madness", and that life for him became "almost unbearable . . . He had to face again the fact that his role had involved him in an empty and dishonourable fraud. How much should he tell? Should he say openly that the British would have promised the Arabs almost anything in order to get them to revolt? . . . Should Lawrence say in *Seven Pillars* that because he knew Britain had no intention of allowing the Arabs to have a government of their own, his part in the conspiracy was a shameful one . . . It is clear from this that Lawrence decided against telling the full story of Britain's actions in Arabia and his own part in them he found too shameful to tell . . . "[3]

It becomes necessary to reconcile the accusation that "Britain had no intention of allowing the Arabs to have a government of their own" with the fact that she had afforded recognition to the Kingdom of the Hejaz and supported it with every type of subsidy at a time when virtually every other Arab group had refused to accept its claims to independence: had created the "sovereign state, independent and free" of Iraq following its period of nominal independence under a British Mandate; while at the same time laying the foundations of a third Arab kingdom by creating and sustaining the Emirate of Transjordan. Was Lawrence indeed "near to madness", as Knightley and Simpson would have us believe, when after his return from Jordan at the end of his period there as Chief British Representative he declared his satisfaction with Britain's treatment of the Hashemites?

The alleged "deeply emotional state" in which Lawrence was immersed when he was writing *Seven Pillars* is not revealed in the published letters of that period. In the month following his July 1922 resignation there are four addressed to Edward Garnett, busily concerned with printing and binding: the last written a few days before his entrance into the R.A.F. Of greater significance in any consideration of his "emotional state" is the letter dated 17.viii.22 which he wrote to Bernard Shaw, written, as it happens, on the same day as his first letter to Garnett that month. The letter to Shaw signalled the commencement not only of an extensive correspondence with Shaw but also of a deep friendship with Mrs. Charlotte Shaw which was maintained until Lawrence's death.

"I hate letter-writing as much as I can",[4] he wrote to Bernard Shaw in his first letter: a declaration which reads oddly against Sir Edmund Craster's comments in his review of *The Home Letters of T.E.Lawrence and his Brothers*. "Lawrence was a prodigious letter-writer", wrote Craster: "Bruce Rogers, Liddell Hart and Robert Graves have each of them published in separate volumes the letters they received from him. The Bodleian Library has the volume of the letters to his mother and 17 volumes of letters which will not be available for publication until the year 2000". His letters to Charlotte Shaw are held in the Department of Western Manuscripts of the British Museum, and there is a further collection of Lawrence letters in the Houghton Library of Harvard University. At Oxford the Library of All Souls College has a collection of the letters he wrote to Lionel Curtis, while the Ashmolean Museum Library harbours his letters of the Carchemish period. Those seventeen volumes in the Bodleian which Craster mentions contain thousands of letters; the Library of Jesus College has the letters to Robin Buxton; and at the University of Texas, Austin, Humanities Research Center, the Lawrence Collection contains hundreds of his letters. Many others have found their way into private collections, and countless numbers may have shared a fate similar to that of those he wrote to Storrs ("Sixty or seventy letters – I never counted them – from T.E.Lawrence"), which were destroyed when

Government House in Cyprus was burnt to the ground by a mob itself inflamed by a consuming Philhellenism. Not a bad total for a man who claimed to hate letterwriting: and possibly an example of the Lawrentian complex which prompted Christopher Sykes to pronounce emphatically if unkindly: "the fact that the man was a complete liar".

A mass of correspondence from the short Uxbridge period has survived. The last letter in the Garnett collection with the Uxbridge address is dated 27.x.22, but the succeeding flow of letters, mostly from Farnborough, continued unabated until the end of the year. For the most part they are concerned with what he chooses to call "the architecture of the book", the book in question being, of course, *Seven Pillars*, while "architecture" there refers to the design of the text and the general format, together with the illustrations which were a special feature in the published work. His letters in this group are all written in a lively and vigorous fashion, and Lawrence's handling of the problems which emerged as the work progressed reveals no hint of the mental condition suggested by Knightley and Simpson when they wrote: "The clinical picture of Lawrence at this time is that of a man suffering from depressive illness, an illness in which guilt and self-reproach are prominent features and madness not far away".

According to Mack, Eric Kennington and other friends considered that Lawrence "appeared steadier and more poised in his trim Air Force uniform". There is most certainly an astonishing lack of proper reserve in the manner in which he wrote to Air Vice-Marshal Sir Oliver Swann on September 1st, 1922, commencing "Dear Swann" and causing the Air Vice Marshal to comment: "One would think from the letters that I was a close correspondent of Lawrence's, possibly even a friend of his. But, as a matter of fact, I never met him until he was brought to me at the Air Ministry and I was ordered to get him into the R.A.F. I disliked the whole business, with its secrecy and subterfuge: I discouraged communication with or from him".

When it is recalled that the letter, although it bore the signature of "T.E.Lawrence", came to Swann from A/C2 No-352087 John Hume

Ross, the name under which Lawrence had enlisted on the previous day, the impertinence and impropriety of the manner of its address border on the incredible. The new recruit addresses the Air Vice-Marshal as "Dear Swann", condescendingly entrusts him with a couple of messages for the Chief of the Air Staff ("Would you tell the C.A.S., etc.? Please tell the C.A.S . . . ") and ends on a note reassuring informality: "Don't bother to keep an eye on what happens to me."[5] One may guess why Lawrence was quickly transferred from Uxbridge to the Farnborough School of Photography, which apparently he reached on November 8th. On the following day he wrote again to Swann ("Dear Swann, I expect my move here is your doing"), and again Swann did not reply. Undeterred he addressed his next letter to Swann, on November 19th, to his home.

Further evidence of Lawrence's behaviour during his brief spell at Uxbridge has been provided by his C.O., Squadron-Leader G.F.Breese, R.N.A.F., who, shortly after Lawrence's enlistment was receiving complaints about the new recruit Ross. He was said to be slovenly and resentful of discipline, among other things. Eventually the C.O. received from Ross a request for a private interview. What followed is best told in the Squadron-Leader's own words. "Ross twisted and turned like a ballet dancer, kept looking at me shyly and with a broad grin and then said (looking at the floor), 'I suppose you know who I am?' . . . and I replied: 'Oh yes, you're A/C2 Ross from No.8 Squad . . . what do you want to see me about?' Another spasm of twisting and turning, looking all round the office, anywhere but at me, and then shyly again, "I think they should have told you who I really am'. 'Well', I said, 'suppose you tell me who you think you are and what you want to see me about . . . Have you got some woman trouble?' This remark apparently galvanised him to action; he declared most vigorously that there was nothing of the sort but in point of fact he was a great writer of books; he still did not tell me his name, but asked if he could be given a private room in which to do some writing."[6]

His expeditious transfer to Farnborough must have come as a relief to all concerned. Throughout the following twelve months his letters are for the most part concerned with his book. For a time he continued in some cases to sign "T.E.L.", mostly for those who knew him by no other name; then, gradually, reduced it to "T.E." for old friends, and finally completely abandoned the "L" or the "Lawrence". During the transition period one letter was signed "T.E.S.(ex J.H.R.ex T.E.L)". It was dated 3.viii.23, and may be regarded as signalling his renunciation of the "Lawrence of Arabia" identity. The title had not been his invention but had been conferred, unsought, upon him. Yet he cannot be absolved from the charge that he contributed to the creation of the legend. Mack believed that "the Lawrence legend grew directly out of the elements of his personal psychology" but also that its creation and popularizing were hastened by Lowell Thomas's illustrated lectures, films and writings.[7] But he does not deny that Lawrence was attracted by the glorious image of himself as "the Uncrowned King of Arabia" that was played on the screen and embellished by Lowell Thomas, although at the same time "he was also genuinely repulsed by it".[8]

Chapter Twenty One

The genesis of the legend

The reader will recall General Rankin's acid comment in his *Melbourne Argus* letter about Lawrence that "but for Lowell Thomas he would never have been heard of." On the other hand Thomas wrote in the Foreword to his book that: "not only did Lawrence little dream that I might one day be 'booming him', as he describes it, but it had never even occurred to me that I should be so doing." This might well have been the case, for when Thomas presented his famous film lecture at Covent Garden, it was first featured as

> *America's Tribute to British Valour*
>
> *With Allenby in Palestine, including*
>
> *The Capture of Jerusalem and the*
>
> *Liberation of Holy Arabia*

without any mention of Lawrence in the advertising, but it soon became clear that great public interest was being aroused by what *The Sphere*, four days after the first performance, referred to as "the Strange Story of Colonel Thomas Lawrence, the Leader of the Arab Army," and the title was extended to "With Allenby in Palestine and Lawrence in Arabia."

Lawrence attended some of the performances. Mack states that Lawrence "knew Thomas's picture of him to be false . . . because it was a make-believe, commercial glorification", while Lawrence himself wrote about Thomas to an acquaintance saying "He has invented some silly phantom thing, a sort of matinee idol in fancy dress, that does silly things and is dubbed 'romantic.'[1] In retrospect, it is reasonable to assume that the "Lawrence of Arabia" theme, developed out of the recognition of the interest in Lawrence, of considerable value to an astute showman, and did not emerge in the first place from Thomas's visit to Arabia.

Thomas had been one of a party of American newspapermen who were sent out on a propaganda mission to the battle areas through the initiative of Lord Beaverbrook. The Western Front in Europe failed to provide the quality of drama he was seeking and, with the help of John Buchan, he went on to Allenby's headquarters in the Middle East. "One day not long after Allenby had captured Jerusalem" his "curiosity was excited by a single Bedouin, who stood out in sharp relief from all his companions. He was wearing an *agal*, *kuffieh*, and *abba* such as are worn only by Near Eastern potentates. In his belt was fastened the short curved sword of a Prince of Mecca, insignia worn by descendants of the Prophet . . . As the young Bedouin passed by in his magnificent royal robes, the crowds in front of the bazaars turned to look at him.

Posing for posterity.
"as I looked a perfect idiot (see page 176)..."
(Letter to H.R. Hadley, September 2nd 1920)

"It was not merely his costume, nor yet the dignity with which he carried his five feet three, marking him every inch a king or perhaps a caliph in disguise who had stepped out of the pages of *The Arabian Nights* . . . My first thought as I glanced at his face was that he might be one of the younger apostles returned to life." It is small wonder that Thomas's intense interest should have been aroused by one who portrayed in his single person the noble attributes of a Prince, a king, a caliph and an apostle. "I was certain I could obtain some information about him from General Storrs, Governor of the Holy City, and so I strolled over in the direction of his palace . . . "[2]

The "General" and the "palace" are nice touches, and should prepare the reader for the quality of Thomas's prose and his standards of accuracy. Storrs had received the appointment of Military Governor of Jerusalem, with the local rank of Lieutenant-Colonel, on the 28th December, 1917, less than four weeks before Thomas arrived in Palestine. His "residence" was "a suite of rooms in Fast's Hotel", while the Governorate was described by Storrs as being "established in a long row of uncomfortable offices on the first floor of Hugh's Hotel."

However, we are told that Storrs was able to reveal to his visitor "seated at the same table where von Falkenhayn had worked out his unsuccessful plan for defeating Allenby . . . the Bedouin prince, deeply absorbed in a ponderous tome on archeology." One can appreciate the drama of that moment.

Enter Thomas. "Salaam 0 Shaikh! What's that you're reading?"

Lawrence. "I am reading an archeological tome."

But Storrs does confirm that Lawrence would visit him and stay, "reading always Latin or Greek . . . We had no literary differences," though nowhere in his own writings does Storrs express any interest in archeology; but by now the reader will have got the idea: the "archaeological tome" goes well with the mysterious prince, the "General" and the "palace".

"And that," continued Thomas "was how I first made the acquaintance of one of the most picturesque personalities of modern times, a man who will be blazoned on the romantic pages of history with Raleigh, Drake, Clive and Gordon . . . quietly, without any theatrical headlines or fanfare of trumpets, he brought the disunited nomadic tribes of Holy and Forbidden Arabia into a unified campaign against their Turkish oppressors, a difficult and splendid stroke of policy, which caliphs, statesmen, and sultans had been unable to accomplish in centuries of effort! Lawrence placed himself at the head of the Bedouin army of the Shereef of Mecca, who was afterwards proclaimed King of the Hedjaz. He united the wandering tribes of the desert, restored the sacred places of Islam to the descendants of the Prophet, and drove the Turks from Arabia forever. Allenby liberated Palestine, the Holy Land of the Jews and Christians. Lawrence freed Arabia, the Holy Land of million of Mohammedans."[3]

It is difficult to imagine Lawrence's reaction to this lyrical nonsense, because he knew better than almost anyone that where the restoration of the Holy Places was concerned, Mecca had been "liberated" by the Sharif months before he had appeared on the scene; that Medina was never liberated at all, and remained in possession of the Turks even beyond the signing of the armistice; and that the "third sacred city of Islam", Jerusalem, had been "liberated" by Allenby's forces without any sort of participation on the part of Lawrence, and in spite of the fierce opposition of the Palestinian Arab Regiments of the Turkish Army, who inflicted grievous casualties on the British in the battles which had frustrated the allied advance on Jerusalem.

Lawrence did say, writing in 1927, of Thomas's book, that it was "silly and innaccurate: sometimes deliberately inaccurate", and on a most important issue insisted to E.M.Forster, "My height is five foot five and a half inches!" That there were earlier misgivings about the publicity he was then receiving or possibly the character of that publicity - is revealed in a letter which he wrote in 1920 to an acquaintance who had requested "a photo", saying that "they were done by that wild American, Lowell Thomas who came to Akaba and took us all . . . However as I looked a perfect idiot in most of those he published, there probably isn't much lost."[4]

Few will quarrel with this reaction of Lawrence to the camera portraits. Nearly a score of them are included in the Thomas biography: "Lawrence, the 'uncrowned king of the Arabs'"; "Lawrence the mystery man of Arabia"; "Lawrence looking 'like the reincarnation of one of the prophets of old'"; "Lawrence the king-maker", and so on. For the most part they possess the style and character of studio portraits: in some he is tense, in others simpering or posturing, sheepish or embarrassed, as well he might be. And yet Mack claims that he was "cooperative . . . seemed to enjoy posing in his 'Sherifian regalia'." On the other hand Thomas wrote of him, "He was so shy that when General Clayton, or some other officer sought to compliment him he would get as red as a schoolgirl and look down at his feet. Several years ago, in Calcutta, Colonel Robert Lorraine, the actor-airman, said to me, 'But if Lawrence is so modest and shy, how did you get so many photographs of him?' Out of justice to Lawrence this should be explained: We saw considerable (sic) of Lawrence in the desert, and although he arranged for us to get both 'still' and motion pictures of Emir Feisal, Auda Abu Tayi, and the other Arab leaders, he would turn away when he saw the lens pointing in his own direction . . . But after using all the artifices that one learns as a reporter . . . I finally manoeuvred Lawrence into allowing Chase to take a 'sitting shot' on two different occasions. Then, while I distracted the Colonel's attention . . . Chase hurriedly took a dozen pictures from as many different angles in less time than it usually takes a studio photographer to set up and expose two plates . . . I realized that Lawrence was one of the most romantic figures of the war, and that we had a great scoop".[5]

A very circumstantial account, but it does not explain the manifestly careful poses, usually with the Mecca dagger conscientiously presented, and at least a dozen different backgrounds. This is not to suggest that at the time these pictures were taken it was known that they would eventually illustrate a biography. Films were made for news-reels, and the stills would seek a market in journals and newspapers. The success of the film lectures would certainly encourage the writing of a book on their theme; and the author was able to dedicate the work to the "Eighteen Gentlemen of Chicago" who, Thomas wrote, "supplied the funds for the undertaking."

CHAPTER TWENTY TWO

"With Lawrence of Arabia":
Lowell Thomas composes a novel history.
Lawrence's own responsibility for the legend.

The English edition of Lowell Thomas's *With Lawrence in Arabia*, which was published in May, 1925, contained the following disclaimer: "The Publishers desire to state that Colonel Lawrence is not the source from which the facts in this volume were obtained, nor is he in any way responsible for its content." But anyone familiar with *Seven Pillars*, or its 1927 abridgement, *Revolt in the Desert*, and the accounts of the desert war contained in Liddell Hart's biography of Lawrence and in other books, must be aware that these contain a great deal of material which is common to them all. They even share almost identical style and language. It would present no difficulty to produce a volume along the lines of the Parallel Bible which, as many readers will know, prints synoptic passages from separate bible books side by side to represent their common character. But it would be a very large volume indeed if it covered all the works mentioned above, and still a very considerable one even if it were limited to *With Lawrence in Arabia* and *Seven Pillars*.

Such a work would present a tiresome and thankless task, and we must here be content with a brief sample of what it might contain. Thomas informs us that Lawrence "as a part of his reading . . . made an exhaustive study of military writers, from the wars of Sennacherib, Thotmes and Rameses down to Napoleon, Wellington, Stonewall

Jackson and von Moltke . . . Among his favourite books was Marshal Foch's Principe de Guerre; but he remarked to me on one occasion in Arabia, that his study of Caesar and Xenophon had been of more value to him in his desert campaign, because in the irregular war which he conducted against the Turks he found it necessary to adopt tactics directly opposed to those advocated by the great French strategist."[1]

"With Lawrence of Arabia"

In *Seven Pillars* Lawrence tells us: "In military theory I was tolerably read, my Oxford curiosity having taken me past Napoleon to Clausewitz and his school, to Caemmerer and Moltke, and the recent Frenchmen. However, Clausewitz was intellectually so much the master of them, and his book so logical and fascinating, that unconsciously I accepted his finality, until a comparison of Kuhne and Foch disgusted me with soldiers, wearied me of their officious glory, making me critical of all their light[2] . . . The algebraical factor had been translated into terms of Arabia, and fitted like a glove. It promised victory . . . I went to Xenophon and stole, to name it, his word *diathetics*, which had been the art of Cyrus before he struck."[3]

Film: "Lawrence of Arabia" (1962)

Liddell Hart enters this debate. "The original Napoleonic system was obscured by the Napoleonic legend. In this darkening of military thought there developed a swing of the pendulum back to immobility – due to the new theory of mass, on which fresh weights were piled by Napoleon's disciples, beginning with Clausewitz and culminating with Foch . . . That theory evolved from the reveries of Lawrence as he lay on his sick-bed in Abdulla's camp. His thoughts travelled back to the military books he had read while at Oxford."[4] These included Napoleon, Moltke, "and some of the post-1870 French military writers",[5] together with Henderson's *Stonewall Jackson*. There is much more of this, which the reader must be spared, as he finds himself wondering what Feisal, let alone Allenby, may have thought of all this.

Liddell Hart's book, published fourteen months before Lawrence's death, far from containing any disclaimer, discloses that Lawrence supplied the author "with many notes and comments that help to explain his ideas and actions, as well as the course of events." He also submitted "to prolonged and repeated cross-examination on questions of fact."[6] In addition to this Hart had available to him the texts of the 1926 edition of *Seven Pillars* and *Revolt in the Desert*. In contrast, *With Lawrence in Arabia* was written and published before these others, so that much of the material which we now know to be common to all three works represents, as it were, a first appearance. If Lawrence is acknowledged to be the source, as of course he must be of the later books, he then must assuredly be also, the source, despite the publishers' disclaimer on his behalf, of the first.

This was confirmed in a letter written in December, 1950, from Lowell Thomas to Richard Aldington, which said of Lawrence: "He helped me in a lot of ways on the lecture that I gave a couple of thousand times. He also worked with me on my book. At that time he was exceedingly anxious that no one should know this."[7] It is now known that this subterfuge was practised by Lawrence in at least two other cases. *Lawrence and the Arabs*, by his friend Robert Graves, contains the statement for the author: "unfortunately, owing to pressure of time, my completed typescript could not be submitted to

Shaw (the name Lawrence was then using) before publication, and I apologise to him for any passages where my discretion has been at fault." But later Graves wrote, "Lawrence read and passed every word of the book, though he asked me to put a sentence in my introduction making it seem that he had not."[8] And although Liddell Hart accepted the responsibility for the contents of his book it is clear that certain passages in it were written by Lawrence.

Mack went to the trouble of visiting Thomas and questioning him about "Lawrence's relationship with (him) and his attitude toward the elaborate and fanciful romanticization of his exploits" and writes "that Lawrence cooperated with him in the creation of his own legend."[9] Thomas further disclosed that when he was working on the biography and living in the London area in 1921 "Lawrence walked twelve miles to the edge of London and back several times" to help him with his book. Mack came to the conclusion that Lawrence "knew Thomas's picture of him to be false" but was at the same time attracted by the glorious image of himself as the "Uncrowned King of Arabia." Lawrence wrote to Sir Archibald Murray in January 1920 concerning statements appearing in Thomas's writings, which he claimed to find embarrassing, and said that he had refused to correct galley proofs because they contained so many misstatements that he "could not possibly pass one tenth of it." Leaving aside for the moment those statements concerned with Murray's role in the war, the question arises as to the responsibility on the part of Lawrence for the enormous amount of misinformation incorporated in the pages of *With Lawrence in Arabia*, much of which could only have emanated from Lawrence himself. After the war Thomas came to England "in the hope," he wrote, "of being able to learn something concerning his (Lawrence's) career, prior to 1914, which might throw a light on the formative period when Destiny was preparing him for his important role."[10]

It would appear that he learnt quite a lot, especially about the Lawrence family: the "celebrated ancestor, Sir Robert Lawrence, who accompanied Richard the Lion-Hearted to the Holy Land, seven hundred and thirty years ago and distinguished himself at the Siege of

Acre, just as the youthful T.E.Lawrence accompanied Allenby to the Holy Land and distinguished himself in its final deliverance. The brothers, Sir Henry and Sir John Lawrence of Mutiny fame, pioneers of Britain's empire in India, were among his more recent predecessors." Unhappily, Lawrence's father's name was Chapman, and the only Lawrence forebear he could truthfully boast was his mother, who was the illegitimate child of one John Lawrence, the eldest son of a Lloyds surveyor named Thomas Lawrence, in whose house Sarah Lawrence's mother had been a servant.

The story of the Chapman family has been related elsewhere, and has no useful place in the present narrative. Our concern is properly with the substance of a book which succeeded in creating a mighty legend which in its turn served to distort the facts and possibly influenced the course of twentieth century history. The impertinence in the paragraph we have just quoted, where Lawrence is represented as "accompanying" Allenby to the "Holy Land" will be seen, if one ploughs through the remaining pages, as a characteristic example of Thomas's treatment of the subject. Nearly every other character closely associated with Lawrence who is introduced into the narrative is made to appear subservient, or accessory, to Lawrence. Hogarth, who was appointed Director of the Arab Bureau in Cairo is introduced by Thomas as "a man who had an important influence over (Lawrence's) entire life down to the present day, and who even came out to Egypt during the War and acted as his intimate counsellor during the Arabian campaign." In case this description might be considered ambiguous, Thomas finally puts Hogarth in his place by showing him in one of the illustrations over a caption which reads: "Colonel Lawrence conferring with one of his advisers at the Arab Bureau in Cairo."[11]

It would not be sensible to attempt to list every solecism in Thomas's book in this present work: it would be both extensive and tiresome. One or two examples of the style of writing may suffice to inform the reader of the quality of the narrative. We are asked to believe that in 1912, at a time when the control of the harbour of Alexandretta, on the Mediterranean coast, was under international discussion, Lawrence, then a twenty-four year-old archaeologist "immediately hurried down to Cairo, demanded an audience" (which of course, could hardly be refused by the *de facto* Governor of Egypt) "with Lord Kitchener, and asked K. of K. why Germany had been permitted to get control of Alexandretta, the vital port to which Disraeli referred when he said that the peace of the world would one day depend on the control of that point on the coast of Asia Minor to which the finger of Cyprus pointed. Kitchener replied: 'I have warned London repeatedly, but the Foreign Office pays no attention. Within two years there will be a World War. Unfortunately, young man, you and I can't stop it, so run along and sell your papers'."[12]

Kitchener could not have foreseen that two years later Lawrence would attempt to enlist in his "Mob", only to be rejected by "members of the Army Medical Board (who) looked at the frail, five-foot-three, tow-headed youth, winked at one another, and told him to run home to his mother and wait until the next war. Just four years after he had been turned down as physically unfit for the ranks, this young Oxford graduate, small of stature, shy and scholarly as ever, entered Damascus at the head of his victorious Arabian army. Imagine what the members of the medical board would have said if some one had suggested to them in 1914 that three or four years later this same young man would decline knighthood and the rank of general, and would even avoid the coveted Victoria Cross and various other honours!"[13]

"But, with many other scientists, scholars, and a few young men of exceptional ability, such as Mark Sykes, Aubrey Herbert, Cornwallis, Newcombe and others, he was summoned to headquarters in Cairo by Sir Gilbert F.Clayton" (who was incidentally at that time plain Colonel Clayton, but, as we have seen, Thomas did not place much store by accuracy)."Though he was then only twentysix years old, he was already familiar with Turkey, Syria, Palestine, Arabia, Mesopotamia, and Persia . . . He not only spoke many of the languages, but he knew the customs of all the different nationalities and their historical development.

"To begin with, he was placed in the map department, where generals spent hours poring over inaccurate charts, discussing plans for piercing vulnerable spots in the Turkish armour. After working out a scheme they would turn, not infrequently, and ask the insignificant-looking subaltern if, in view of his personal knowledge of the country" (he had in fact not yet set foot in any of the battle areas,) "he had any suggestions to offer. Not infrequently his reply would be:

"While there are many excellent points in your plan, it is not feasible except at the expense of great loss of time in building roads for transport of supplies and artillery, and at needless expense of lives in maintaining lines of communication through the territory of hostile native tribes." "Then, as an alternative, he would point out a safer and shorter route, with which he happened to be familiar because he had tramped every inch of it afoot while hunting for lost traces of the invading armies of Assyrians, Greeks, Romans, and Crusaders . . . Later on in Arabia, Lawrence frequently outwitted the Turks because of this same superior knowledge of the topography of the country. He was better acquainted with many distant parts of the Turkish Empire than were the Turks themselves."[14]

After all this extravagant hyperbole one could well wonder at the author's reactions to the modest chapter-heading in *Seven Pillars*; "Book I. MY FIRST VISIT TO ARABIA" - in the autumn of 1916. But never mind the anachronisms, the narrative is more important, and Thomas eventually comes to the first crisis."When Lieutenant Lawrence arrived at Jeddah, the situation was critical. It was at this stage in the campaign that Lawrence decided to disregard Foch's dictum that the object of modern war is to locate the enemy army and annihilate it. He came to the conclusion that to win a war against the Turks, or any other well-trained troops in the desert, it would be better to imitate the tactics of Hannibal and other military leaders of pre-Napoleonic wars."[15]

At least, no anachronism there, because Hannibal may surely be regarded as pre-Napoleonic. But even with Hannibal as your mentor, you still need an army, and fortunately destiny had ensured that in the hour of need Lawrence would be in the right place. Thomas's statement that "the General Staff at headquarters in Cairo raised no objection to Lawrence's remaining in Arabia when he failed to return at the end of his furlough"[16] reads oddly against Lawrence's confession that after becoming "quite intolerable to the Staff . . . they . . . at last determined to endure me no longer.[17]" Perhaps the Thomas version may be accepted as a kinder paraphrase. At all events Lawrence was there in time to apply his special methods for creating a fighting force. Thomas explains; "It was by the process of accretion that Lawrence and Feisal built up their army. With only two companions the former started out across the desert. He stopped at every nomad encampment, and, calling the headmen together, in faultless classic Arabic he explained his mission". And that was how the Arab Army was created.

Thomas and his cameramen arrived at Aqaba, by all accounts, during March 1917. Ten years later Lawrence, writing to Ralph Isham, told him : "Of course, as you know, Lowell Thomas was not with me on any ride or operation in Arabia. I do not know how long he was in the country, for he arrived when I was up-country, and I had gone up again before he left. I expect he was there some ten or fourteen days, in all; of which we were together in Akaba for perhaps three."[18] This would not have afforded sufficient time for Thomas to acquire the material which he used for his book, and he claims that he was able to resort to Lawrence's "fellow adventurers, Colonel Wilson, of the Sudan, Newcombe, Joyce, Dawnay, Bassett, Vickery, Cornwallis, Hogarth, Stirling, etc.", but it is clear that a great deal of the material, by its very nature, could have come only from Lawrence himself.

Chapter Twenty Three

"Objective truth";
Britain's actions and Lawrence's part in them.

The Lawrence who emerges from the preceding chapters bears little resemblance to the romantic hero apotheosised by Lowell Thomas. Those who prefer to be allowed to regard his memory with veneration must either come to terms with the truth, or accept the legend with the sense of realism with which Robert Bolt, who wrote the screenplay, *Lawrence of Arabia*, has been able to reconcile himself. Bolt, according to *The Times* of July 30, 1988, declared "that he gave up the attempt to reach objective truth and 'eventually took *Seven Pillars* and pretended that that was what really happened'."

In this way the film preserves the legend for those who find the fiction to be more acceptable – more satisfying perhaps – than the facts. After all those biographies, and the continuing dissension between his admirers and his detractors, it may be easier for the ordinary person to regard Lawrence as a character part historical and part legendary, taking his place in our annals with the Arthur who had a Round Table, the Alfred who burnt the cakes, the wicked King John and the Lion-Hearted Richard, Bluff King Hal and Good Queen Bess.

The legendary Lawrence is easier to comprehend than the Lawrence who, in John Mack's words,"provides accounts which throw the spotlight on himself and credit him with a central place in actions whose grandeur is raised to epic proportions" even though "this self-elevation is invariably matched with countervailing passages of self-disparagement, and proclamations of the baseness of his position and of his deceit, which become a kind of litany." Thus *Seven Pillars* is seen as "a psychological document rather than as a literary work" and "the glorification of himself, and of the great events of the Arab Revolt in which he took part, seems to serve to overcome his low self-regard." The distortions in the book do not come from a simple alteration of facts; they "result from Lawrence's need to elevate the tale to epic proportions and to make of himself a contemporary legendary figure." This, then, is the figure which becomes readily acceptable to the playwright, and far easier for the comprehension of his audiences than the Lawrence Trinity: "the private Lawrence, Lawrence as a real person, and the mythological Lawrence of legendary heroism." But both his admirers and his detractors refuse the legend: the first acclaim the heroism as reality, the others see in him a man whose "role had involved him in an empty and dishonourable fraud."[1]

What then was "the real story of Britain's actions in Arabia", and why should it not be told? The real story is that Britain found herself at war with Turkey, when that country combined against her together with her most formidable enemy in Europe, and then remembered that she had refused to arm the Sherifians against the Turks when both powers were at peace, but recognised the sense of native support in those areas important to the proper defence of her Near East interests, and was justified now in responding to the Arabs. It is not true that she "would have promised them almost anything in order to get them to revolt";[2] and it is on clear record that the handful which raised the flag of rebellion went into action without the prior knowledge of the British, choosing their own time and motivated by their own ambitions. It was these who were free in their promises to Britain in return for the recognition of their expectations, saying that "it is to the Arab's interest also to prefer the assistance of the Government of Great Britain in consideration of their geographical position and economic interests" and expressing disappointment at the British reluctance "to promise almost anything" in return.

Right hand photo is of Irish-born actor, 27 year old Peter O'Toole in the title role of Sam Spiegel's film production of the famous Lawrence of Arabia.

On Left: Lawrence of Arabia (Thomas Edward Lawrence)

It is undisputable that Britain poured into that ungrateful area untold millions in gold and food and the requirements of war, and that there she sacrificed the lives of tens of thousands of British and Commonwealth fighting men. And in the final reckoning she left behind her independent Arab states, with their own Governments: all built on the final but costly success of British arms.

And what was Lawrence's part in this "shameful fraud"? In the pages of *Seven Pillars* he says that he believed in the need to replace the Turks in their Arabian empire not by European or Western Powers but by those who "had served a term of five hundred years under the Turkish harrow, and had begun to dream of liberty . . . we who believed we held an indication of the future set out to bend England's efforts towards fostering the new Arabic world in hither Asia."[3] From the very outset, he made every effort to identify himself with the British group, whom today we would label "Arabists", who were brought together under the British administration, to form the Arab Bureau, concerned with the promotion of Arab political and economic interests. "We called ourselves 'Intrusive' as a band " wrote Lawrence; "for we meant to break into the accepted halls of English foreign policy, and build a new people in the East, despite the rails laid down for us by our ancestors."[4] And when he felt that the General Staff were trying to keep him "away from the Arab affair" he contrived to elude them with "stratagems . . . I justified myself by my confidence in the final success of the Arab Revolt if properly advised" he wrote. "I had been a mover in the beginning; my hopes lay in it."[5]

One would have to look very far to find a favourable Arab appreciation of Lawrence's devotion and proved loyalty to the Arab cause. Abdulla writes of Lawrence's arrival "to supervise the wrecking of the railway" and goes on to say "I did not like his intervention as I was suspicious of his influence among the tribes". Abdulla maintains that "the general dislike of Lawrence's presence was quite clear . . . Lawrence appeared only to require people who had no views of their own, that he might impress his personal ideas upon them." But when Abdulla wrote those words he must have been fully aware of his indebtedness to Lawrence for the part he played in securing Transjordan for him and for serving him faithfully there in the troublesome period following the summer of 1921 as Chief British Representative, at a time when Abdulla's maladministration had created great difficulties in his country.

Lawrence stayed on until December the 8th of that year. St. John Philby, who succeeded him, had nothing but praise for the work he had done, writing: "He is excellent, and I am struck with admiration of his intensely practical, yet unbusinesslike methods." On his return to England Lawrence felt able to recommend to Churchill that Transjordan "be treated as an independent state, freed of control by the High Commissioner of Palestine, and that Abdullah be allowed to stay as the head of the new country." A further example of his "shameful" part in the alleged "conspiracy"?

What emerges from the whole history of the post-war settlement is the base ingratitude of the Arabs in general and the Hashemite family in particular. Storrs has described a meeting with King Hussein in Amman in 1924, at a time "when Sir Herbert Samuel (at that time the High Commissioner for Palestine) was straining to promote an understanding between him and Ibn Saud . . . We talked with him for long hours in bitter cold, and he kept turning to Clayton and me, repeating that we were the authors of all his troubles and difficulties: which consist, as you know, in a Crown for himself, a Crown for Feisal, and a coronet for Abdallah."[6]

It was not many years before that coronet too became a royal Crown. Feisal's Crown had been assured in the deliberations of the Cairo Conference of 1921, where, as Lawrence wrote to Mrs. Bernard Shaw, "all the Mespot officials (were swung by Gertrude Bell) to the Feisal solution, while Winston and I swung the English people." St. John Philby was one of the Englishmen who was opposed to that choice, but admitted that Lawrence was "an uncompromising champion of Arab independence" although "trammelled by the obsession that the future of Arabia must be worked out under the shadow of Sharifian hegemony." Philby was of course stating what we all now know, but it seemed to cut little ice with the Sharifians. "I myself incline to doubt" wrote Storrs "whether King Husain ever loved Lawrence. There were moments when he and his sons suspected him of working against them, and more than once let fall hints . . . that he should not be allowed to mingle too much with Arab tribesmen. Feisal spoke of him to me with a good-humoured tolerance which I should have resented more if I had ever imagined that Kings would like King-makers."[7]

Chapter Twenty Four

War in Mesopotamia.
The tragedy of Kut

After the capture of Baghdad in March, 1917, Britain addressed the peoples of Mesopotamia, reminding them that the Arabs of the Hejaz had "expelled the Turks and Germans who oppressed them and have proclaimed Sharif Hussain as the King and His Lordship rules in independence and freedom and is the ally of the Nations who are fighting against the power of Turkey and Germany . . . It is the desire and hope of the British peoples and nations in alliance with them that the Arab race may rise once more to greatness and renown among the peoples of the earth and that it shall bind itself to this end in unity and concord . . . Therefore I invite you to participate in the management of your civil affairs in collaboration with the Political Representatives of Great Britain who accompany the British army so that you may unite with your kinsmen in the North South East and West in realising the aspirations of your race."[1]

The British should then have well known - as they became later aware – that these references to Hussain had failed to take into account "the feelings of Arab leaders such as Ibn Saud, who not only refused to recognise the right of Sharif Husain to speak or negotiate on behalf of the Arab people, but were actively hostile to his pretensions. This hostility was accentuated by the somewhat overbearing attitude adopted by Sharif Husain in correspondence, and by the jealousy with which the very large subsidies he received in the form of gold, arms, and munitions were regarded by Ibn Saud and others. We had already found that the Sharif Husain carried no weight in Mesopotamia: his pretensions were ridiculed, and his claims to speak on behalf alike of the Sunni and Shi'ah elements were vehemently denied."[2]

The identification of Sharif Hussain with "the Arab Revolt" meant nothing to the Mesopotamians, who contributed no part towards it, any more than did the peoples of Syria or Palestine, or of the Yemen or the Shammar or the Nejd. In short, "the Arab Revolt" was no more than a Sharifian essay to achieve a dominant supremacy over all the tribes and peoples of and adjoining the Arabian peninsula; and insofar that its opening shots were of necessity aimed at the Turks it may have been entitled to claim for itself the credit for an Arab revolt. It has suited the aims of Arab nationalism or Pan-Arab hegemony to immortalise the legend in writings which tell of *al-Thawret al'Arabiyet al-Kubra* ("the Great Arab Revolt"), but the records of the war histories of the period and the recollections of the many individuals who played major roles in the conflict lend them little support. Nevertherless, thoughout the years which have followed, the legend has received universal acceptance, and has been usefully exploited to further the claims of those who have found it profitable to invoke it in their demands for territories and for political privilege. At the Paris Peace Conference Feisal spoke about the victories of his armies, and the 100,000 warriors he had thrown into the conflict: a reckoning which prompted Allenby to convey to Woodrow Wilson that this number far exceeded any muster of which he was ever aware; while Feisal's figure of "20,000 having been killed" prompted Lloyd George to suggest that there is usually "something romantic about Oriental arithmetic."[3] "Mousa felt impelled to modify the casualty list, writing of the "ten thousand (who) died for the cause they cherished."

So the Mesopotamian campaign has to be regarded as a conflict which took place in an area separate from "The Palestine Campaigns" (the title of Wavell's history, in which the Mesopotamian campaign receives less than five lines of print). As Elizabeth Monroe has pointed out, the British Government and the Government of India "tended to look on the Middle East not as a single region but as a desert with two edges, one belonging to the Mediterranean and the other to the Indian Ocean.[4] The Anglo-Indian invasion of Mesopotamia was an initiative of the Government of India, motivated to a considerable extent by their determination to give protection to those areas – reaching northwards from Aden and including its Protectorate together with the Arab Principalities of the Arabian coast to the shores of the Persian Gulf – which had over the years been reinforced to shield her other interests in Asia. These were designed also to support British measures to counter the growing encroachment of Germany in the region which extended to Persia from the Eastern Mediterranean.

It is clear that the Government of India had been well prepared for the sequence of events which followed the closing of the Dardenelles by the Turks on the 27th of September, 1914; and on that very day the British Political Resident in the Persian Gulf received from Ibn Saud copies of the telegrams which had been sent by Enver Pasha, advising the despatch of arms and ammunition to be used against the British, and Turkish officers to train his Arabs. The Anglo-Persian Oil Company was exporting oil at the rate of over a quarter of a million tons per annum, and in that interest alone it was important that Abadan should receive protection against any Turkish threat. On the 29th September British warships were positioned in the Shatt-al-Arab: a precautionary measure which was ill-received by the Turks, and arguments arose as to whether the Shatt-al-Arab was in Turkish or international territorial waters.

While these proceeded the First Brigade of Indian Expeditionary Force 'D' sailed under sealed orders from Bombay, leaving there on October the 16th and anchoring at Bahrain on the 23rd. Six days later the warships Goeben and Breslau bombarded Russian ports on the Black Sea; and on the same day Force 'D' left its anchorage for Fao, on the Turkish shore of the Shatt-al-Arab, where it landed on November 6th, war having been declared on Turkey on the previous day. Within a few days fighting broke out, and the invading Anglo-Indian forces reported on November 11th their first casualties in the campaign.

The full story of the war in Mesopotamia is available in the Official Histories, supplemented by the personal reminiscences and records of many of the participants, and is beyond the scope of the present work, which is concerned with the examination of the relationship between the political and military activities on the two fighting fronts – the Palestinian and the Mesopotamian – and the theme of "Arab Revolt" against Turkish Rule. But it might not be unprofitable to consider some of the differences in the nature of the two campaigns.

In the east the Government of India launched offensive action from the very outset, carrying the war into the territories occupied by the enemy, while in the west the British stood on the defensive and had to suffer the early attacks of the Turco-German forces. It will be recalled that it took more than three years for the British to battle across the Sinai Peninsula before they could attempt the invasion of Palestine. Another significant contrast lay in the behaviour of the native populations. At no time during its four-year haul from Cairo to Damascus did the Allied forces find themselves under threat or in conflict with either the tribes or the townspeople. It is true that the Palestinian Arab Regiments in the Turkish Armies fought only too well against the British, but their civilian compatriots proved completely apathetic during the British advance, seemingly indifferent to the prospect of exchanging their Turkish masters for new rulers.

The Mesopotamians were far from apathetic in the face of the invading forces. These invaders were infidels, undeserving of mercy, and they received none. The British did their utmost to establish a promising relationship between the natives and their new masters, and when their troops occupied Basra on November 23rd Sir Percy Cox issued a proclamation announcing that "the wish of the British Government is to free the Arabs from the oppression of the Turk and to bring them advancement, prosperity and trade."[5] The Arab response to this was recorded by Arnold Wilson: "Bitter experience of Arab hostility, Arab thefts, and Arab rapacity occasionally tempted departmental chiefs to embark without full consideration upon policies the repercussions of which might well endanger a delicate political structure."⁶

It might well be said that the substitution of British rule for that of the Turks, together with the disappearance of the Turkish administration and Police Force did in fact imbue the local Arabs with an appreciation of a newly-found freedom, for when the British entered Basra they found the Arabs busily engaged in looting, while armed bands of robbers infested the dategroves all the way down to Fao and pirates had made their appearance on the Shatt-al-Arab. The Turks were not slow in their reaction to the situation. "During January" wrote Wilson "the efforts made by the Ottoman Government to give the contest the character of a Holy War against the infidel began to bear fruit. The *Jihad* had been preached in every mosque in Syria and Mesopotamia and emissaries had been busy among the tribes and in the towns urging them to do battle in the name of the Faith. The effect of the campaign was ostensibly greatest among the Shi'ah of the Mesopotamian delta whose only gods, to quote a Turkish writer, 'were gifts and success'."⁷ These appeals to the religious susceptibilities of the natives did not go unheeded. The Bani Turuf, the Bani Salih, the Bani Tamim and the Bani Sikain rose against the British, sending detachments to join the Turks at Illa near Kut Nahr Hashim, while on February 5th the Bawi made their contribution to this Arab Revolt by cutting the Anglo-Persian Oil Company's pipe-lines and telephone wires. The Ch'ab of Fallahiya and the Mirs of Hindian, together with the people of Ram Hormuz joined the other tribes in an overwhelming support for the Turks.

Their ardour for revolt was not necessarily a measure of their dependability as on more than one occasion the Turks found to their cost. The Turks had assembled at the end of March a force of 9,000 regular troops at Shu'aiba and Ahwaz, supported by 21,000 Arabs. Together they outnumbered "the British, 14,400 strong, but when the fighting commenced on April 12th the Arabs held back, preferring to await the outcome of the battle. The fighting went badly for the Turks, with the result that on the evening of the 13th the Arabs discreetly withdrew from the battlefield. They returned to the scene after the Turkish Commander, Sulaiman Bey al'Askari, anticipating defeat, committed suicide. The fleeing Turkish soldiery, as they toiled through the mud along the shores of the Hammar Lake, were butchered without mercy by the Muntafiq bands, and only a mere remnant under Sulaiman al 'Askari's lieutenant, Ali Bey, reached the shelter of the *sarai* at Nasiriya. Never again did the Turks invite the Arabs to cooperate in military organized operations."[8]

The British victory at Shuaiba was not achieved without cost. They suffered losses of 1,257, and on the last day of the fighting a young British officer, Captain F.L.Dyer, who had strayed, unarmed, from the battlefield, fell into Arab hands and was promptly slaughtered. Encouragement for this savagery came from a zealous Sheikh, Ghadhban, who offered a reward of several gold pieces for every British or Indian head brought in to him, a benificence which ensured the horrid mutilation of every unfortunate who fell into Arab hands They gleaned a dreadful harvest on March 2nd, when General Robinson's force lost 62 killed and 127 wounded when fighting against vastly superior numbers.

There is confirmation from Lawrence on Turkish army attitudes to the Arabs, writing to his mother on his way home from Basra in May, 1916, that "the ill-feeling between Arabs and Turks has grown to such a degree that Halil cannot trust any of his Arabs in the firing line";[9] while his subsequent report in the *Arab Bulletin No 23* stated; "Halil Pasha, Commander-in-Chief of the Turkish Forces in Iraq, spoke very freely on the question of the Arab attitude. At first he proposed the exchange of Indian sick for Arab prisoners of war; but later he went back on this, and refused to accept Arabs in exchange at all . . . he did not want them . . . . ninety per cent of Arabs were bad. He said their only desire was to get taken prisoner, and that the whole lot of them were undesirable."[10] In another report Lawrence expressed his disillusionment with the prospects of finding support for the "Arab Revolt" in the area:"I have been looking up pan-Arab party . . . it is about 12 strong. Formerly consisted of Sayed Taleb and some Jackals. The other BASRA people are either from NEJD, interested in Central Arabia only and to be classed with Arabia politically, or peasants who are interested in date palms, or Persians."[11]

Despite this curt dismissal Sayed Taleb was destined to emerge after the end of the war as a formidable figure in Mesopotamian politics, though earning not British support but the most intense British hostility for his views.

Wilson (Lieutenant-Colonel Sir Arnold T. Wilson, K.C.I.E., C.S.I., C.M.G., D.S.O., and, later, the perhaps more pedestrian M.P.) served throughout the Mesopotamian campaign as Political Officer with the British Expeditionary Forces and, after the war, as Acting Civil Commissioner in Mesopotamia. In the course of his distinguished career he had also functioned as Political Resident in the Persian Gulf and His Majesty's Consul-General for Fars, Khuzistan and other places. To whatever attributes these responsibilities demanded was added a literary ability of high standard and considerable industry. He wrote a history of the Persian Gulf and produced a Bibliography of Persia, but his most important book for the reader researching the course of the Middle East fighting is his *Loyalties: Mesopotamia 1914-17*.

After he had been instructed in June 1915 to join the forces under General Gorringe, who had been ordered to take Nasariya (some 100 miles north-west of Basra) he became closely involved with the military situation and was able to report at close hand on the political issues which developed. As the only Arabic-speaking officer with the Division which, under General Nixon, was authorized to begin the operations, he went forward on June 22nd with reconnaissance parties on the slow advance up the Euphrates, on which Nasariya, like Basra, lay, and drew first blood in an encounter with a Turkish sergeant and a private, whom he shot and wounded. When he returned later to the scene he saw, to his horror, "that the Arabs had been busy. The two Turks lay on the opposite side, stripped naked with their throats cut."[12]

It was not long before he found that these outrages reflected the normal behaviour of the native population during the upheaval of the conflict: "Incidents such as these afterwards came within the experience of practically all members of the civil administration employed in Mesopotamia outside the large towns . . . the Army, staff and regimental officers alike, could scarcely be blamed for regarding Arabs, collectively, as incorrigible thieves and murderers, faithless and mercenary. Again and again they found the wounded slaughtered, the dead dug up for the sake of their clothes and left to the jackals. "[13]

After the British took Nasariya, at the cost of over 500 casualties, the control of virtually the entire province of Basra passed into their hands, and the General Staff in India began to look towards Kut-al-Amara, which stood on the Tigris river roughly half way between Nasariya and Baghdad. Kut was destined to play a tragic role in the history of the campaign. The first move towards its capture was made on the 28th of September, 1915, at a position held by the Turks across the Tigris eight miles to the south of the town. In its ultimate outcome it was successful, but at great cost: 1,229 in British killed and wounded.

During the course of the fighting the War Office received information to the effect that substantial reinforcements would be reaching the Turks on the Mesopotamian fronts by the following January, and it was decided that there should be no delay in the British advance towards Baghdad. General Nixon accordingly ordered a concentration of his forces at Aziziya, about fifty miles south-east of Baghdad, more than halfway to the capital from Kut. This move was completed by October 10th, and on the nineteenth of the following month Nixon decided to commence his advance towards Baghdad. Progress at first was rapid, and a British force under General Townshend reached Ctesiphon, some sixteen miles from Baghdad. The Turkish army awaiting them there numbered 20,000, and inflicted enormous losses on the British and Indian regiments engaged in the battle. Of Townshend's total force of 12.000 men, 4,200 were killed or wounded: of the total number of 317 British officers 130 were killed or wounded; and of 235 Indian officers only 111 survived.

The Turks counter-attacked at midday, and by dusk the British were forced to break off the battle. They renewed their efforts to strike back on the following morning, but the Turks held their ground. Townshend was forced to retreat on the third day of the battle November 25th, and the Turks, now aided, for the first time, by their own aircraft, pursued him down the river. "The retreat continued during the 1st and 2nd December, and Kut was entered early on the 3rd: the Turks had been outdistanced and our only assailants were the Arabs, who harried our columns, pillaging and killing stragglers in the darkness and harrying the field ambulance when they got a chance."[14]

As could be expected, the Germans reported the outcome of these battles with satisfaction, dwelling particularly on the behaviour of the Arabs during the British retreat. The German report brought forth a response which is worth recording. "On the 13th December the Secretary of State for India informed the House of Commons that he had every reason to believe that the (German) statements that friendly Arabs had turned against the British troops during this action were quite untrue." Wilson's wry comment on this was: "The statement was in its literal sense correct, for the Arabs in question were not and never had been friendly, but it was misleading."[15] It is possible that students of the record of British-Arab attitudes might find some echo in Elizabeth Monroe's statement, some thirty-five years later, about the "band of British public servants whose predilection for Arabs . . . caused them to view Arab resistance with indulgence."[16]

Such indulgence was not shared by Wilson. He records that when the remnants of Townshend's forces entered Kut the Arab population numbered between five and six thousand. "Some were expert thieves, and twelve were shot by court martial for pillaging stores; others were in communication with the enemy."[17] Their offences were not exclusively directed at the British: "Arab women and children going to the Tigris for water were freely shot at, both by Turks and Arab irregulars.[18] But as time went on, and the stores of food became depleted, the troops faced increasing hardships", deprivations which the civilians were somehow spared, according to the report of one British survivor, who wrote that "although we had to feed hundreds of the Arab population – many of them gratuitously – few ever showed signs of starvation, even up to the end. The children, fat as butter, showed no signs of shortage of food."[19]

By the end of April it was clear that Townshend's beleagured force could not expect either rescue or even survival except by way of surrender to the besiegers. An effort was made to purchase their freedom: Townshend offered to surrender his forty guns to the Turks and pay them one million pounds in sterling if his men were allowed to go free on parole. The offer was passed through the Turkish commander, Khalil Pasha, to Enver Pasha, whose response was that Turkey did not want money, and that "10,000 Turkish lives had been sacrificed at Kut."

In their desperation the British increased their offer to two million pounds, but met with the same rejection as before. It was then that the British sent out in their effort to negotiate a settlement the delegation of the three officers, one of whom was Lawrence. The other two were Captain Aubrey Herbert, a Member of Parliament, and Colonel W.H.Beach, head of the Intelligence Branch I.E.F.'D'. "The choice of Aubrey Herbert was a natural one. As a Member of Parliament he carried some authority in addition to his military status: he was well-known as a Turkophile, spoke Turkish well, had many friends in Constantinople and was said to have been personally acquainted with the Turkish commander, Khalil Pasha".[20]

Lawrence was apparently sent out "to find out whether the Tribes on the Turkish lines of communication could be induced to revolt" and to negotiate "with Arab elements in Turkish army with a view to detaching them from Turks and making afterwards side with Arab movement."[21] As the Kut garrison surrendered on April 29th, and Lawrence was back in Cairo about the middle of the next month, it appears to be incredible that he could undertake, or be expected to undertake, the sensitive and intricate tasks which involved the locating, identifying and suborning of potential Arab rebels. Sir Percy Cox, the chief political officer in Iraq, reported on Lawrence's activities, such as they were, and said of the mission, "I cannot as a political officer of the Government of India afford to be identified with it,"[22] while Hubert Young made his own acid comments on Lawrence's attitudes and general behaviour during the brief period he spent in Basra, describing him as "thoroughly spoilt and posing".[23] But we know from Lawrence's own reports that even if the brevity of his stay in Basra inhibited more than the briefest contacts with potential dissidents, he found time to investigate and comment on the quality of the lithography, the quayside berthing and storing problems, the railways and the medical authorities as well as the conduct of the campaign. He may not have succeeded in performing successfully his chosen assignment but, as we have seen, he did not permit this failure to prevent him from making suggestions to those responsible for the many deficiencies he uncovered.

Chapter Twenty Five

*A catalogue of dreadful atrocities:
the martyrdom of the British captives.*

From Kut there went into Turkish captivity some 12,000 men, of whom more than 4,000 died, mostly through the horrifying neglect and shameful cruelty they were called upon to endure. Wilson tells us that nearly seventy per cent of the British rank and file "left their bones in Turkey . . . The occupation of Kut by the Turks was accompanied by scenes of indiscipline, violence, and savage brutality. Officers of the highest rank and men, sick and wounded, were pillaged by Turkish soldiers and Arabs under the eyes of their officers, their boots and blankets stolen, and their food seized, any resistance being met by merciless bludgeoning."[1]

In military terms a disaster, a reversal: in terms of human suffering an episode of almost unbearable poignancy. There had been no neglect on the part of the British Generals in charge of the campaign in their efforts aimed at the relief of Kut. Throughout January they had mustered whatever forces they could assemble to enable them to apply pressure against the Turkish besiegers, but even the weather conspired against them, frustrating their designs. An attack had been planned by General Aylmer on the 19th, but on that day the weather conditions were so appalling that the action had to be postponed until the twenty-first. It met with failure. The British casualties on that day amounted to close on 2,700 – probably more than half their total strength – and on the following day they sent a flag of truce to the enemy requesting a cessation of hostilities so that the wounded could be collected and the dead buried. They should have known better. "Scarcely had the flag been hoisted in our trenches when Arabs swarmed out of the Turkish lines, and began to rob wounded and dead alike and in some cases to stab and cut the throats of wounded men, whenever they could do so unobserved. Officers and men, unarmed because of the flag of truce, went to the rescue of their comrades only to be assaulted and robbed by Arabs, who prowled around, tireless in their foul lust for property and human life."[2]

But Kut could not be left to its fate. At the close of the first phase of fighting Aylmer's casualties amounted to 8,000 killed and wounded, but he made a further attempt, in March, to establish contact with the Kut garrison. This operation, which commenced on the 8th, ended quickly in further disaster, with the same horrendous sequel as the previous failure. "Arab marauders were busy on the battlefield, pillaging the dead, stripping and sometimes killing wounded men: the stretcher-bearers had to be accompanied by armed parties, whose attempts to drive away the Arabs frequently drew on them outbursts of rifle fire from the Turkish trenches, causing many casualties. When dawn broke the Arabs were still on the battlefield, cheerfully risking their lives in the all-absorbing pursuit of pillage. No object seemed too trifling for them: the blankets and clothes in which the dead had been buried, perhaps months before, were keenly sought for."[3] Once again Aylmer was forced to withdraw. His last effort had resulted in a further 3,500 casualties, with some units losing more than a quarter, others as much as one third, of their strength.

Inevitably Aylmer's catalogue of failures resulted in the loss of his command, and a new force of 30,000 rifles together with 127 guns was assembled under General Gorringe for a final effort to break through the Turkish siege. Despite the numerical superiority of the British – for the enemy had no more than 20,000 troops and 88 guns – the attempt failed. The Turks were strongly entrenched on both banks of the Tigris: for three weeks the battle ebbed and flowed, with the British losses amounting to 10,000 men. On April 25 it was announced that there would be no more frontal attacks: on the 29th General Townshend surrendered. The dreadful siege was ended: for the survivors an even worse ordeal was to commence.

"Khalil Pasha was warned by General Townshend that the men of the garrison were too emaciated to walk: he promised in a written reply that every care should be taken of them, and that they should be transported by steamer to Baghdad and thence by carts. As a matter of fact he must have already given orders that all but the officers, and a few men who could not stand, were to proceed by road, for during that night and the following day the greater part were marched up-river for the eight miles to Shamram, where they were to lie, exposed to wind and rain, ringed round by sentries. The journey took eight hours, at the end of which, and for some days later, the prisoners were given a few Turkish ration biscuits, which had apparently been rejected as unfit for issue to troops. They were made 'of the coarsest unhusked barley, not unmixed with earth, as hard as iron, and many of them green with mould'. These biscuits were ravenously devoured by the starving men, over three hundred of whom died in the agonies of gastro-enteritis during the first days at Shamram . . . Few of those who died at Shamram were buried: their bodies were cast into a nearby ravine, where in July 1917 some of their skulls were found . . . After a few days at Shamram the Turks realised that few of their captives would reach Baghdad alive unless further food was sent, and General Gorringe was permitted to send up some supplies; but before these rations arrived many of the men had sold boots and clothing to Arabs for a few handfuls of dates and black bread. On 6th May the rank and file left Shamram under an escort of Arab cavalry."[4]

These dreadful reports were not allowed to reach the British public. "So little were the British Government told as to the actual treatment by the Turks of the wounded at Kut that Lord Desart in the House of Lords on 16th May 1916 stated that it was now known 'that those who are sick and wounded have been handed to the British authorities by the Turks, to whom in this respect I think one should pay a tribute in comparison with other of our enemies'.⁵ "But in due course the truth emerged through witnesses and survivors, and the *Official History* of the campaign reported: "The march itself was a nightmare. The Arab soldiery used sticks and whips to flog the stragglers on, and although in some cases they kept the promise given to the British officers that men who fell out from sickness would be put on camels and donkeys, many died by the roadside."

Captain E.O.Mousley survived the siege and was able to record his personal experience of the aftermath. "We tingled with anger and shame at seeing on the other bank a sad little column of British troops who had marched up from Kut driven by a wild crowd of Kurdish horsemen who brandished sticks and what looked like whips. The eyes of our men stared from white faces, drawn long with the suffering of a too tardy death, and they held out their hands towards our boat. As they dragged one foot after another some fell, and those with the rearguard came in for blows from cudgels and sticks. I saw one Kurd strike a British soldier who was limping along, he reeled under the blows . . . It seemed that half their number were a few miles ahead and the rest strewed the road to Kut. Some have been thrashed to death, some killed, and some robbed of their kit and left to be tortured by the Arabs. I have been told by a sergeant that he saw one of the Sumana crew killed instantly by a blow on the head from a stirrup iron swung by a Kurdish horseman for stopping on the road for a few seconds. Men were dying of cholera and dysentery and often fell from sheer weakness . . . Every now and then we stopped to bury our dead . . . Enteritis, a form of cholera, attacked the whole garrison after Kut fell, and the change of food no doubt helped this . . . A man turned green and foamed at the mouth. His eyes became sightless and the most terrible moans conceivable came from his inner being . . . They died, one and all, with terrible suddenness. One night several Indians were missing . . . jumped overboard to end their wretchedness. Major . . . was, so soon as we disembarked, left lying uncovered from the sun on a stretcher, covered by thousands of flies. Now and then a wasted arm rose a few inches as if to brush them off but fell back inadequate to the task . . . One saw British soldiers in a similar state dying of enteritis with a green ooze issuing from their lips, their mouths fixed open, in and out of which flies walked . . . Details of other similar cases I won't write about."[6]

When the survivors reached Baghdad they were placed in an unsheltered enclosure on the right bank of the Tigris, where many died. Those who could still walk were soon sent northwards, and Captain Shakeshaft, of the 2nd Norfolks, who recorded the journey in his diary, has described their arrival at Tikrit, nearly one hundred miles north of Baghdad. "We met a number of unfortunate British and Indian soldiers who were standing together at the door of a miserable yard, where they were herded together. They looked ghastly. The Arabs used to bring milk and eggs to sell and asked exorbitant prices; consequently they would soon have no money and would die of starvation and neglect . . . Sometimes, when a sick man would crawl out of the hovel they lived in, Arabs would throw stones and chase him back into the yard."[7]

Meanwhile the compatriots of these doomed martyrs seemed at home to bask in an almost ecstatic euphoria. "I look on Mesopotamia," declared one Member of Parliament "as the prize for which the Indian Army is fighting. I hope to see a Mesopotamia in future with its irrigation works and canals all in working order under the British Government. I hope to see the banks along its rivers populated and cultivated by flourishing Indian colonies transported from the banks of the Indus."

Hansard records the date of that panegyric: the 22nd March 1916, when Aylmer was frantically and desperately attempting the rescue of the Kut garrison. One wonders how it was possible that the British people and their representatives in Parliament could remain in such complete ignorance of the unspeakable tragedies which were being enacted in this land of fair promise. Wilson blamed the censorship for this state of affairs. "It soon became clear that it was being used less to prevent information reaching the enemy than to prevent the public in

India and at home becoming aware of the appalling sufferings that were being endured by our troops. The expression 'friendly Arabs' drew a warning that no turn of phrase should be used which implied that all Arabs were not friendly. When our wounded were murdered and the graves of our dead despoiled by Arabs they were described as 'Kurds and others' and 'marauders in Turkish pay.' "[8]

Chapter Twenty Six

*Triumph of an Arab Revolt;
The British create the Arab State of Iraq.*

British troops entered Baghdad on the eleventh of March, 1917, and eight days later General Maude issued a proclamation to the worthy citizens, reminding them of the historic bond which had existed between them and the Dominions of the King of England, and inviting them "to participate in the management of civil affairs in collaboration with the Political Representatives of Great Britain".[1] Moreover, it expressed the "hope of the British people and Nations in alliance with them that the Arab race may rise once more to greatness and renown amongst the people of the Earth and that it shall bind itself to this end in unity and concord."[2]

Although the proclamation was formally addressed "To the People of the Baghdad Wilayet" it was at the same time distributed by His Majesty's Government throughout the neutral and eastern countries. Its extravagant wording was criticized in quarters in which the British Cabinet, who were responsible for its composition, had hoped that it would be enthusiastically received. Its effusive references to "the aspirations of the Arab race" may possibly have been directed towards the people of Syria and Palestine, for at the time of its publication military preparations were being completed for the opening phases of the Allied invasion of Palestine.

The British occupation of Baghdad served to secure their

possession of Lower Mesopotamia, but vast areas beyond the city remained in the possession of the Turks. A British advance into these enemy territories necessarily involved extension of the lines of supply and communication. The physical character of the territory favoured the defenders: the slow progress against them was effected only at the grievous cost of heavy casualties. The two-day battle which resulted in the British capture of Samarra, about seventy-five miles north-west of Baghdad, on April 23rd, cost the attackers two thousand men in killed and wounded.

Beyond Samarra there lay sixty miles of desert, waterless away from the river courses of the Tigris and the Euphrates, and raised by the heat of the midday sun to temperatures of 160°-120° in the shade where available.

It was the middle of October before General Maude's forces reached Falluja, some thirty-five miles west of Baghdad. The slowness of this advance was attributed to the unbridled lawlessness which prevailed in the desert region between the two rivers. Wilson reported that "the population as a whole had contrived to provide itself with modern weapons and abundance of ammunition, to such effect that the price of a Mauser or Lee-Enfield, which before the War stood at £20 or £25, had dropped to £5 or less. British and Turkish rifles had been picked up on fields of battle or stolen on the lines of communication in thousands; ammunition had been accumulated on a scale hitherto undreamt of. In the quest for arms the Arab showed qualities of courage, cunning and perseverance which, if turned to a better cause, would have ensured success in any walk of life. In one British camp over 70 boxes of over 1,000 rounds each were dug up and stolen from under the noses of the sentries."[3]

The military authorities attempted to deal with this situation by purchasing rifles and ammunition from any tribesman who would sell. But "the measure did more harm than good . . . The rifles and ammunition freely issued to our allies on the Syrian side, together with captured Turkish arms, soon filled the gap, and the money we paid went to purchase more and better rifles."

General Maude was not unaware of this problem, and tried to counter it by trading and making friends with the Arabs. In the words of the Official History: "It appeared that our policy was tending towards enlisting the tribes under our banner, though it was not clear exactly how it was proposed to use them. They were quite unreliable, and though they might fight for us one day, they were quite likely to take up arms against us the next. They had, moreover, little or no fighting value; because – while expert as desert marauders – they would take full toll from a demoralized retreating army – they were quite ineffective, though tiresome, against unbroken regular troops."[4] The British failure to seize the Turkish stronghold at Ramadi, some thirty miles to the west of Falluja, on July 11th, 1917, provided an illustration of this last description of Arab tactics. After suffering severe casualties, "the force withdrew from opposite Ramadi before dawn on the 13th. The Turks did nothing to impede the retirement, but the Arabs, some 1,500 strong, made repeated attacks on the rearguard and persevered, undeterred by heavy losses, till the force reached Dhibban – march of about 25 miles to the east – during the evening of the 13th."[5]

It could be maintained that the British forces in Mesopotamia were in reality engaged in fighting two separate enemy groups: the regular Turco-German armies, and the Arab tribes who were seemingly unresponsive to the fine sentiments which had been addressed to them and their brethren in the Official Proclamation of March 15th, and although in September 1917 it was estimated that for every Turk under arms the British possessed two combatants and four non-combatants on their ration strength, with three guns on the British side against one with the Turks, it was found necessary to further reinforce General Maude. From France he received a regiment of cavalry and horse artillery and from India two cavalry regiments, together with an additional Flying Squadron. He was now able to continue his offensive, making good progress throughout the month of October, and probably heartened by the tidings of the last day of that month that Allenby had captured Beersheba and taken 1,800 prisoners: a success doubly welcome because it reduced the possibilities of counter-attack on his left flank from the direction of the Syrian theatre of war. But another whole year had to pass before the fighting ceased in response to the armistice which was signed on November 1st, 1918.

With the defeat of the Turkish and German armies the fate of the Ottoman Empire was sealed. With Russia out of the picture its dismemberment would largely be determined between Britain and France. But despite the Sykes-Picot Agreement and the presumed essence of the Entente Cordiale there soon appeared murmurs of dissent and more than a hint of conflict between the two allies on the sharing of the spoils. Sykes-Picot had agreed that the British zone would comprise the *vilayets* of Baghdad and Basra, but now, as we have earlier noted, Britain demanded Mosul, which had been promised to the French.

There was dissension, too, between the Government in London and the Government of India concerning the character of the new regime which would be planned for Mesopotamia, for India, which had contributed so largely in human and material resources to the final victory, had received no specific consideration in the Sykes-Picot deliberations, and it now appeared that despite the importance of her political, economic and strategic interests in Mesopotamia, her claims were not to be taken into account. As we have seen, the first of the Allied troops to enter that theatre of war were the soldiers of the Indian Expeditionary Force who invaded Mesopotamia: vast numbers of their dead lay entombed in the soil of that conquered territory. Throughout the entire campaign reinforcements and supplies reached the battlefields from the Indian mainland, and the Indian and Burmese Regiments had shared in full the dreadful sufferings of the other British units during the battles and afterwards when they fell into enemy hands. India had sent troops to fight in the Palestine campaigns: twenty battalions to contribute to the reorganization of the Egyptian Expeditionary Force, while Indian cavalry divisions played an important part in the great offensive which brought the

Middle East wars to an end.

"India was being bled white by the incessant demands of Mesopotamia for men and munitions . . . It seems clear that Mesopotamia had by this time become, like Syria and Palestine, an objective in itself, apart from the main campaign in Europe, for Turkey was at this time engaging on both fronts larger British Forces than her own, greatly to the benefit of her European allies."[6] Assuredly she had well earned the right to lay some claim before those arbiters, who now assumed the authority to determine the fate of a great territory.

Whatever dissension arose between India and Whitehall on the future of Mesopotamia faded into the background as the Arabs of that country united to advance the most vociferous claims to the greatest possible share of the spoils of victory: based not of course on the grounds of their cooperation with the armies which had defeated and ejected their Turkish oppressors but on promises of Arab independence contained in wartime Allied declarations. In his exchange of letters with the Sherif Hussain in 1915 McMahon had written: "With regard to the *vilayets* of Baghdad and Basra, the Arabs will recognise that the established position and interests of Great Britain necessitate special administrative arrangements (an earlier translation of the Arabic of the letter had read "special measures of administrative control") in order to secure these territories, from foreign aggression, to promote the welfare of the local populations and to safeguard our mutual economic interests."

The Mesopotamian Arabs appeared to adopt the view, and not without good reason, that they were not party to that presumption, and preferred to invoke the 1918 "Declaration to the Seven Syrians" which promised that the British Government would recognise the complete and sovereign independence of the Arabs inhabiting those areas emancipated from Turkish control by the action of the Arabs themselves during the war and support them in their struggle for freedom. It also referred to areas 'occupied by the Allied forces during the present war' where it would be Britain's 'wish and desire' that the future government should be based on 'the principle of the consent of the governed'.

Notwithstanding the appalling record of the Mesopotamian Arabs during the course of the conflict, they united in their demands for "complete and sovereign independence", the Sunni minority (though despite their numerical inferiority the arbiters of Arab nationalism in the country) combining with the Shia majority and other elements to foment increasing discontent with the policies of the British administration. Iraqi officers in Damascus sent arms and money in support for the local demands for Arab government at Baghdad. The publication there on May 3rd, 1920, of the news that Britain had accepted the mandate for Iraq encouraged the view of the dissidents that Britain could not be relied upon to fulfil her alleged promises. The mandate for Iraq allotted to Britain resulted from the formula approved at the San Remo Conference of April 1920 which effectively distributed the political, strategic and economic control of the former Turkish territories between Britain and France. Syria and Lebanon went to France: Palestine and Mesopotamia to Britain. It was a measure which satisfied the British Government's determination to hold fast to the essentials of imperial defence, especially in the region of the Persian Gulf, while at the same time it appeared to avoid any accusation that it was acquiring more territory. While this interpretation may have offered some reassurance to British critics of imperialism, the Arabs refused to see the measure in any light other than an artifice to maintain British control of their country.

Despite the warnings of the growing unrest conveyed to London by Gertrude Bell and others the agitation, now carried into the countryside in order to arouse the tribes, and to religious centres in an attempt to give it the character of a *jihad*, burst on June 30th into the great Arab Revolt. This was the real thing, not the feeble flicker of the candle in Storrs' description of the etoliated Hashemite venture of 1916. But that, at least, however ineffective in its initial stages, was directed against Britain's adversary, Turkey, while the June 1920 attack at Rumaitha, signalled the people's uprising against the British.

Despite this, in the popular mind the "Arab Revolt" means only the story of the desert fighting in the Palestine campaigns of 1916-1918: the thought that the real Arab Revolt was the Mesopotamian conflict with the British administration would uncomfortably disturb a cherished legend.

In their effort to restore a measure of peace to the country 30,000 troops and an air squadron were brought in from India. At home Lawrence re-entered the arena in a series of letters to the press and other writings. Within three weeks of the commencement of the rebellion *The Times* allowed him to express his view of the situation which had developed. In this letter he admitted that Mesopotamia had "never fought the Turks", commented on the reinforcement of the garrison ("our garrison will run into six figures next month") and the increasing cost of the occupation ("The expense curve will go up to 50 million pounds for this financial year") and complained about the "Englishness" of the administration.

"I would make Arabic the Government language," he wrote. "This would impose a reduction of the British staff, and a return to employment of the qualified Arabs."[7] This last raised the ire of Gertrude Bell, who wrote in her diary on September 5th: "The thing isn't made any easier by the tosh T.E.Lawrence is writing in the papers . . . I can't think why the India Office lets the rot pass uncontradicted. T.E.L.again: when he says we have forced the English language on the country it's not only a lie, but he knows it is. Every jot and tittle of official work is done in Arabic; in schools, law courts, hospitals, no other language is used. It's the first time that has happened since the fall of the Abbasids . . . " and a further entry in her diary of September 19th declared: "I can't believe T.E.L. is in ignorance, and I therefore hold him to be guilty of the unpardonable sin of wilfully darkening counsel. We have a difficult enough task before us in the country; he is making it more difficult by leading people to think that it is easy."[8]

Although the rebellion did not collapse until late in October it proved to be an effective move towards political changes in the country. On November 11th Sir Percy Cox, the new High Commissioner, announced the formation of the provisional Arab government, under a council of state in which all classes and sects would be represented. With it came the promise of administrative reorganisation, the creation of a permanent government, the drafting of an electoral law and the inauguration of an assembly.

In his preface to *Loyalties*, Arnold Wilson dwelt on the sacrifices which marked the bloody road which led so painfully and at such enormous cost to the delivery from Turkish rule of the people of Mesopotamia. He recalls the death in that country of many of his dearest friends together with "the great company of 60,000 men who perished with them[9] . . . To the memory of those who suffered and died needlessly in the torrid wastes of Mesopotamia the truth, so far as it may be known, is also due."

"Died needlessly"? Neither their deaths nor their painful sufferings were planned by the governments who sent them to a foreign land with the aim of destroying or expelling the occupying power, but those fates were implicit in their mission. What did they know of the interest of their governments in the Anglo-Persian Oil Company; or of the findings of the Admiralty committee of 1903 which led by 1912 to the widespread naval change to liquid fuel; of the need to guard the approaches to Abadan, or to ensure that the Germans would not be allowed to proceed with their plans for the construction of a railway to Baghdad? Perhaps it was not their's to question why, or they may have imagined their mission was to deliver a subject people from oppression.

For the crimes which were committed against them history records no retribution. The dead were buried, or left unburied; it was of little consequence. What was important was the creation of an administration which would have the appearance and character of a native institution while at the same time serving the vital interests of its sponsors. It was decided that the Mesopotamia *vilayets* should be combined into a kingdom, that the king should be democratically chosen by means of a plebiscite, and that he would be the Amir Feisal, selected in advance of the plebiscite at a Cairo conference in March 1921. Three months later Feisal arrived in Basra, accompanied by his personal adviser, Kinahan Cornwallis, and within three weeks of his arrival the council of state passed a unanimous resolution declaring him King of Iraq.

This brief summary fails to convey the whole story. There is more to tell. "There was to be a plebiscite to approve his nomination, but there would be a wink in the eyes of the ballot officers.[10] Feisal won his plebiscite hands down, his candidature being approved, according to official estimates, by 96 per cent of the populace. To be sure, his most pertinacious rival for the throne had been arrested and deported to Ceylon, and the electorate was in any case given no chance to vote for anyone else, and most independent analysts offer rather more sober estimates of the vote, and one prominent member of the British High Commission protested against what he considered a rigged election."[11]

The prominent member of the British High Commission was H.St.John Philby, who has left his own account of the incident. "The crux of all our cabinet-making centred round the Presidency of the Council and the Ministry of the Interior. On the merits Saiyid Talib was the obvious man to hold both posts, as the interior was the vital portfolio and could very suitably be combined with the Presidency. Had we adopted this course, Saiyid Talib would quite clearly have been designated in advance as the future head of the State, whatever the title of this office might have been – probably President of the Republic for, apart from a handful of important adherents of the Sharifian cause, the feeling in Mesopotamia at this time was definitely in favour of a republic and adverse to a monarchy."[12]

Saiyid Talib was at the time Minister of the Interior: Philby held the post of Advisor to the Ministry. He continued, "While we had been striving might and main to give effect to the policy of His Majesty's Government as decided upon in August, other forces were coming into play in far-away Whitehall to scrap that policy, lock, stock and barrel. Mr. Winston Churchill had become Colonial Secretary, and had taken over all Middle East commitments of the Government for review and settlement. He had invited Lawrence to be his *fidus Achates* and, promises or no promises, Lawrence was determined to strike a last doughty blow for his friend, Faisal, then languishing in Italy."[13] When Feisal was invited to pay his official visit to Iraq Saiyid Talib invited to a dinner-party "all the consular or diplomatic representatives at Baghdad, the leading business-men of the European community and a number of local notables." At the end of the dinner the host made an announcement. "The gist of his speech was that, rumours of the appointment of Faisal as prospective King of 'Iraq having been widely current, he wished to make it clear to those present and to the British Government that the people of 'Iraq did not want Faisal and would not tolerate his imposition on them.[14]

Saiyid Talib would hardly have been prepared for what followed. He was invited to take tea with Lady Cox on the Saturday following his dinner-party, and at the Alwiya Club on that same evening an officer related to Philby how "Saiyid Talib had, by Sir Percy Cox's orders, been kidnapped while a guest in his house, and had been carried off in an armoured car to a launch waiting downstream to take him to Basra and internment in Ceylon."[15]

Philby goes on to relate his conversation with Cox after Feisal's arrival in Baghdad, telling Sir Percy, "Of course Faisal has realized that, if the elections are free, he stands little chance of success. In fact I told him that quite frankly." "I know you did, " said Cox, "but surely you understand now what the British Government want." "Of course I do," I replied. "I have realized that for a long time in spite of all the assurances that you have given me to the contrary. What I can't understand is why the Government, if it wants and intends Faisal to be King, doesn't appoint him in a straightforward manner instead of insisting on the farce of an election. Anyway, I am too deeply committed by the assurances I have given all round to take part in rigging the elections."[16] He resigned.

The plebiscite on which Feisal was elected contained the single question: "Do you want Faisal to reign over you?"'. "Ninety-six and a half per cent of the *ad hoc* electorate answered that question in the affirmative."[17] Feisal was crowned King of Iraq on August 21st, 1921. Britain had sponsored a second Hashemite Kingdom in the Middle East. The third was yet to come.

Chapter Twenty Seven

The Hashemite brothers are awarded their awaited thrones.
Death of Lawrence.

The Lawrence who accompanied Churchill to the Cairo Conference of 1921 was no longer that legendary "Lawrence of Arabia" who had, we were told, "brought the disunited nomadic tribes of Holy and Forbidden Arabia into a unified campaign . . . a difficult and splendid stroke which caliphs, statesmen and sultans had been unable to accomplish in centuries of effort."[1] Of course he did nothing of the sort, diligently recording that very failure in the pages of the epic which during the year of the conference was nearing completion. The "wild ass of the desert" had returned to harness: he was a servant of his government, a political advisor in the Middle East Department of the Colonial Office.

Little more than four years had passed since his first meeting with Feisal, the Hashemite with, in Lawrence's view, "the necessary fire . . . to give effect to our science." Whatever that might mean in plain English, it signalled Lawrence's extraordinary dedication to Feisal and his family, seemingly undaunted by his dislike of the father, the mutual antipathy with Abdulla, and the Tefilah perfidy of Zaid. The reader will no doubt recall his earlier plans to ensure that rule in the conquered areas would be awarded to his favoured Hashemites: Syria to Feisal, Lower Mesopotamia to Abdulla and Upper Mesopotamia to Zaid. Feisal's expulsion from Syria by the French had put paid to such plans, but provided Arnold Wilson with the opportunity to suggest to the government, in July 1920, that Feisal should be appointed to rule in Iraq. This was favourably received in London: the subsequent talks in Cairo merely confirmed the Middle East Department memorandum: "We consider that Feisal should be the ruler, and that the first steps to ascertain from Sir Percy Cox that he can *ensure* (added italics) the Council of State selecting him."

Lawrence could have desired nothing better than this, but his ardour encouraged him to suggest to Feisal the advisability of an immediate personal meeting between the two to "explain details". The Colonial Office could not permit this to take place: it would have been both premature and unwise, and could have been interpreted as an offcial signal from the government, but it afforded a yet further illustration, if one were necessary, of Lawrence's devotion to Hashemite interests. But without further delay an opportunity presented itself to enable him to demonstrate yet again that loyalty, for during the conference Abdulla decided to march into Trans-Jordan, a move which prompted the French in Syria to prepare a military attack on his party.

This crisis was solved by a measure which anticipated Article 25 of the League of Nations Mandate for Palestine, separating the mandated territory into two parts divided by the line of the River Jordan. The ten thousand square miles west of the river would retain the designation of Palestine: the thirty-four and a half thousand square miles to the east would become an Arab State, over which Abdulla would rule with the support of British subsidies. Lawrence was of course delighted: this would be that third Arab State under Hashemite rule. Abdulla responded with proper oriental restraint: he would accept, but perhaps the British would at the same time add the whole of Palestine to the area they were offering him, and then under his rule the difficulties which had arisen between the Arabs and the Jews there would disappear.

Churchill's unwillingness to accept this generous offer was

alleviated by his recommendation of "an immediate advance up to £5,000 to Abdullah for his personal expenses, quite apart from administrative or military expenditure, in Transjordania."

Hussein in the Hejaz, Feisal in Iraq, Abdulla in Transjordan: the advocates of Arab independence should have been delighted with this progress. The rejoicing was, however, not universal. From the neighbouring Sultanate of the Nejd, Ibn Saud looked sourly on the favours which the British were so generously conferring on his rivals and foes. He felt slighted. He had been committed to British interests by a treaty signed by both parties in December 1915 and ratified in the following July over the signatures of Percy Cox and the Viceroy of India. It confirmed Ibn Saud's possession of Nejd and other territories, but committed him, in the words of its clause VI, "to refrain from all aggression, or interference with, the territories of Kuwait, Bahrain, and all the Shaikhs of Qatar and the Oman Coast, who are under the protection of the British Government, and who have treaty relations with the said Government; and the limits of their territories shall be hereafter determined."

All the places mentioned in this clause lay to the east and north-east of Ibn Saud's territories, leaving him free to pursue his quarrels with the Shammar and the Hejazis without being in breach of the treaty. His clashes with King Hussein were mainly in the year following the end of the 1914-1918 war concerned with an oasis, Khurma, which was situated near the ill-marked borders of Nejd and the Hejaz. Hussein had persisted' in his claims to the place, and on a number of occasions had attempted to seize it by force but had been driven off by the inhabitants. Finally he appealed to the British Government, and Curzon called a meeting at the Foreign Office in London which was attended, according to St. John Philby, who was also present, by "an imposing array of generals, admirals, Under-Secretaries of State and Hubert Young as Secretary."[2]

Curzon told the gathering that the government had promised both parties to settle the dispute, and that Hussein was pressing for a settlement, "as he is entitled to do . . . There is indeed room for differences of opinion on the merits of the case. Now in all these Arabian problems our policy is a Husain policy. It is a matter of expediency also. We must be satisfied that our man, if we decide in his favour as we would like to do, will win if it comes to a fight."[3] The admirals and generals agreed unanimously that the British-trained, British equipped and British-armed regulars of the Hejaz would have no problem in dealing with "a rabble of Wahhabi fanatics" and on the strength of this decision Hussein was formally authorized to occupy the disputed territory. His army, led by Abdulla, reached the area without incident, and established itself in a strongly-fortified position in preparation for the final attack. But on May 19th, Ibn Saud's "rabble of Wahhabi fanatics" swept down on the camp in the early hours of the morning and annihilated the defenders. Abdulla and his staff escaped on horseback to Taif.

Hussein protested to his British paymasters, and Curzon essayed attempts to redeem the situation by means of British military intervention, but now the generals changed their tune and refused approval of this policy. The Hejazis curbed their former enthusiasm for armed action against Ibn Saud, and he was left free to pursue his own vendetta against Ibn Rashid and his Shammar. But new British plans for trans-Arabian ground and air routes called for the pacification of the area. This could best be guaranteed by means of a friendly overture to Ibn Saud, sweetened by the promise of a yearly subsidy of £100,000 provided that he kept to his bargain. However, in order to avoid "jealousy and unfavourable comment, King Hussein would have to be given an equal subsidy."

Lawrence was empowered to negotiate with the King the new treaty which would incorporate the proposed measure, and on July 8th he left for Jedda. The talks which followed provided a severe test for Lawrence's Hashemite dedication, and soon he was to report that "the old man is conceited to a degree, greedy and stupid, but very friendly and protests devotion to our interests". The King was at the same time not entirely oblivious to his own interests, accepting during the talks a "loan" of 80,000 rupees from Lawrence, who wrote that "he was in urgent need of it, and so proportionately grateful". The nature of the "need" was revealed before long, when it became known that Hussein had bought ten aeroplanes, some of which came from Italy: a circumstance which encouraged the ever-resourceful Lawrence to cover his *faux pas* by explaining that "perhaps it is not understood . . . what rubbish the Italian aeroplanes here are . . . and how disgusted King Hussein will shortly be with his very expensive purchases. I think it is an admirable lesson for him".

Lawrence's views concerning Hussein's "urgent need" of money recalls a passage from Storrs' reminiscences of the King's exile to Cyprus in 1925, following Ibn Saud's invasion of his country. "King Husain was popularly supposed to have brought with him (in petrol tins) some of the hundreds of thousands of sovereigns wherewith Great Britain had subsidised the Revolt in the Desert . . . At all events the old King had the wit whenever his sons visited him in search of revenue, to forestall their demands by appealing for a loan for himself – as King Faisal complained once during a round of golf-croquet on Mount Troodos."[4] It would appear from this that his own family felt able to share the "popularly supposed" inheritance of the British taxpayers' benefactions.

Lawrence went on to Jordan where in his new appointment as Chief British Representative he had little difficulty in obtaining Abdulla's agreement to the conditions laid down by the Colonial Office for their sponsorship of the Emir's rule. This duty successfully completed, Lawrence returned to England, resigned from the Colonial Office, and by all accounts immersed himself in the completion of his epic *Seven Pillars*.

Towards the end of the year he wrote that he "was happy to withdraw from a political milieu which had never been congenial".[5] He was still a young man: at 34 there was the prospect before him of years to which he could devote his undoubted talents. The story of his life from the time of his resignation from the Colonial Office until his death is the subject for a full biography, and has been recounted many times. In these pages we will resume the narrative with an excerpt from a letter he wrote on December 20th, 1934 to John Buchan: "my R.A.F. twelve-year engagement is within a few weeks of running out, I have not tried to extend for 24 years . . . but if I could have remained perpetually young, nothing would have pleased me better . . . Some day I'm going to ask another favour - that you will read my notes on the making of an airman, about 60,000 words of typescript, that date from 1922".[6]

Those few lines must surely convey an acceptable impression of the way he had spent those twelve years. There can be no reason to doubt that in the main he had been satisfied with his service life, and that he had been able to indulge in the particular activity for which he was gifted, that of writing. Apart from those "60,000 words of typescript" (ultimately published under the title of *The Mint*) there are more than 400 letters of that period appearing in the David Garnett edition: there were of course many more besides.

Five weeks later he wrote to A.E.Chambers about his cottage. "My plans are to leave the R.A.F. early in March, and make my way slowly to Cloud's Hill."[7] By March 6th he was in London, complaining in a letter to Ernest Thurtle that "My Dorset 'fastness' is beset they tell me, by pressmen: so I wander about London in a queer unrest . . . "[8] and after he arrived at the cottage he was impelled to write to the Hon. Esmond Harmsworth, at that time the Chairman of the Newspaper Proprietors Association. "You may have heard that about a month ago I was discharged from the R.A.F. upon completion of my engagement for twelve years with the colours . . . returned to this cottage, which has been mine for many years, with the intention of settling quietly in retirement. Unfortunately, the quietude has been a complete failure. Reporters and press photographers have visited the place in some numbers . . . Their eagerness to find me drove me out: and after I had gone it led them to break the tiles of my roof, split the door and trample all over my patch of land in search of me. I have had to ask the local police to patrol the place, in my absence. I am writing to ask if your association can help to relieve me of some of this attention . . . "[9]

But on April 1st he wrote to John Buchan: "My life? Not too good. The Press were besetting this cottage when I reached it. I went to London for a while: they desisted. I returned: they did . . . The most exigent of them I banged in the eye."[10]

Five weeks later he was complaining to both H.S.Ede and George Brough that "his enemies, the Press" were still pursuing him, but wrote to Lady Astor on May 8th that "wild mares would not at present take me away from Clouds Hill. It is an earthly paradise and I am staying here till I feel qualified for it."[11]

Five days later he was thrown from his motor-cycle and died on the 19th.

The funeral of Thomas Edward Shaw took place at Moreton in Dorset on May 21st. Several photographs of him over the years he spent in the R.A.F. have survived. One, taken at the end of February, 1935, as he was leaving the force, is reproduced in Knightley and Simpson's biography. "He packed his bags," the authors wrote, "put on his trouser-clips and a check muffler and got on his bicycle. He paused by a wall at Bridlington to let a friend photograph him – an ordinary-looking man of forty seven with deep lines round his mouth and eyes."[12] He could have been anybody: anybody, that is, except the legendary Lawrence of Arabia.

But it seems that in death he was transformed. Storrs and Newcombe and Kennington were among the pall-bearers at the funeral: Storrs had stayed beside the coffin until it was screwed down, and recalls " . . . his countenance was not marred . . . It was somehow unreal to be watching beside him in the cerements, so strangely resembling the *abba*, the *kuffiya* and the *aqal* of an Arab Chief . . ."

In death the worn features of the middle-aged ex-serviceman were transmuted into the configuration of a noble warrior, the legendary

Lawrence whose effigy would be long preserved in flawless Portland stone. Kennington carved the memorial: "a figure shaped in the pure tradition of the Knight of Dorchester. Lawrence lies lightly, his head resting on the *maklufa* camel-saddle, clasping his curved Meccan *hangar* sheathed: about his body the Bedouin *aba*, around his head the flowing *kuffiya* secured by the knotted *aqal* . . . Lawrence lies, once more an Arab chieftain and warrior, enshrined tranquil and beautiful in the deep Saxon peace of St. Martin."[13]

POSTSCRIPT

The defeat of Turkey in 1918 was followed by the dismemberment of the Ottoman Empire. Under the Treaty of Sevres, signed on August 10, 1920, the Ottoman government was committed to surrender all her Arab provinces and to recognise the Allied arrangements for their disposal, which resulted in a compromise between distribution of imperial "zones of interest" in favour of France and Britain and the promise of a measure of independence in some areas. For Syria, the Lebanon and Palestine (both of which under Turkish rule were effectively parts of Syria), Transjordan (formerly part of the Vilayet of Syria), and Mesopotamia (later Iraq), a system of Mandates was introduced under the Covenant of the League of Nations to take care of those territories which at the time were considered to be unprepared for independence.

The San Remo Conference of April 1920 awarded the Mandates for Palestine (including Transjordan) and Iraq to Great Britain: for Syria and Lebanon to France. In time these mandates were all terminated: that for Iraq in 1930, Syria and Lebanon in 1936, Transjordan in 1946, and Palestine in 1948. The first three became founder members of the United Nations Organisation in 1946: Transjordan was admitted to the U.N. in December, 1955.

This brief outline of the transition of these territories from Ottoman domination to independent Arab states can convey nothing of the strife and confusion which attended their progress towards autonomy. In Syria there had from the beginning been strong resistance to the idea of

French administration, and in 1920 a body calling itself the "General Syrian Congress" elected the Hashemite Prince Feisal King of the country, intending that this would include both Lebanon and Palestine in a Greater Syria, but within a few weeks of this declaration French troops entered Damascus, and Feisal went into exile. The French military government lasted for six years and was succeeded by an elected assembly. France endeavoured to retain her economic and other privileges in the country, but finally succumbed to the growing strength of the separatist movements and withdrew in 1946.

From 1940 onwards, following the assassination of the pro-Hashemite Shabandar by political opponents, the history of the country is one of continual strife. In March 1949 the commander-in-chief of the armed forces, General Za'im, deposed the President and Parliament, but, four or five months later, was himself deposed and, together with his Prime Minister, executed. Za'im was succeeded by Sami al-Hinnawi, who was in turn dismissed in the December of the same year by Colonel Shishakli. Shishakli established a dictatorial regime which was finally overthrown in February, 1954, when he was replaced by President al-Atassi. In the mean time the Ba'th party was gaining strength in the country.

A Syrian Army officers' coup in September 1961 was followed by another in March 1962, a Ba'th coup in March 1963 and an unsuccessful Nasserist attempt to overthrow the regime in July '63. In the spring of 1964 merchants' and landowners' riots were put down with great brutality, and in both 1965 and 1966 further coups resulted in the establishment in power of the Alawites, a minority group which has remained in control of the country.

The history of Iraq over the same period reflects the general instability of the Arab states created after the First World War. The Hashemite regime established by the British in 1921, however, survived until the revolution of July 1958, when the young King and his family were treacherously murdered. Qassem, the leader of the group of "Free Officers" who were responsible for this crime and who was appointed Prime Minister survived, first an attempt by his deputy, Colonel Araf, to assassinate him: a further attempt on his life in the December of the same year by the Rashid Ali group: a rising of anti-Communist officers in March, 1959: and a Ba'thist attack in October 1959. Each of these attempts was repulsed with heavy bloodshed, but finally Qassem, together with three of his closest collaborators, was killed in February 1963. General al-Bakri come to power after two successive coups in July 1968: his vice-president was Saddam Hussein.

The seemingly perpetual struggle for power reached a further crisis in June, 1979, when Saddam's supporters placed al-Bakri under house arrest. From the moment of Saddam Hussein's assumption of power the conflict between the Sunni minority which he represented and the Shia under the leadership of the Ayatollah Baqir al-Sadr became intensified. Saddam arrested and executed five Shia ulema, and in 1980 had al-Sadr and his sister put to death. These killings were but a prelude to the slaughter which was to follow. The war between Iraq and Iran was said to have cost a million casualties. Amongst those who were killed were the deserters, totalling 30,000 in all, recaptured and executed. The subsequent invasion of Kuwait and the resultant Gulf War bring the bloody history of Iraq to the present date.

We have seen how brief was the Hashemite rule in Syria, and its termination in Iraq after its duration of some 37 years. Between these two countries the Kingdom of Jordan, occupying some 37,000 square miles to the south of Syria and to the west of Iraq, has been successful in remaining under Hashemite rule since its beginnings in 1921. Its present ruler, Hussein, thus represents the sole remaining Hashemite monarch of the dynasty founded by his great-grandfather and namesake in 1916.

Reference Notes

In the notes on the text the following abbreviations have been used:

Aldington	LAWRENCE OF ARABIA: A biographical Enquiry by Richard Aldington. Collins 1955
Allenby	ALLENBY: Soldier and Statesman by Field-Marshal Viscount Wavell of Cyrenaica. Harrap 1944
Letters	THE LETTERS OF T.E. LAWRENCE: Edited by David Garnett. Spring Books 1964
Loyalties	LOYALTIES: Mesopotamia 1914 - 1917: by Lt. - Col. Sir Arnold Wilson, K.C.I.E., D.S.O Oxford University Press. London 1930
Mack	A PRINCE OF OUR DISORDER: The life of T.E.LAWRENCE by John E. Mack. 1976
Memoirs	MEMOIRS OF KING ABDULLAH OF TRANSJORDAN Edited by Philip P. Graves. London 1950
Morris	THE HASHEMITE KINGS. By James Morris, Faber, 1959
Monroe	BRITAIN'S MOMENT IN THE MIDDLE EAST 1914 - 1956 By Elizabeth Monroe. Methuen 1964
Mousa	T.E. LAWRENCE: An Arab View: By Suleiman Mousa Oxford University Press. London 1966
Orientations	ORIENTATIONS by (Sir) Ronald Storrs The Definitive Edition. Nicholson & Watson 1945
Secret Lives	THE SECRET LIVES OF LAWRENCE OF ARABIA By Phillip Knightley and Colin Simpson. 1969
Seven Pillars	SEVEN PILLARS OF WISDOM: A triumph By T.E. Lawrence. First Public Edition 1935
'T.E. Lawrence'	'T.E. LAWRENCE' In Arabia and After By Liddell Hart. Cape 1935
Thomas	WITH LAWRENCE IN ARABIA. By Lowell Thomas 23rd Impression. Hutchinson. n.d.
Three Deserts	THREE DESERTS. By Major C.S. Jarvis, C.M.G., D.S.O. Murray, 1951
Arabian Days	ARABIAN DAYS: An Autobiography By H. St. J. Philby Hale 1948.

CHAPTER ONE (Pages 17 to 22)

Notes for Pages

1. Named after Sir Mark Sykes and Charles Francois George – Picot, the chief British and French negotiators, the Agreement was incorporated in an Anglo-French memorandum drawn up on 9th March 1916. It provided for the division of the non-Turkish provinces of the Ottoman Empire: the Arabian peninsula was to become independent: Palestine west of the Jordan River was to be placed under an international regime: Britain was to control Haifa and Acre together with the area between these two towns.

   The French sphere was to include two zones: one, designated as a French zone of influence, would comprise Damascus, Homs, Hama and Aleppo together with the interior regions of Syria up to and including the Mosul District in the east; while Cilicia in Asia Minor and the whole of coastal Syria would be placed under direct French control.

   The British sphere was to include the Negev desert in Palestine, and the area east of the Jordan River and central Mesopotamia up to the Persian border, while the Basra and Baghdad provinces would come under direct British control. Semi-independent Arab states or a confederation of Arab states might be established in the areas of the two zones of influence, with France and Britain supplying advisers and receiving economic privileges.

2. *Letters*, p. 193. Written from the *Grand Continental Hotel, Cairo* and dated *18th March* (1915).

3. *Letters*, p. 182.

4. After the capitulation of France in June 1940 French administrators and officers in Syria and Lebanon under General Dentz threw in their lot with the Vichy authorities. German and Italian troops were stationed in the Levant, while Syria and Lebanon were expected to serve as the bridgehead of a fully-fledged invasion of the Middle East by the Axis forces.

CHAPTER TWO (Pages 23 to 30)

1 *The Palestine Campaigns*, p. 9.
2 *Letters* p. 187.
3 *The Palestine Campaigns*. p. 149.
4 *Letters*, p. 186.
5 He was eventually recalled, and set off for Cairo together with Lawrence on December 9th, 1914
6 "*T.E.Lawrence,*" p. 95.
7 Ibid, p. 96
8 This letter was written to a British Foreign Office staff member: it bears no date, but is attributed to November, 1919.
9 *T.E.Lawrence" to his biographer Robert Graves*, p. 16
10 Ibid pp. 16-17.
11 Mousa, p.6.
12 *Letters*, p. 191.
13 *Letters*, p. 190.
14 *The Palestine Campaigns*, p. 30.
15 Ibid, p. 31.
16 *Loyalties*, p. 26
17 "*T.E.Lawrence*", p 437.
18 *Loyalties*, p. 161.
19 *Letters*, p. 197.

20 *Loyalties,* p. 29.
21 Ibid, p. 35
22 Sir Reginald Wingate, Sirdar and Governor-General of the Sudan; appointed High Commissioner of Egypt, replacing McMahon, in Oct., 1916

CHAPTER THREE (Pages 31 to 36)
1 Secret Lives, pp. 5-6.
2 Mack, pp. 415-6.
3 Ibid, p. 452.
4 Aldington, p. 331.
5 Ibid, p. 332.
6 Ibid, p. 333.
7 *Secret Lives,* p. 38.
8 Ibid, p. 164.
9 Mack, p. 96.
10 Lincoln Steffens: "Armenians are Impossible: An Interview with Lawrence of Arabia." *Outlook and Independent,* October 14, 1931, pp. 203-223.
11 *Seven Pillars,* p. 33.
12 *Letters,* p. 577.
13 Elizabeth Longford: *A Pilgrimage of Passion: The life of W.S. Blunt* p. 418.
14 Mack, pp. 457-8.

CHAPTER FOUR (Pages 37 to 48)
1 *Letters,* p. 199.
2 *Orientations,* p. 122.
3 King Abdullah of Transjordan: *Memoirs* (London 1950), p. 112.
4 Ibid, p. 71.
5 *Orientations,* p. 123.
6 Ibid, p. 149.
7 Ibid, p. 152.
8 James Morris : *The Hashemite Kings,* p. 34.
9 Ibid, pp. 37-38.
10 *Correspondence between Sir Henry McMahon and The Sherif Hussein of Mecca.* Miscellaneous No. 3 (1939). London: H.M.S.O., pp. 3-4.
11 Ibid, pp. 4-5.
12 Ibid, pp. 5-6.
13 Ibid, pp. 7-8.
14 Ibid, p. 10.
15 Ibid, pp. 11-12.
16 Ibid, p. 13.
17 Ibid, pp. 14-15.
18 Ibid, pp. 15-16.
19 *Orientations,* pp. 153-4.
20 *McMahon Letters,* p. 18.
21 Mousa, p. 15.

22 *Orientations*, p. 155.
23 Ibid, p. 156.
24 Ibid, p. 159.

CHAPTER FIVE (Pages 49 to 56)
1 Mack, p. 143.
2 Ibid, pp. 138.
3 *Letters*, p. 202.
4 *Orientations*, p. 184.
5 Brian Gardner, *Allenby* p. 132.
6 *Seven Pillars*, p. 63.

CHAPTER SIX (Pages 57 to 62)
1 *Orientations*, p. 171.
2 Ibid, p. 172.
3 Ibid, p. 174.
4 Ibid, p. 176.
5 Ibid, p. 177.
6 Ibid, p. 178.
7 Ibid, p. 179.
8 Ibid, p. 184.
9 Ibid, p. 185.
10 Ibid, p. 186.
11 Ibid, p. 187.

CHAPTER SEVEN (Pages 63 to 68)
1 Mousa, p. 29.
2 *Orientations*, xv.
3 Ibid, p. 165.
4 Mousa, p. 30.
5 *Memoirs* (Abdullah), p. 157-8.
6 *The Palestine Campaigns*, p. 155.
7 *Memoirs* (Abdullah), p. 160.

CHAPTER EIGHT (Pages 69 to 74)
1 *Seven Pillars*, p. 64.
2 Ibid, p. 67.
3 Ibid, pp. 68-71.
4 Mousa, pp. 30-31.
5 *Orientations*, p. 190.
6 *Seven Pillars*, p. 114.
7 Ibid, p. 110.
8 *Memoirs*, p. 155.
9 "T.E. Lawrence", p. 181

10 Ibid, p. 90.
11 *Seven Pillars*, p. 94.

CHAPTER NINE (Pages 75 to 80)

1 Ibid, p. 133.
2 Ibid CHAPTERS XXIII - XXXVIII, pp. 140-164.
3 Mousa, pp. 47-49.
4 *Seven Pillars,* pp. 140-141.
5 Bray: *Shifting Sands (1934),* pp. 122-123.
6 Ibid, p. 127.
7 *Seven Pillars,* p. 160.
8 Ibid, p. 161.
9 Ibid, p. 142.
10 Ibid, pp. 163-164.

CHAPTER TEN (Pages 81 to 88)

1 Brémond: *Le Hedjaz dans la Guerre Mondiale*, p. 196
2 *Seven Pillars*, p. 228.
3 Ibid, p. 263.
4 Ibid, p. 272.
5 Ibid, p. 273.
6 Ibid, CHAPTERS XXXIX-LV, PP. 227-317.
7 Ibid, P. 232.
8 Ibid, p.268.
9 Ibid, p. 269.
10 Ibid, p. 276.
11 Ibid, p. 277.
12 *Letters*, pp. 225-6.
13 Mousa, pp. 74-5.
14 Ibid, p. 76.
15 Ibid, p. 77.
16 Ibid, p. 72.
17 *Secret Lives*, p. 162.
18 Mousa, p. 69.
19 Ibid, p. 70.
20 Ibid, p. 71.

CHAPTER ELEVEN (Pages 89 to 94)

1 *Seven Pillars*, p. 323.
2 Antonius: *The Arab Awakening* (1938), p. 322.
3 *Seven Pillars*, p. 325.
4 Ibid, pp. 326-7.
5 Ibid, p. 435.
6 Jarvis: *Arab Command* (1946), pp. 41-42.
7 Ibid, p. 46.

CHAPTER TWELVE (Pages 95 to 100)

1. *The Palestine Campaigns*, p. 83.
2. Ibid, p. 83.
3. Ibid, p. 96.
4. *Seven Pillars*, p. 348.
5. Ibid, p. 349.
6. Ibid, p. 359.
7. Ibid, p. 371.
8. Ibid, p. 376.
9. Ibid, p. 344.

CHAPTER THIRTEEN (Pages 101 to 110)

1. *Seven Pillars*, p. 380.
2. Ibid, p. 381.
3. Ibid, p. 387.
4. Ibid, p. 392.
6. Ibid, p. 402.
6. Ibid, pp. 404-405.
7. Ibid, p. 406.
8. Mousa, p. 105.
9. *Seven Pillars*, p. 411.
10. Ibid, p. 388.
11. Ibid, pp. 412-413.
12. Ibid, p. 413.
13. Ibid, pp. 417-418.
14. Ibid, p. 423.
15. Ibid, p. 424.
16. Ibid, p. 457.
17. Ibid p. 458.

CHAPTER FOURTEEN (Pages 111 to 122)

1. *Seven Pillars*, p. 463.
2. Ibid, p. 463.
3. Ibid, p. 464.
4. Ibid, pp. 465-6.
5. Ibid, p. 468.
6. Mousa, pp. 131-2.
7. *Seven Pillars*, p. 456.
8. Ibid, p. 473.
9. Ibid, pp. 474-5.
10. *Arab Bulletin, No. 79.*
11. *Seven Pillars,* p. 483.
12. Mousa, pp. 139-140.
13. Ibid, pp. 142-143.

14. *Seven Pillars*, p. 485.
15. Ibid, p. 486.
16. Ibid, p. 490.
17. Ibid, p. 496.
18. Ibid, p. 499.
19. Ibid, p. 500.
20. Ibid, p. 502.

CHAPTER FIFTEEN (Pages 123 to 130)

1. *Seven Pillars*, p. 503.
2. Ibid, p. 506.
3. *The Palestine Campaigns*, p. 182.
4. *Seven Pillars*, p. 514.
5. *The Palestine Campaigns*, p. 183.
6. *Arab Command*, p. 32
7. *Orientations*, p. 153 (footnote).
8. *Seven Pillars*, p. 516.
9. Ibid, p. 523.
10. *Arab Command*, p. 34, recording that "the Beduin took no part in the actual engagement but charged in immediately the place fell in a widely-gesticulating mob to sack the station stores".
11. Ibid, p. 35.
12. *The Palestine Campaigns*, pp. 184-5.
13. *Seven Pillars*, pp. 525-6.
14. *Allenby*, 213. (footnote).

CHAPTER SIXTEEN (Pages 131 to 140)

1. *Seven Pillars*, p. 527.
2. Ibid, p. 532.
3. Ibid, p. 533.
4. Ibid, p. 534.
5. Ibid, p. 539.
6. Ibid, p. 540
7. Ibid, p. 541.
8. Mack, p. 240.
9. *Seven Pillars*, p. 631.
10. Ibid, p. 633.
11. Mack, p. 239.
12. Mousa, p. 199.
13. *Seven Pillars*, p. 632.
14. Mack, p. 240, p. 242.
15. Ibid, p. 247
16. *Seven Pillars*, p. 444.
17. Ibid, p. 445.
18. Ibid, p. 447.
19. See *Letters*, p. 80

20. Mack, p. 420.
21. Ibid, p. 33.
22. Mousa, p. 115.
23. Ibid, p. 118.
24. *Secret Lives*, p. 204.
25. In the early part of 1968 a 64-year-old Scotsman, John Bruce, disclosed to the *Sunday Times* that between 1923 and 1935 Lawrence had employed him to administer floggings.
26. Mack, P. 433.

CHAPTER SEVENTEEN (Pages 141 to 146)

1. Mack, p. 224.
2. Ibid, p. 225.
3. Aldington, p. 337.
4. Mack, p. 195.
5. *Seven Pillars*, p. 236.
6. Ibid, p. 311.
7. Ibid, p. 392.
8. Ibid, p. 292.
9. Ibid, p. 199.
10. Ibid, p. 200.
11. Ibid, pp. 621-2.

CHAPTER EIGHTEEN (Pages 147 to 154)

1. *Seven Pillars*, p. 636.
2. Ibid, p. 634.
3. Ibid, p. 638.
4. *Three Deserts* (1951 edn.) pp. 280-283.

CHAPTER NINETEEN (Pages 155 to 164)

1. *The Palestine Campaigns*, p. 203.
2. Ibid, p. 226.
3. Ibid, p. 229.
4. Mack, p. 167.
5. Mousa, p. 202.
6. Dane, Vol. II, p. 161.
7. *Seven Pillars*, p. 660.
8. Chauvel report of October 22, 1929. General H.G. Chauvel commanded the Desert Mounted Corps in the final Order of Battle.
9. *Seven Pillars*, p. 555.
10. Ibid, p. 556.
11. Mack, p. 248.
12. *Letters*, pp. 265-9.
13. Ibid, p. 270.
14. *Secret Lives*, p. 53.
15. *Letters*, pp. 670-1

CHAPTER TWENTY (Pages 165 to 170)
1. *Letters*, pp. 345-6.
2. *Secret Lives*, p. 153.
3. Ibid, p. 154.
4. *Letters*, p. 356.
5. Ibid, pp. 363-5.
6. Aldington, 1957 printing, p. 383.
7. Mack, p. 221.
8. Ibid, p. 276.

CHAPTER TWENTY ONE (Pages 171 to 178)
1. Mack, P. 227.
2. Thomas, pp. 15-17.
3. Ibid, p. 18.
4. *Letters*, p. 319.
5. Thomas, p. 290.

CHAPTER TWENTY TWO (Pages 179 to 188)
1. Thomas, p. 23.
2. *Seven Pillars*, p. 188.
3. Ibid, pp. 194-5.
4. "T.E. Lawrence", p. 164.
5. Ibid, p. 165.
6. Ibid, p. 8.
7. Aldington, p. 108.
8. Ibid, p. ????
9. Mack, p. 275.
10. Thomas, p. 21.
11. Ibid, p. 236.
12. Ibid, p. 25.
13. Ibid, p. 37.
14. Ibid, p. 38.
14. Ibid, p. 73.
16. Ibid, p. 75.
17. Ibid, p. 77.
18. *Seven Pillars*, p. 63.

CHAPTER TWENTY THREE (Pages 189 to 194)
1. *Secret Lives*, p. 154.
2. Ibid, p. 153.
3. *Seven Pillars*, p. 57.
4. Ibid, pp. 58-9.
5. Ibid, p. 63.
6. *Orientations*, p. 444.
7. Ibid, p. ????

CHAPTER TWENTY FOUR (Pages 195 to 206)

1. *Loyalties*, p. 238.
2. Ibid, pp. 304-305.
3. *The Truth about the Peace Treaties* (David Lloyd George), p. 1041.
4. Monroe, pp. 12 and 13.
5. *Loyalties*, p. 11.
6. Ibid, p. 12.
7. Ibid, p. 22.
8. Ibid, p. 23.
9. *Letters*, p. 206.
10. Ibid, pp. 208-9.
11. Telegram MS3, 9/4/16. FO 141/461/1198 fo. 247. Lawrence to G.F. Clayton.
12. *Loyalties*, p. 54.
13. Ibid, p. ???
14. Ibid, p. 89.
14. Ibid, footnote.
16. Monroe, p. 117.
17. *Loyalties*, p. 92.
18. Ibid, p. 94.
19. Barber; *Besieged in Kut and After*.
20. Aldington, p. 149.
21. "T.E. Lawrence", pp. 98-9.
22. *Loyalties*, p. 98.
23. *The Independent Arab*, pp. 72-73.

CHAPTER TWENTY FIVE (Pages 207 to 212)

1. *Loyalties*, p. 99.
2. Ibid, pp. 110-111.
3. Ibid, p. 118.
4. Ibid, pp. 130-131.
5. Ibid, p. 131.
6. *Secrets of a Kuttite* (1922).
7. Diary of Capt. Shakeshaft (2nd Norfolk) quoted by Moberly: *Campaign in Mesopotamia 1914-1918* (1913-1927).
8. *Loyalties*, pp. 165-6.

CHAPTER TWENTY SIX (Pages 213 to 224)

1. Loyalties, p. 238.
2. Ibid, 139.
3. Ibid, 259.
4. *Official History*, Vol. IV.
5. *Loyalties*, p. 170.
6. Ibid, pp. 270-271.
7. *Letters*, pp. 307-8.
8. Burgoyne, *Gertrude Bell*, II, 163-163.

9. *Loyalties*, p. xiv.
10. Morris: *The Hashemite Kings*, p. 85.
11. Ibid, p. 87.
12. Philby (St. J.) *Arabian Days*, p. 192.
13. Ibid, pp. 195-6.
14. Ibid, p. 197.
15. Ibid, p. 198.
16, Ibid, p. 204.
17. Ibid, p. 205.

CHAPTER TWENTY SEVEN (Pages 225 to 232)
1. Thomas, p. 18.
2. *Arabian Days*, p. 175.
3. Ibid, p. 176.
4. *Orientations*, p. 497.
5. *Letters*, p. 346.
6. Ibid, pp. 836-37.
7. Ibid, p. 841.
8. Ibid, p. 860.
9. Ibid, p. 861.
10. Ibid, p. 863.
11. Ibid, p. 872.
12. *Secret Lives*, pp. 265-6.
13. *Orientations*, pp. 454-5.
14. Mack, pp. 457-8.

BIBLIOGRAPHY

ABDULLAH (King of Transjordan) *Memoirs*, ed Philip Graves. Cape. London 1950

ALDINGTON, Richard. *LAWRENCE OF ARABIA: A Biographical Enquiry*. Collins. 1955

ANTONIUS, George. *THE ARAB AWAKENING*. Hamish Hamilton. London 1938

ARAB BULLETIN, THE. The Papers of the Arab Bureau, 1916-1918 (Foreign Office)

BARROW, George. *THE FIRE OF LIFE*. Hutchinson. London 1943

BRÉMOND, Edouard. *LE HEDJAZ DANS LA GUERRE MONDIALE*. Payot. Paris 1931

BROWN, Malcolm and CAVE, Julia. *A TOUCH OF GENIUS: The Life of T.E. Lawrence*. London 1988

BUCKLEY, Christopher. *FIVE VENTURES*: Iraq, Syria, etc. H.M.S.O. London 1954

BURDETT, Winston. *ENCOUNTER WITH THE MIDDLE EAST*. Deutsch. London 1970

CORRESPONDENCE BETWEEN SIR HENRY McMAHON AND THE SHERIF HUSSEIN OF MECCA Cmd. 5957, H.M.S.O. London 1939

CROSSMAN, Richard. *PALESTINE MISSION: A PERSONAL RECORD*. n.d. London (1946)

DANE, Edmund. *BRITISH CAMPAIGNS IN THE NEARER EAST 1914-1918*

DUGDALE, Blanche. *ARTHUR JAMES BALFOUR*. 2 vols. Hutchinson. London 1936

FALLS, Captain Cyril, and BECKE, Major. A.F. *MILITARY OPERATIONS EGYPT & PALESTINE*. Vol.II. H.M.S.O.1930

GARDNER, Brian. *ALLENBY*. Cassell. London 1965

GARNETT, David. (ed) *THE LETTERS OF T.E.LAWRENCE*. Spring Books. London. 1964

GLUBB, J.B. *BRITAIN AND THE ARABS*. Hodder and Stoughton. London 1959

GRAVES, Robert. *LAWRENCE AND THE ARABS.* Jonathan Cape. London 1927

GRAVES, Robert. and LIDDELL HART, B.H. *T.E. LAWRENCE TO HIS BIOGRAPHERS.* Cassell. London 1963

GREAT BRITAIN AND EGYPT 1914-1951: Information Papers No. 19 Royal Institute of International Affairs. London 1952

HOWARTH, David. *THE DESERT KING: A LIFE OF IBN SAUD.* Collins. London 1964

JAMES, Lawrence. *THE GOLDEN WARRIOR, The Life and Legend of Lawrence of Arabia.* London 1990

JARVIS, C.S. *ARAB COMMAND: The Biography of Lieutenant-Colonel F.G. Peake.* Hutchinson. London 1942. *THREE DESERTS* John Murray, London 1936

KEDOURIE, Elie. *THE ANGLO-ARAB LABYRINTH: The McMahon-Husayn Correspondence and its Interpretations, 1914-1939.* Cambridge University Press. *BRITAIN AND THE MIDDLE EAST 1914-1921.* London 1956

KIMCHE, Jon and David. *BOTH SIDES OF THE HILL: Britain and The Palestine War.* Secker & Warburg. London 1960

KIRKBRIDE, Alec. *A CRACKLE OF THORNS* John Murray. London 1956

KNIGHTLEY, Phillip, and SIMPSON, Colin. *THE SECRET LIVES OF LAWRENCE OF ARABIA.* Nelson. London 1969

LAWRENCE, A.W. (ed) *LETTERS TO T.E. LAWRENCE* Jonathan Cape. London 1964

LAWRENCE, T.E. *THE MINT.* Jonathan Cape. London 1973. *ORIENTAL ASSEMBLY.* Williams & Norgate. London 1939. *REVOLT IN THE DESERT.* Jonathan Cape. London 1927. *SEVEN PILLARS OF WISDOM.* Jonathan Cape. London 1935.

LIDDELL HART, Basil H. *'T.E.LAWRENCE': In Arabia and After.* London 1934

MACK, John E. *A PRINCE OF OUR DISORDER: The Life of T.E.Lawrence.* Weidenfeld and Nicolson. London 1976

MACKWORTH, Cecily. *THE MOUTH OF THE SWORD.* Routledge. London 1949

MATHESON, Christopher. *IMAGES OF LAWRENCE.* London 1988

MEINERTZHAGEN, Colonel R. *MIDDLE EAST DIARY 1917 to 1956.* London 1959

MONROE, Elizabeth. *PHILBY OF ARABIA.* Faber. London 1973. *BRITAIN'S MOMENT IN THE MIDDLE EAST 1914-1956.* Chatto and Windus. London 1963

MORRIS, James. *THE HASHEMITE KINGS.* Faber. London 1959

MOUSA, Sulieman. *T.E.LAWRENCE: An Arab View.* Translated by Albert Butros. Oxford U.P. 1966

PALESTINE ROYAL COMMISSION REPORT: July 1937 H.M.S.O. London 1937

PARKES, Dr. James. *WHOSE LAND? A History of the Peoples of Palestine.* Gollancz, 1949. Revised ed Penguin. London 1970

PHILBY, H. St. John. *ARABIAN DAYS.* Robert Hale. London 1948

PIRIE-GORDON, C.H.C. (ed) *A BRIEF RECORD OF THE ADVANCE OF THE EGYPTIAN EXPEDITIONARY FORCE: July 1917 to October 1918.* H.M.S.O. London 1919

RICHARDS, Vyvyan W. *PORTRAIT OF T.E.LAWRENCE.* Cape. London 1936

SACHAR, Howard. *THE EMERGENCE OF THE MIDDLE EAST, 1914-1924.* Knopf. New York 1969

STEIN, Leonard. *THE BALFOUR DECLARATION,* Valentine, Mitchell. London 1961

STORRS, Ronald. *ORIENTATIONS.* Nicholson and Watson. London 1937

SUGARMAN, Sidney. *THE HASHEMITE DEBT TO LAWRENCE OF ARABIA* International History Magazine: Editions Horizon Lausanne, July, 1973. *THE TRUTH ABOUT T.E. LAWRENCE AND THE ARAB REVOLT.* J.O. and Middle East Review. 12th September 1969

TABACHNICK, Stephen E. and MATHESON, Christopher. *IMAGES OF LAWRENCE.* London 1988

TEMPERLEY, H.W.V. (ed) *A HISTORY OF THE PEACE CONFERENCE OF PARIS.* Oxford University Press. London 1924

THE PALESTINE CAMPAIGNS. Constable. London 1928

THOMAS, Bertram. *ARABIA FELIX.* Scribner's. New York 1932

THOMAS, Lowell. *WITH LAWRENCE IN ARABIA.* Hutchinson. London 1924
 Vol.I, 1917; Vol.II. *THE TIDE OF VICTORY* London 1919

WAVELL, Archibald. *ALLENBY: A STUDY IN GREATNESS.* Oxford University Press. 1941. *THE PALASTINE CAMPAIGNS.* Constable. London 1928

WEINTRAUB, Stanley and Rodelle. *PRIVATE SHAW AND PUBLIC SHAW.* London 1963

WILSON, A.T. *LOYALTIES: MESOPOTAMIA 1914-1917.* London 1931

WILSON, Jeremy. *LAWRENCE OF ARABIA: The Authorised Biography.* London 1989

WINGATE, Sir Ronald. *WINGATE OF THE SUDAN.* Murray. London 1955

WOODWARD, E.L. and BUTLER, R. (eds) *DOCUMENTS ON BRITISH FOREIGN POLICY 1918-1939.* Series 1, Vol. IV. London 1952

YARDLEY, Michael. *BACKING INTO THE LIMELIGHT: A Biography of T.E. Lawrence.* London 1985

YOUNG, Hubert. *THE INDEPENDENT ARAB.* Murray. London 1933

ZEINE, Zeine N. *THE STRUGGLE FOR ARAB INDEPENDENCE.* Beirut. 1960

Index

A

Abd el Main (Mayein, Muein etc.) 117
Abd el Kader 105
Abdullah (Abdullah etc.) Emir, later King of Jordan 12, 15, 38, 39-41, 48, 57-60, 63-65, 67-70, 92, 161, 163, 192, 227
Abu Lissan (Aba el Lissan, Abu Lissal) 16, 86, 109-110, 132
Abu Tayeh (Abu Tayi) tribe 92, 93, 114
Achmed (Ahmed) Salim. *See Dahoum*
Aden 18, 19, 42
Akaba. *See Aqaba*
Ageila, Ageyl 77, 81, 83, 142
Alawites 163, 234
Aldington (Richard) 15, 32, 141, 182
Aleppo 44, 45, 155, 163, 164
Ali, Emir 12, 42, 73, 132, 161
Ali Haidar (Sherif of Mecca) 75
Allenby (General Sir Edmund) 96, 101, 103, 106, 109, 113, 123, 126, 131-133, 157, 158, 215
All Souls College, Oxford 167
Amman 113, 123, 124, 125, 129, 159
Antonius (George) 38, 39
Anzac Mounted Division 124
Aqaba 15, 24, 25, 81, 83-5, 87, 89, 91, 103, 113, 117, 123, 125, 132, 143, 159, 175, 187.
Arab Bulletin, The 91, 114, 200
Arab Revolt, The 11, 125, 196, 198, 200, 219
Arfaja 83
Armenians 34
Auda Abu Tayi 81, 83, 85, 89-92, 159

Auja (River) 109
Australians 149, 155
Aylmer (General) 207, 208, 211
Azrak 103, 106, 126, 133, 136

B

Baalbek 85
Baghdad 44, 195, 202, 209, 211, 213, 216, 217, 220
Bani Salih 199
Bani Sikain 199
Bani Tamim 199
Bani Turuf 199
Barrow (Major-General Sir George) 134, 147, 148, 149
Basra 44, 198-201, 205, 216
Beersheba 23, 24, 95, 103-5, 216, 217
Beirut 21, 44
Bir ibn Hassani 75
Blunt (Wilfred Scawen) 35
Bray, Captain (later Major) N.N.E. 77, 78
Breese, Squadron-Leader G.C. 169
Bruce (John) 139
Buxton 167
Buxton's Camel Corps 99

C

Cairo 41, 48, 87, 123, 136, 159, 204
Cairo Conference 225-6
Caliphate 47
Carchemish 24, 25, 27

Chauvel, General Henry 151, 157, 158

Churchill, Winston S. 145, 164, 165, 193, 222, 226

Clayton, Colonel G.H. 40, 53, 54, 71, 84-6, 89, 90, 123, 158, 176, 185, 193

Cox, Sir Percy 49, 198, 205, 220, 222, 226

Craster, Sir Edmund 167

Curzon (Lord) 227

Curtis, Lionel 167

Cyprus 19, 168, 229

D

Dahoum 27, 32, 33, 86

Daily Telegraph, The 148

Damascus 20, 38, 48, 85, 86, 103, 123, 134145, 148-50, 155, 156, 157, 159, 163, 164

Dane, Edmund 156

Dardenelles 40

Da'ud 103, 104, 109, 139, 141-3

Davenport, Major 75

Dawnay, Alan 126

Dawnay, Guy 187

Deraa 92, 109, 131-4, 136-40, 145, 147-9, 156, 157

Desart, Lord 209

Dhiab, Dhiabat 86

Dhiban 215

Druses 35, 161, 163

Dumaniyeh 86

E

Egypt 18, 23, 159

Enver Pasha 145, 204

Es Salt (Salt) 124, 128, 158

Euphrates 201, 214

F

Faisal. *See* Feisal

Faiz el Ghussein 139

Farraj 103, 104, 109, 126, 139, 141-3

Fawaz el Faiz 31-2

Feisal 15, 58-60, 71, 77-80, 85, 86, 89, 92-3, 96, 106, 123, 126, 151-2, 157-60, 162, 196, 221-3

Fontana (Mrs) 25, 29

France 17, 18, 20, 23, 65, 124, 157, 161

G

Gallipoli 29

Gardner (Brian) 53

Garland (Major H.) 72, 75

Garnett, David 20, 137, 159, 168

Gaza 23-5, 95, 96, 105, 108, 109

Germany 19

Gibraltar 18, 19

Graves, Robert 27, 85, 112, 115, 163, 167, 182

Gueira, Guweira 86, 90, 91, 96, 117

H

Haifa 19, 133

Hamilton (General) 29

Hart, Basil Liddell. *See* Liddell Hart

Hashemites 41, 57, 161, 166, 223

Hauran 103

Haza (Sheikh) 127

Hedjaz. Hejaz 12, 19, 38, 41-2, 45, 51-2, 151, 153, 161, 166.

Hedley, Colonel Coote 26, 71

Herbert Aubrey 49, 185, 204

Hindian 199

Hittites 33, 34

Hogarth, David G. 20, 26, 28, 29, 48, 123, 184, 187

Home Letters of T.E. Lawrence 167

Houghton Library 167

Howeitat, Huweitat 81, 83, 86, 89-91, 96, 114

Humber (H.M.S.) 98

Hussein, Sherif, (later King) 12, 19, 37-9, 41-5, 50, 67, 132, 152, 160, 163, 194-6

Hussein-McMahon Letters 41

Hussein Mabeirig 73

I

Ibn Rashid 29, 72

Ibn Saud 19, 29, 161, 193, 195, 196, 228

Idrisi 59

Illa 199

Imam Yahya 47

India 19, 197

Irak, Iraq 13, 35, 44, 50, 163, 166, 218

J

Jaffa 109, 113

Jarvis, Major C.S. 92, 147

Jedda, Jeddah, Jidda 38, 53, 54, 57, 59, 60, 73, 76, 186, 228

Jefer 86

Jemal 145, 158

Jerusalem 18, 95, 109, 113, 124, 174, 175

Jordan 166

Joyce, Lieutenant-Col. P.C. 75, 89, 92, 110, 150, 187.

K

Kaf 86

Khuidr 103

Kitchener, Lord 23, 25, 27, 38-40, 48, 185

Knightley, Phillip 31, 86, 139, 159, 161, 166, 168.

Kosseir 80

Kress von Kressenstein 52, 95

Kurds 35, 137, 163, 210

Kurna 79

Kut (Kut-al-Amara) 195, 201, 203, 204, 207, 209-11

Kut Nahr Hahgim 199.

L

Lawrence, Professor Arnold Walter 27, 138, 139.

Lawrence, Sarah Junner (nee Maden) 136, 138, 139

Lawrence and the Arabs (Graves) 182

Lawrence of Arabia (Film) 189

Lawrence of Arabia (Aldington) 32

Lebanon 18, 47, 157, 158

Letters of T.E. Lawrence, The 20, 159, 160, 165

Liddell Hart, Basil 26, 29, 30, 71, 73, 115, 149-50, 167, 179, 182

M

Maan 91, 98, 101, 110, 113, 123

McMahon, Sir Henry 37, 42-5, 49, 160

McMahon-Husseon Correspondence 41, 217

Mack, Dr. John E. 31, 34, 49, 134, 135, 137, 138, 141, 146, 156, 168, 171, 183, 189

Mafrak 93

Mahmud 103

Malta 18

Matar 103

Mecca 12, 38, 39, 42, 59, 67, 152, 160, 175

Medina 38, 39, 45, 48, 51, 76, 101, 113

Mediterranean Expeditionary Force 52

Melbourne Argus 150

Mesopotamia 13, 19, 20, 28, 29, 34, 75, 161, 164, 195-6, 198

Mint, The 230

Mohammed el Dheilan 90

Mohammed Said (Emir)158

Monroe, Elizabeth 196, 203

Morris, James 41, 42

Mosul 20, 45, 163, 216

Motlog (Sheikh) 118

Mousley, (Captain E.O.) 210

Mousa, Suleiman 27, 48, 64, 70, 77, 85-6, 105, 107, 112, 114-6, 135, 139, 156, 196

Mudawwara 97-9, 114, 117, 124

Murray, General Sir Archibald 50, 52, 53, 183

Murray, Sir John 67, 70, 95, 96.

Mutawalis 163

Muthakkarati (King Abdullah) 63

N

Naseeb al-Bekri 85

Nasir, Sherif 81, 83, 85-7, 118, 145-6

Nebk 83, 85, 86

Nejd (Najd) 12, 77, 196, 201

Newcombe, Capt. S.F. 24-6, 77, 79, 150, 185, 187

Nicholson, Sir Arthur 53

Nimrin 128

Nuri Pasha Said 134

Nuri Shaalan 83, 91

O

Ottoman Empire 18, 19, 160. *endent*
Oxford Companion to English Literature 32

P

Palestine 12, 19, 20, 34, 103, 105, 109, 153, 161, 198
Palestine Exploration Fund 23-5
Paris Peace Conference 13, 162, 196
Peake, F.G. 92, 93, 125, 127, 128
Persia 28, 42
Persian Gulf 18, 197, 201, 218
Philby, H.St. John 193, 221, 227
Prince of Our Disorder (Mack) 31

R

Rabegh, Rabugh 45, 58, 66, 72, 73, 75
Rafa 24
Rahail 103
Ram Hormuz 199
Ramadi 215
Ramleh 113, 127
Rankin, Maj.-Gen. George 150, 151, 171
Remtha 134
Revolt in the Desert (Lawrence) 179, 182
Robinson, General 29, 200
Ross, John Hume 168-9
Royal Air Force 167, 168
Ruhi 46
Russia 29, 216

S

"S.A." 27, 33
Saad 143
Said Ali Pasha 58
Sayed Taleb 201, 221-2
Secret Lives of Lawrence of Arabia, The 31
Serahin, Serhan 106, 108, 109
Seven Pillars of Wisdom, (Lawrence) 27, 32, 35, 36, 50, 69, 84, 93, 102, 103, 107, 108, 111, 115, 116, 124, 138, 142, 148, 152, 160, 166, 167, 180, 182, 186

Shatt-al-Arab ,197, 199
Shaw, George Bernard 167
Shaw, Mrs. Charlotte 167, 193
"Shaw, T.E." 183
Sheik Achmed (Sheikh Ahmed) 27, 32, 33
Shia 47, 161, 196, 199, 218
Shu'aiba 199, 200
Simpson, Colin 31, 139, 159, 161, 166, 168
Sinai Desert 23, 25, 40
Steffens, Lincoln 34
Stirling, Major W.F. 50, 187
Storrs, (Sir) Ronald 37, 38, 40, 41, 46, 48, 51, 52, 54, 57-9, 63, 68, 70-2, 95, 167, 174, 194
Suakin 57
Suez Canal 18, 24
Swann, Air Vice-Marshal Sir Oliver 168, 169
Sykes, Christopher 168
Sykes, Lieut.-Col. Sir Mark 53, 185
Sykes-Picot Agreement 19, 157, 158, 163-4, 216
Syria 12, 19-21, 25, 35, 85, 153, 157, 160-2

T

Tafas 134-6, 145-6
Tafila, Tafileh 113-8, 124
Taif 12, 72
Talal 135
T.E. Lawrence to His Biographers 85
Tell el Shehab 103
Texas, University of 167
Tigris, The 202, 203, 211, 214
Tikrit 211
Times, The 13, 33, 163, 189, 219
Times Literary Supplement, The 157
Togatga 97
Townshend, General 49, 202-4, 209
Trans-Jordan 139, 153, 164, 166
Trucial Coast 19
Turkey 20, 29, 37, 39, 155, 159
Turki 105

U

Umtaiye 134, 145

Urfa 137
Uxbridge 168

V
Vickery 77-9, 187

W
Wadi Diraa 83
Wadi Ithm 25
War Office 26
Wavell (Field-Marshall Lord) 23, 25, 67, 95, 125, 128-9, 155-7
Wejh 75-7, 79-81, 84, 89, 90, 142
Wilderness of Zin, The 25
Wilson, Sir Arnold 198, 199, 201, 203, 207, 214, 220, 226
Wilson, Lieut.-Col. C.EE. 29, 57, 76, 187
Wilson, President 196
Wingate, Gen. Sir Reginald 30, 40, 53
With Allenby in Palestine, (Thomas) 171
With Lawrence in Arabia, (Thomas) 179, 182
Woolley, Leonard 24-6

Y
Yale, William 165
Yarmuk 101-3, 108, 109, 114, 118, 124, 136
Yemen 12, 47
Yenbo (Yanbo) 38, 75, 76, 78
Young, Major Hubert 227

Z
Zayd, Zeid 48, 73, 114, 116, 118
Zeitun 98
Zelebani 97
Zuweida 97